John Taylor, Emil Friedrich Kautzsch

An Outline of the History of the Literature of the Old Testament

With chronological tables for the history of the Israelites, and other aids to the

explanation of the Old Testament

John Taylor, Emil Friedrich Kautzsch

An Outline of the History of the Literature of the Old Testament
With chronological tables for the history of the Israelites, and other aids to the explanation of the Old Testament

ISBN/EAN: 9783744796187

Printed in Europe, USA, Canada, Australia, Japan

Cover: Foto ©Lupo / pixelio.de

More available books at **www.hansebooks.com**

AN OUTLINE OF THE HISTORY

OF THE

LITERATURE OF THE OLD TESTAMENT

WITH

CHRONOLOGICAL TABLES

FOR THE

HISTORY OF THE ISRAELITES

AND OTHER AIDS TO THE

EXPLANATION OF THE OLD TESTAMENT.

BY

E. KAUTZSCH,

PROFESSOR OF THEOLOGY AT THE UNIVERSITY OF HALLE.

REPRINTED FROM THE "SUPPLEMENTS" TO THE TRANSLATION OF THE OLD TESTAMENT EDITED BY THE AUTHOR.

TRANSLATED BY JOHN TAYLOR, D.LIT., M.A.

NEW YORK: G. P. PUTNAM'S SONS
LONDON: WILLIAMS & NORGATE

1899.

PREFACE.

THE publisher and the editor of "Die Heilige Schrift des A. T." (edited by E. Kautzsch, with the co-operation of Professors Guthe, Kamphausen, Kittel, Marti, Rothstein, Rüetschi, Ryssel, Seigfried and Socin; second edition, with many corrections, Freiburg and Leipzig, 1896), have been repeatedly urged to print separately these "Supplements" to the work, and the appeal has been specially supported from England. They have not acceded to it without careful consideration. With the exception of minor corrections and additions (especially of references to the most recent literature), together with an alteration in the arrangement, this separate edition differs from the last impression only in the following points. The division of the six periods into numerous smaller sections with special titles, and the employment of headlines to each page has made it easier to trace the Outline of the History of Old Testament Literature (p. 1 ff.). On p. 93 a discussion of the Song of Moses (Deut. xxxii.) has been inserted, and at p. 97 f. a notice of the so-called Ebed-Jahweh poems. From p. 120 onwards repeated reference has been made to Prof. Ed. Meyer's important work, "Die Entstehung des Judenthums" (Halle, 1896).

On pp. 225-247, there is an addition to the matter previously contained in the "Supplements," in the form of a Survey of the constituents of the Sources of all the historical books from Genesis to 2 Kings, together with Ezra and Nehemiah. This was requisite because we could not take it for granted that the readers of our Reprint would use along with it the Translation (see above), in which the various documents are distinguished by marginal letters. The Survey now added is naturally in general agreement with those assumptions of literary criticism on which the Translation and the Outline are based. But the renewed weighing of the critical problems and the employment of contributions to the analysis of the sources made by others since 1894, have led to corrections of all kinds, and in some cases (especially with regard to the Third Book of Moses) to more precise results concerning certain strata of the Sources.

With regard to the standpoint here occupied in literary criticism and theology I must again refer to the concluding words of the "Outline" (p. 164 ff.). Nothing can alter the fact that scientific problems, once recognized as such, are not stilled until they have been solved, or until, at least, the limits within which they can be solved have been determined. That is true of the problems of theological science and consequently of those of Biblical Investigation, as well as of all others, and one of the signs of a church's vitality is that it leaves honest inquiry unhampered and has confidence in the power of Truth, which will triumph in the end. But a church which cannot bear to have the traditions of its faith scientifically tested, and fancies that by majority-resolutions in synods it can arbitrarily maintain a view of Scripture which contradicts Scripture itself, pronounces its own sentence. If people wish to tie men's consciences for ever to traditional views they must be able to meet the objections raised against the tradition. Attempts to do this have not been wanting, and we shall always welcome them, so long as they recognize facts and are content to moderate the excess of critical zeal and to put down an unseemly kind of discussion of the questions involved in Biblical inquiry. But some facts have been finally settled, such as the construction of the Pentateuch and the Historical Books out of different documents, some of them varying widely from each other. And if we are required, even with reference to them, to destroy our sense of truth and give the lie to indisputable results for the sake of groundless prejudices, we protest, in the name of Evangelical liberty, and that the more vigorously seeing that all previous attempts to cover such a demand with a show of erudition have failed utterly and miserably.

E. KAUTZSCH.

HALLE, *February*, 1897.

TRANSLATOR'S NOTE.

The Rev. J. H. Stowell, The Manse, Lightcliffe, has most kindly placed his MS. translation of the "Abriss" at my disposal during the revision of the proof-sheets of this volume. This does not involve him in any responsibility for the rendering, but it obliges me to cordial thanks.

J. T.

November 11th, 1898.

TABLE OF CONTENTS.

	PAGE
PREFACE	V

I. HISTORY OF THE LITERATURE OF THE OLD TESTAMENT.

§ 1. *The Pre-monarchic Period.*

1. The Relics of ancient popular poetry.

    (*a*) The Book of the Wars of Jahweh—The Triumphal Song of "Them that speak in Proverbs"—The Song of the Well—The Book of the Upright Ones   1

    (*b*) The Song of Lamech—The passage concerning the Holy Ark—Exod. xvii. 16—The Song of Deborah—Jotham's Fable .   3

2. The Relics of ancient stories and legends—The literary works ascribed to Moses   5

§ 2. *The Period of the Undivided Monarchy.*

1. David's Elegies on Saul and Abner—Possible Psalms of David—Nathan's Parable—Solomon's Speech in dedication of the Temple—Possible remnants of Solomon's Writings . .   10

2. Other possible literary memorials of the period of David and Solomon (especially the "Blessing of Jacob" and the original form of the Balaam-Discourses) .   14

§ 3. *The Period of the Divided Monarchy until the Destruction of Samaria.*

 1. General—The "Hero-Stories" of the Book of Judges—The "Jerusalem-Source" in the Second Book of Samuel—The "Saul-Stories" and the "David-Stories" . . 18

 2. The Beginnings of the Legal Literature: The Book of the Covenant . 29

 3. The Jahwistic Historical Work—On the History of Pentateuch Criticism . 31

 4. Other Relics of the Literature of the ninth and eighth centuries (1 Sam. iv. 1 ff.)—"The Blessing of Moses"—The Mirror of the Prophets—1 Kings xx. 22, &c. . . 40

 5. The Historical Work of the older Elohist—The more recent Biographies of Samuel and Saul . 43

 6. General Remarks on Prophetism . 46

 7. The earliest Literary Prophets: Isa. xv. f., Amos, Hosea . . . 50
 8. Isaiah—Micah . 53

§ 4. *From the Destruction of Samaria to the Exile.*

 1. Nahum—Zephaniah . 59

 2. The Historical Work of the Jehovist—Deuteronomy . 61

 3. The Book of Kings . 68

 4. Habakkuk—Jeremiah . 74

§ 5. *The Period of the Exile.*

 1. Ezekiel . 86

 2. Lamentations . 91

3. The Close of the Deuteronomistic Historical Work	94
4. Deutro-Isaiah (and Trito-Isaiah)	96
5. Isa. xxxiv. f., xiii. f., xxi. 1-10	99
6. The Law of Holiness	100

§ 6. *The Post-Exilic Period.*

1. Haggai and Zechariah — Malachi	103
2. The Priests' Code and the Law Book of Ezra—The Close of the Pentateuch and of the Historical Work extending from Gen. i. to 2 Kings xxv.	106
3. The Work of the Chronicler (Ezra, Nehemiah, and Chronicles)	121
4. The Book of Ruth—The Book of Esther	129
5. The After-Growths of the Prophetic Literature (Obadiah, Joel, Jonah, Isa. xxiv. to xxvii., Zechariah ix.-xiv.)—The Close of the Canon of the Prophets	132
6. The Book of Daniel	138
7. The Poetical Books.	
(*a*) The Psalter	141
(*b*) The Song of Songs	148
8. The Monuments of the Wisdom Literature.	
(*a*) Proverbs	151
(*b*) The Book of Job	154
(*c*) Ecclesiastes	162
Conclusion	164
II. CHRONOLOGICAL TABLES FOR THE HISTORY OF THE ISRAELITES FROM MOSES TO THE END OF THE SECOND CENTURY, B.C.	167

III. MEASURES AND WEIGHTS, MONEY, COMPUTATION OF TIME IN THE OLD TESTAMENT.	PAGE
1. Measures and Weights	206
2. Money	210
3. Computation of Time	212
IV. LIST OF OLD TESTAMENT PROPER NAMES, ACCOMPANIED WITH AN EXACT TRANSLITERATION OF THEIR HEBREW FORMS	216
V. SURVEY OF THE COMPOSITION FROM DIFFERENT DOCUMENTS OF SEVERAL BOOKS OF THE OLD TESTAMENT	225
INDEX	248

I.

HISTORY OF THE LITERATURE
OF
THE OLD TESTAMENT.

§ 1. THE PRE-MONARCHIC PERIOD.

1. THE RELICS OF ANCIENT POPULAR POETRY.

a. **The Book of the Wars of Jahweh.—The Triumphal Song of "Them that speak in Proverbs."—The Song of the Well.—The Book of the Upright Ones.**

IN Israel, as in other nations, the earliest literary period was preceded by one of song and legend. The conditions on which, in every age, the appearance of a real literature depend—above all, the wide diffusion of the arts of writing and *reading*, the settled life and comparative prosperity of the people—did not exist in Israel till near the end of the so-called age of the Judges, certainly not during the Journey through the Desert or whilst the tribes were incessantly struggling for existence after the immigration into Canaan.

We do not mean to deny that in these earlier times songs and legends were eagerly repeated. But the subjects they dealt with can only be determined from the subsequent literature, and that in two ways: first, from the actual records of later date, containing the remnants of the old popular poetry, as these could be gathered from the mouth of the people or of the professional singer; secondly, from the free adaptations and developments of ancient songs and legends which are also preserved in the subsequent literature.

As to the first kind, the actual records of ancient popular poetry, we have at least two explicit testimonies that in very early times attention was paid in Israel to the collection of such reliques. At Num. xxi. 14, the "Book of the Wars of Jahweh" is quoted as the source of a very obscure fragment of song given there. The pæan of "Them that speak in proverbs," on the overthrow of the Moabites, Num. xxi. 27 ff., is possibly taken from the same book; perhaps also the so-called "Song of the Well," v. 17 f., and some other fragments, such as the groundwork of Exod. xv. 1 ff., and the "Song of Miriam," of which Exod. xv. 21, appears to have given only the beginning. All these traces point to a collection of songs celebrating the heroic deeds of the people, and especially of Jahweh, as the God of War, and the real commander in the battles which had to be fought for the conquest and retention of the land which He had promised. Another collection, "The Book of the Upright Ones" (literally, "of the Upright One") is mentioned twice. The precise meaning of the title is disputable. It either designates songs about brave and pious members of the nation, or else "of the Upright Ones" is a designation of the people of Israel itself (hence, "The Book of Israel"). Both passages put it beyond doubt that here again a *collection of songs* is meant: at Joshua x. 12 f. it is quoted as the source of two verses in which Joshua celebrates Israel's complete victory over the Amorites; at 2 Sam. i. 18 as the source of David's elegy on Saul and Jonathan. The latter example shows that the collection contained artistically cultivated poetry as well as folk-songs, and these belonging to an age when the foundations of a real literature had already been laid. Indeed, if it be a correct conjecture that in the original text of 1 Kings viii. 13 (on which cf. below, p. 13) "The Book of the Upright Ones" and not "The Book of Songs" is quoted, the collection cannot have been arranged earlier than the time of Solomon.

When we turn to the remains of the popular poetry which

were subsequently written down, we cannot sufficiently regret that so few fragments have been preserved, and these, in part, badly disfigured and hard to interpret. This is due to a twofold cause. The oldest connected presentations of the history of the people could point to those collections of ancient song as accessible to every one. A brief quotation sufficed to recall the whole of the passage in question as it stood in "The Book of Songs." Besides this, there is another circumstance on which sufficient emphasis cannot be laid for the understanding of Old Testament literature. The composition, and certainly the final collection and canonization of this literature were effected, one might say, exclusively from the religious standpoint, in the interest of religion. What wonder that, on the whole, when the final redaction was made, everything was omitted—and, indeed, expunged—which seemed to serve only for the satisfaction of worldly curiosity or actually to excite a carnal national conceit?

b. **The Song of Lamech. — The Passage concerning the Holy Ark.—Exod. xvii. 16.—The Song of Deborah.— Jotham's Fable.**

In addition to the fragments already mentioned (Exod. xv. 1 ff. and 21; Num. xxi. 14 f., 17 f., and 27 ff.; Joshua x. 12 f.), the following fragments and sections must be assigned to the pre-monarchic time:—

1. The so-called "Song of Lamech" (Gen. iv. 23 f.), apparently an ancient folk-song, uttering an arrogant boast of the possession of weapons and constant readiness for bloody revenge. This little three-verse song is already stamped with all the marks of Hebrew poetry—precise parallelism between the two halves of each verse, exalted, rhythmical language, and the use of special words belonging to the dialect of poetry.

2. The poetic fragment, Num. x. 35 f. (taken, perhaps, from the "Book of the Wars of Jahweh"). The great antiquity of

this verse is clearly seen from the manner in which the holy ark is spoken of as a pledge, not to say a representation, of the personal presence of Jahweh — an idea which we shall find supported by other ancient witnesses.

3. The poetic fragment, Exod. xvii. 6: of this we shall speak again later.

4. The so-called "Song of Deborah" (Judges v. 2 ff.). The ascription of this "Song to Deborah" (at v. 1, in conjunction with Barak!) may be due simply to a misunderstanding of v. 7 ("till I arose, &c." instead of "till thou arosest;" or, with the Greek Bible, "till she arose"). In point of fact, the view that she was the author is excluded by the address to Deborah in v. 12. But it has never been denied that this is a poem of priceless worth, almost contemporaneous with the events it describes, flowing out of impressions experienced by and still vivid to the writer himself. Doubtless the text has suffered severely, as is usually the case with such remnants from the pre-literary period: in fact, v. 8-14 are nothing but a heap of puzzling ruins. But the portion which can certainly be understood fully justifies the verdict that this is genuine, splendid poetry, which enables us to conjecture how much that was equally important has vanished without leaving a trace. The insight, however, which the song gives us into the historical, and particularly the religious, conditions of that far-off century is of infinitely more importance than its æsthetic value. We are looking on a time when the people are severely oppressed, reduced to forty thousand capable of bearing arms, but possessing none (v. 8). The roads are deserted because no man is sure of his life (v. 6), till Deborah, by inspiriting speech, and Barak, by courageous action, rouse their own and the adjacent tribes to a fight for freedom. Obviously it is still a time of confusion and disintegration. Only the northern tribes, who are immediately threatened by the Canaanites, with their nearest relatives, bestir themselves for the fight. Strange to say, there is not a word of Judah. But, on the other hand, the scorn poured on Reuben, who merely gave the matter serious consideration and then

preferred to listen to the sound of the shepherd's pipes, shows that something better might have been expected from him—that it was his duty to think of the distress of his compatriots. He was connected with them by a tie which ought to show itself stronger than any human covenant or agreement—the worship of the same God. The fight was for the victory of *His* side: *His* was the glory of the victory gained (v. 2, 3, 31). In His awful majesty He left Mount Sinai, His holy dwelling-place, to appear in person on the field of battle (v. 4 f.), and His curse deservedly falls upon the city (v. 23), which "came not to the help of the Lord amongst the mighty," the Lord who is the champion of His people.

5. Jotham's Fable (Judges ix. 8 ff.) is of quite another character, but an equally striking and indubitably genuine product of the pre-monarchic time. The technical structure of the fable is here found in such perfection and imbued with so fine a sarcasm as again to suggest the conjecture that this form of composition must have been long and diligently cultivated.

2. THE RELICS OF ANCIENT STORIES AND LEGENDS.—THE LITERARY WORKS ASCRIBED TO MOSES

(especially Exod. xvii. 14 ff., the Book of the Covenant and the Ten Commandments).

As a second source for ascertaining the traditions which come from the pre-literary period of the people we have referred to the adaptations and developments of ancient stories and legends which are preserved—often in duplicate—in the literature proper. It belongs to the nature of the case that we here move on far less certain ground than before. That is to say, in any individual instance it is difficult to decide which traits of a narrative are derived from the original tradition, and which from the later development, or possibly even from very late reflection. But we are not without criteria which make it possible to decide up to a certain point. Not seldom in the extant prose narratives there are unmistakable echoes of the early poetical form. This is indubitably the case where the poetical exemplar itself has been preserved, as at Exod. xiv. 29, along with xv. 8; Joshua x. 13b, along with 12b f.; Judges iv. 17 ff., along with v. 24 ff. And in other instances traces of such poetical exemplars are not lacking: thus at Exod. xiv. 24 ff., on the occasion when Pharaoh was destroyed; at Joshua iii. 16, when the Jordan stood still; or vi. 20, when the walls of Jericho fell at the war-cry and sound of the trumpet. In other passages the great antiquity of the narrative is evinced by its correspondence with the primæval traditions of other nations (Gen. iv. 20 ff.), the use of names that are inexplicable or have disappeared elsewhere (Naamah, v. 22), above all, by the intermingling of a mythological element (Gen. vi. 1 ff., xxix. 10, xxxii. 25 ff.) Not unfrequently there is a connection with primæval local traditions (as at Gen. xix.) or historical recollections (as at Gen. xxxiv. 25 ff., confirmed by xlix. 5 ff.). Hence we must ascribe to an actual tradition, handed down from the pre-literary period, the greatest part of the matter furnished by the *ancient* documentary sources (see below) in the Pentateuch and Joshua, although the final development of the patriarchal narratives within the limits of a fixed genealogical system may not have been earlier than the period when literature was cultivated.

In conclusion, we must not shrink from answering a question which will have occurred ere now to many readers. What about the evidences for writings originating with Moses himself? Are not these latter to be regarded as the foundation and starting-point of the entire literature of Israel?

We may here take it for granted that the Pentateuch in its present form raises no claim, either by a title or a signature or in any other way, to be, in its entirety, a work of Moses. Not till the later, post-exilic period, and especially in the Chronicles, do we meet with this idea. On the other hand the Pentateuch no doubt states, in four places, that Moses *wrote* something. At Deut. xxxi. 9, 24, the Deuteronomic writer, a redactor living in the exile, relates that the law of Deuteronomy was written by Moses, and a post-exilic redactor, at Num. xxxiii. 2, asserts that he recorded the names of the Stations in the Desert. Seeing, however, that Deuteronomy cannot have originated before the seventh century and that Num. xxxiii. in all probability belongs to the most recent portions of the Pentateuch, the statements mentioned above must not be taken into account here.

The two other passages are of a different kind. The narrator of Exod. xvii. 14 ff., must have found the express tradition (possibly in the Book of the Wars of Jahweh) that the Amalekites' treachery and probably the threat quoted at v. 16 was recorded by Moses himself in a book (more correctly, perhaps, "on a leaf," according to Num. v. 23, where precisely the same expression is found). But we cannot ascertain anything more precise respecting the scope and the phraseology of this exceptional writing. The narrator of Exod. xxiv. 4 ff., must also have been acquainted with a definite tradition that Moses himself wrote a "Book of the Law of the Covenant." But it is quite another question how much of the phraseology of this so-called "Book of the Covenant" has been preserved in our present Pentateuch. The Ten Commandments used naturally to be thought of first and foremost as the basis of this Book of the Covenant, although the writing down of them is ascribed at Exod. xxiv. 12, xxxiv. 1, not to Moses but to God Himself. But if we admit that the very words of the Ten Commandments were given in Moses' Book of the Covenant and in distinct documentary form on the Two Tables of Stone, how are we then to explain the origin of two forms of the Ten Commandments, those of Exod. xx. and Deut. v., which, with all their agreement, are yet so diverse? It would, in any case, have to be admitted that the original text, especially in the First Table, had been somewhat freely handled. The difficulty becomes still greater if the opinion is correct which Goethe advanced and the majority of students now share. According to it "The Covenant-

Commandments, the Ten Commandments," which Moses is bidden to write (Exod. xxxiv. 27) are the preceding statutes, v. 14-26, which in many ways vary considerably from Exod. xx. (as the older, so-called Jahwistic, Decalogue contrasted with the Elohistic). The passage, Exod. xxxiv. 27 ff., does indeed admit of another explanation. Originally, in a different context, it may have referred to our Ten Commandments; but the redactor did not wish to repeat these in the present context. Even then the question concerning the original Decalogue is still a complicated one and cannot yet be settled.*

Besides the Decalogue, however, the narrator of Exod. xxiv. 3 ff. (cf. v. 3 with xxi. 1) evidently has in view the ordinances of worship and justice in chaps. xx. 24—xxiii. 19, and recent writers are accustomed to limit to this section the name "Book of the Covenant," as the title of the oldest compilation of laws. We may be sure that there are later additions here as elsewhere (most of them recognizable by the use of the plural form of address). But, apart from these, weighty considerations have been adduced against the direct derivation of all these laws from the hand of Moses. A large number of them (especially xxii. 4 ff., 20, 24, 28, xxiii. 9 ff.) are seen at a glance to be a codification of customary laws and maxims which could not have developed till the people had long been settled in the land, cultivating its fields and vineyards.

The result is that whilst nothing can be said against the idea of Moses having written some documents, we must not hope to be able to designate any we possess as certainly Mosaic *in their phraseology*. Obviously this does not preclude the existence of many genuine historical reminiscences in the traditions which deal with the motives for the work of Moses, the work itself, and its fundamental significance for the whole history of Israel. No nation ever gratuitously invented the

---

* On this controversy, besides Dillmann's exhaustive Kommentar zu den Büchern Exodus und Leviticus (Leipzig, 1880), cf. Rothstein, Das Bundesbuch. Halle, 1888: Budde, Bemerkungen zum Bundesbuch (ZATW, 1891, p. 99 ff.): Bantsch, Das Bundesbuch, Exod. xx. 22, xxiii. 33. Halle, 1892: Meisner, Der Dekalog I (der Dek. im Hexateuch). Halle, 1893.

report that it had been ignominiously enslaved by another: none ever forgot the days of its deliverance. And so through all the centuries there survived in Israel the inextinguishable recollection that it was once delivered out of Egypt, the house of bondage, by Jahweh, the God of its fathers, with a strong hand and outstretched arm; that especially at the passage of the Red Sea it experienced the mighty protection of its God. And Jahweh employed as His instrument a man the like of whom was never again found. That man had taught his people to recognize as its highest glory the being called the people *of this God*, as its supreme joy the praising Him and worshipping Him with sacrifices and offerings. And if the oldest tradition regards it as self-evident (Judges xvii. 13) that the priestly service of a member of the tribe of Levi is far preferable to any other, this can only be explained by *one* fact: the tribe of Levi was considered to be the only possessor of the genuine knowledge, derived from Moses himself, of the proper way to worship the God of Israel, to administer justice in His name, and, above all, in special questions and concerns to ascertain His will by means of the holy lot (the "Urim and Thummim").

§ 2. THE PERIOD OF THE UNDIVIDED MONARCHY.

1. DAVID'S ELEGIES ON SAUL AND ABNER.—POSSIBLE PSALMS OF DAVID.—NATHAN'S PARABLE.—SOLOMON'S SPEECH IN DEDICATION OF THE TEMPLE.—POSSIBLE REMNANTS OF SOLOMONIC WRITINGS.

AN event is said to have happened about the middle of the period of the Judges (Judges viii. 14) which enables us to conclude that the art of writing had been gradually disseminated amongst the common people. It is, therefore, easy to understand that it has been thought necessary to date the beginnings of a real literature not later than this period, the second half of the time of the Judges. It must be acknowledged possible that as early as this, perhaps at sanctuaries which had long been famous, such as those at Shiloh and Bethel, amongst a hereditary priesthood of old standing, the writing down of ancient songs or of the histories of these sanctuaries was taken in hand. But no actual proof can be adduced. It would rather appear that we must come down to the time of David for the writing out of the products of those earlier days. If David commanded (2 Sam. i. 18) that the elegy on Saul and Jonathan should be taught to the Judahites this certainly does not preclude his having written it and caused copies to be circulated. But the narrator seems only to have known of its having been written out in the (later) "Book of the Upright Ones."

The doubts occasionally expressed as to the genuineness of the Song * are now set at rest. It has ever been justly

---

* Its erroneous designation as "Song of the Bow," was occasioned by the word "bow" having been brought in from another context to the original text of 2 Sam. i. 18 ("And he commanded to teach [it] to the children of Judah"). This was then taken to be the name of the song that followed.

recognized as a real pearl of Hebrew poetry. And this is true both of its poetical form and of its contents, at once so simple and so stirring. The almost identical lament at the beginning and at the end serve as a framework for six strophes, each consisting of two verses, with two clauses each. The fifth of them corresponds with the first in fine contrast; the second and fourth utter the actual dirge for the dead; the third sings the praise of the fallen heroes. But besides the considerations which affect all the people alike, the poet has a personal right to assert that his pain is deeper than any others feel. *This* pain he expresses in his address to the friend who had been so devoted to him, whose love to him was more wonderful than the love of women. In the first strophe there is only a distant intimation of the gloomy political background: grief for those who had died heroically on behalf of their people causes the abiding distress of the people to be for the moment forgotten. The religious element is quite absent from the song. But what a monument has David here raised to the king from whom he suffered so much, to the heroic youth at his side, and not less, to himself!

No source is mentioned for David's elegy over Abner (2 Sam. iii. 33 f.). This does not give the slightest occasion to doubt its genuineness. The only question is whether, in this single and unquestionably complete strophe we have the whole lament and not merely a fragment (? the opening).

Tradition, as it subsequently meets us, especially in the Chronicles and in the titles of seventy-three * psalms, makes David also the founder and chief representative of sacred song, of psalmody. It has been said that this tradition could not have appeared in such strength and definiteness if it had been without historical foundation. As a matter of fact, the two elegies are sufficient evidences of David's poetical talents, and it is not intrinsically incredible that so zealous a worshipper of Jahweh, the national God, may have treated of spiritual things. But the fact that the

---

* Eighty-three in the Greek Bible.

title, "Of David," is prefixed in the Book of Psalms to many which are demonstrably exilic, or post-exilic, compels us to disregard those titles entirely. This does not preclude the possibility of genuinely Davidic songs, or fragments of them, having been adopted from some pre-exilic book of songs into the later post-exilic collection. But, alas! we have no standard by which to recognize them as Davidic. The *really* strong historical tradition knows David, apart from the above-mentioned elegies, only as a skilful harper (1 Sam. xvi. 18, &c.), perhaps also as an inventor of melodies, or (according to another interpretation of Amos vi. 5),* of musical instruments. In any case, the latter passage does not indicate that he was a master of *sacred* song. It is true that, in the Appendices to the Second Book of Samuel, two songs are expressly ascribed to David (chap. xxii., identical with Ps. xviii., and chap. xxiii. 1-7). Numerous passages in the psalm (especially v. 23 ff., 31, 50 f.) compel us to admit that at most its present form may have arisen from the expansion and adaptation of a Davidic nucleus into a congregational hymn. But the very first verse of the so-called "Last Words" lies open to grave suspicion, partly because it is an obvious imitation of the Sayings of Balaam (Num. xxiv. 3, 5), partly because it makes David call himself "The Darling of the hymns of Israel." And this first verse is so entirely one in spirit and style with those that follow, and can so ill be spared as the presupposition to v. 2, that we have no right to pronounce it an interpolation for the sake of being able to derive v. 2-7 directly from David. The whole can only be understood as a free, poetic reproduction of one of David's utterances. Nathan's Parable (2 Sam. xii. 1-4), on the other hand, must be considered as certainly a remnant from David's time. The technical form of the parable here, like that of the fable at Judges ix. 8 ff., appears in such perfection as to lead to the conclusion that it had been long and abundantly cultivated.

In his speech dedicatory of the Temple, 1 Kings viii. 12 f., we

---

* Cf. *Expository Times*, April, 1898. *Tr.*

have an authentic monument of the time of Solomon. According to the Greek translation (the so-called Septuagint), it was extracted from the "Book of Songs." Probably we ought to follow another reading, "The Book of the Upright"; on this cf. above, p. 2.

But the attempt has also been made to find a reference to a copious literature from the hand of Solomon at 1 Kings v. 9 ff.* This passage speaks, in the first place, of Solomon's extraordinarily great wisdom in all departments. He is further praised as surpassing the wisdom of the dwellers in the East and the Egyptians. This seems to point to astrological (or even astronomical?) and medical knowledge, as well as to the arts of magic and esoteric lore. Yet all these are pure conjectures, especially as we know nothing about the wise men of old time who are mentioned by name at v. 11. Nothing is said about a literature on the above-named subjects; at all events, the very remotest trace of it has disappeared. But when it is added: "He spoke 3000 proverbs, and his songs were 1005," it seems as though an extensive Solomonic literature in another department is implied. Even an approximate number like 3000, to say nothing of a definite one, like 1005, could not be given unless the proverbs and songs were in writing. Was the narrator, then, acquainted with a Solomonic Book of Proverbs and Songs of this compass? Or had these numbers gradually established themselves in the legend of the wise King? The expression which immediately follows: "He spake of trees, &c.," appears again to know only of Solomon's wisdom as manifested in speech. As to the sayings concerning all plants and animals, we must evidently think not of scientific disquisitions, but only of such matters as thoughtful reflections on Nature, or evidences of attentive observation of it. However that may be, we should at best possess but scanty remains of a *literature* of this kind, in case the passages on this subject in the "Proverbs of Solomon" were to be ascribed to him. We must here

* English Versions, 1 Kings iv. 29 ff.

entirely ignore the psalms attributed to him (lxxii., a prayer *for* the King, and cxxvii., in which the "house," v. 1, has been in much too mechanical a way taken to mean the temple).

2. OTHER POSSIBLE LITERARY MEMORIALS OF THE PERIOD OF DAVID AND SOLOMON (ESPECIALLY THE "BLESSING OF JACOB" AND THE ORIGINAL FORM OF THE BALAAM-DISCOURSES).

If, after all, that we cannot prove ancient Hebrew literature to have been considerably enriched with actual *writings* by David and Solomon, it is, nevertheless, a fair question whether other literary monuments must not be assigned to the period of David and Solomon. And, in fact, the conditions for the rise of a real literature must have existed in abundance under David, to say nothing of Solomon. The previous isolation of the tribes, which still continued during the tribal sovereignty of Saul, gave place, after the conclusion of the Civil War, to a strong confederation of the whole people under the mighty and prosperous sceptre of David. The great martial successes of the King, in which the whole Nation had a glorious share, as well as the continued domination over the surrounding peoples, their tormentors of old, must have aroused a national enthusiasm such as had not been known before. Moreover, the time of Solomon was rich in new motive powers: a brilliant court; a splendid royal sanctuary, the seat of that venerable palladium, the ark of Jahweh, served by priests who were numbered amongst the principal officials of the King; manifold contact and active commerce with neighbouring States so highly cultivated as Egypt and Tyre, nay, even (through the voyages to Ophir) with the wonder-lands of the South and the East. Must not all this have impelled men, amidst the blessings of a long-continued peace, to become fully conscious of what had been so painfully won, to look back from the height they had climbed to the battles and victories which had made such an ascent possible, and to fix the still vivid recollection of them in word and writing for the generations to come?

The extent to which this was actually done cannot be strictly demonstrated. But we possess a number of monuments, against the placing of which, at least as early as Solomon's time, no valid objection can be brought. Hence it is best to discuss them here, although we do not thus deny the possibility of a later origin. Leaving aside the collections of songs already mentioned (p. 1 f.), the "Book of the Upright," which in all probability is Judahite, and the "Book of the Wars of Jahweh," we here reckon the two poetical productions, the "Blessing of Jacob" (Gen. xlix. 1-27), and the original form of the Balaam-Discourses (Num. xxiii. 7—xxiv. 19).

Under the form of predictions uttered by the dying patriarch, the so-called "Blessing of Jacob" conveys partly a bitter reproach and partly eulogies and promises of blessing to all the twelve tribes. But the fiction is not so closely adhered to as to prevent the actual standpoint of the poet amidst the tribes long-settled in Canaan from asserting itself repeatedly and frankly. This is especially seen in the reference made to certain historical events; at v. 15 and 23 ff. such events are not predicted, but *narrated* (in the so-called *Imperfectum Consecutivum*).

The sayings are in any case ancient and highly poetic, and the following reasons favour the placing of them in the age of David and Solomon. The outrage on the Shechemites by Simeon and Levi, of which a notice has also been preserved in Gen. xxxiv. seems to be still remembered pretty vividly. At all events it is still clearly known that this was the cause of the almost total destruction of the two tribes which were formerly of equal rank with the rest. But it is very strange that the poet was only aware of the curse which doomed Levi to be scattered in Israel, and says not a word about the future significance of the tribe as heir of the traditions handed down from Moses. Was this possible in an age when the descendants of the tribe of Levi had for a long time, and in high repute officiated at the Royal Sanctuary of Jerusalem? On the other hand, v. 8-12 obviously refer to David's heroic deeds and to the hegemony of Judah, founded by him. If Joseph also (as consisting of Ephraim and Manasseh) is enthusiastically extolled and blessed, this can best be understood of a time when all tribal feuds had died out and one and the same poet could equally rejoice in the fame and felicity of all. For the theory that either the saying about Judah, or that about Joseph, was subsequently added breaks down in face of the fact that the speeches were evidently twelve in number at the first. To prove the later origin of the whole, in the time of the divided kingdom, v. 23 f. has been specially appealed to as an incidental reference to the heroic defence made by the northern kingdom against the Aramæans in the ninth century. But the expression sounds much too general to prevent our thinking just as naturally of glorious fights waged in earlier times by the tribes of Joseph. The designation of Joseph as "Prince amongst his brethren" (v. 26) tells far more heavily against its being dated in the age of David and Solomon. If the word rendered "Prince" must necessarily mean "Wearer of the Diadem," in the strict sense of the expression, the reference to the Ephraimite kingdom founded by Jeroboam I. would be indisputable. But this is not absolutely certain, and the saying concerning Levi would be far more surprising in the ninth century than in the time of Solomon.

In an almost higher degree even than the "Blessing of Jacob" are the four first Balaam-Discourses pervaded with national enthusiasm, the sense of a mighty association of the people, and, above all, exultant gladness, because of the victories won and the overflowing blessings of Jahweh. The reference to David's victories and conquests at xxiv. 17 ff. is unmistakable. The religious element — which in Gen. xlix., apart from the ejaculation, v. 18, only appears in the saying concerning Joseph, v. 24 f.—comes prominently into the foreground in the Balaam-Discourses. As to the rest, if we were willing to assign merely the nucleus of these Discourses to the age of Solomon we should be taking our stand on an almost universally admitted fact. Chap. xxiii. formed in the main a portion of the old Elohistic source, chap. xxiv. 1-19, of the Jahwistic one. And since the contents of the Discourses in the two chapters, with all their divergence, exhibit striking points of contact (cf. especially xxiii. 22 and xxiv. 8), we can scarcely doubt that chaps. xxiii. and xiv. supply two different versions of the same ancient poem. An exact restoration of it is naturally impossible now, but chap. xxiv. must be nearer the original form than chap. xxi. (cf. particularly the bold figure in v. 8b).

§ 3. THE PERIOD OF THE DIVIDED MONARCHY UNTIL THE DESTRUCTION OF SAMARIA.

1. GENERAL.—THE "HERO-STORIES" OF THE BOOK OF JUDGES.—THE JERUSALEM-SOURCE IN THE SECOND BOOK OF SAMUEL.—THE "SAUL-STORIES" AND THE "DAVID-STORIES."

THE division of the kingdom, which occurred about 933, was of profound significance, not only for the external fortunes of the two halves of the kingdom, but also for the development of the literature. A vigorous beginning was made under David by the centralization of military affairs and of the government in Jerusalem, the new capital. And the measures taken by Solomon did their part in enhancing the splendour of this central point at the expense of the remainder of the kingdom. A further advance on this road would have necessarily issued in all the other tribes sinking into insignificant appendages to Judah, and all the ancient sanctuaries being eventually thrown quite into the shade by the splendour of the temple at Jerusalem. The division of the kingdom restored their former self-consciousness to the northern tribes, especially to what had now become the royal tribe of Ephraim: ancient and glorious recollections started into life again, and demanded to be put in writing for the quickening of patriotic feeling. But, above all, Jeroboam I. was careful to create centres for a national worship of Jahweh by raising the long-famous holy places of Bethel and Dan to the position of royal sanctuaries (Amos vii. 13). And thus too were provided central points where a higher culture could be developed in the midst of an honoured priesthood. In setting up the golden calves Jeroboam doubtless did but revive a form of Jahweh worship which was of old standing, but prohibited in the worship at Jerusalem. We nowhere read that this worship itself excited the indignation of an Elijah or Elisha, and their circles. At all events the dwellers in the northern kingdom boldly claimed to belong to the "People of Jahweh." Indeed, the total transfer of the ancient name of honour, Israel, to the northern kingdom, shows plainly that it considered itself the true heir, not only of the power, but also of the glory of the whole people. This is expressed in extremely drastic fashion in King Joash's fable of the thistle and the cedar on Lebanon (2 Kings xiv. 9 ff.). And the Singer of the Blessing of Moses knows of no higher aspiration for Judah than that "Jahweh may bring him back to his people" (Deut. xxxiii. 7).

Judah, in fact, with its small and sparsely populated territory was almost powerless compared with Israel. But its continuance, nay, its ever-growing significance for things spiritual, and for the history of religion, was assured by privileges which were entirely denied to the mightier Israel. We cannot, indeed, follow the current opinion which reckons a purer form of Jahweh-worship amongst the number. The belief that the holy ark was a visible representation of Jahweh must for a long time have been a grossly materialistic one in popular circles. A trace of *this* idea has been preserved in an addition to Jeremiah (iii. 16 ff.), and, unintentionally, even in the so-called Priests' Code (Lev. xvi. 2, &c.). And although King Asa interfered with his mother's idolatry (1 Kings xv. 13) this did not prevent people even in Judah from worshipping Jahweh under the form of an image. Isaiah had to declaim warmly against this error (ii. 8, 18, 20; x. 11; xxxi. 7). It must also probably be attributed to its influence that Hezekiah at length broke in pieces the brazen serpent to which "unto those days the children of Israel did burn incense" (2 Kings xviii. 4).

But in three points Judah actually had the advantage over Israel: Jerusalem, the temple of Solomon, and the uninterrupted rule of the Davidic dynasty. The greatest and most glorious memories of the people continued to be connected with the time when David, after overthrowing all surrounding foes, was enthroned in the tower of Zion and received the homage of distant kings. And the temple of Solomon was still the most splendid sanctuary that had ever been reared for the God of Israel: the holy ark which it enshrined was a monument of that great age when all Israel was led from victory to victory by Jahweh as the God of Battles. The works of art in the temple and the palace were looked on as a kind of wonder of the world. Of Solomon's throne the saying ran "There was not the like made in any kingdom" (1 Kings x. 20). And as to the stability of the dynasty and all the contributions which that can make to the external prosperity and the spiritual advancement of a people, we need only point to *one* fact. Compared with the twelve descendants of David who reigned on Zion down to 722, Israel had nine dynasties, with seventeen kings. Seven of the latter were murdered by their successors: Zimri burned himself and the palace threatened by Omri. In view of such facts we understand how the Judahite view of history would not admit the truth of the Israelite idea that the division of the kingdom was a schism of Judah from the united people. It could see nothing there but a *revolt* of Israel from Judah and the house of David (Isa. vii. 17, 1 Kings xii. 19). Connected with all this is another fact, weightier than anything hitherto mentioned. Judah alone could become the soil from which the idea might spring which has developed the strongest motive power in the religion of Israel, the expectation of the Messianic kingdom. This was chiefly thought of, at all events in the earlier times, as a renewal of the Davidic kingdom under the sceptre of one of his descendants, sent by God and specially equipped by Him: hence the continuance of the Davidic dynasty is its indispensable condition.

Before discussing the literary products of the two kingdoms it must be premised that until we are far advanced in the eighth century it is impossible to date any monument *precisely*. In most cases a latitude of a hundred years or more must be allowed. The only point we can determine with some certainty is the *sequence* of the sources which have been worked up into our present historical books. And, to judge from what we have before us, literary zeal seems to have applied itself first to historical writing. In the northern kingdom it was naturally the reminiscences of the pre-monarchic time, connected with their native soil, which seemed most worthy of record : in Judah the memories of the person and house of the great founder of the Davidic dynasty. Thus there arose in Ephraim the most ancient stratum of the narratives handed down in our Book of Judges (designated in the " Survey," at the close of this book, *H* and *H*^{1}, *i.e.*, Hero-Stories, and in the appendices, chap. xvii.-xxi., *N* and *N*.^{1}), and in Judah the oldest stratum of the narratives about David which we find in the Second Book of Samuel (designated in the " Survey " *Je*, *i.e.*, Jerusalem-Source *).

The " Hero-Stories " are exclusively occupied with the so-called Greater Judges. Ehud (iii. 15 ff.), Deborah and Barak (iv. 4 ff.), Gideon (chaps. vi.-viii., to which the history of Abimelech in chap. ix., a remarkably vivid and ancient narrative, forms a kind of appendix), Jephthah (xi.-xii. 6), and Samson (xiii.-xvi.). In their present form they are furnished with many additions and placed in a framework which is entirely foreign to them. But in almost every case the analysis can be made with certainty although the connection thus reached may not invariably be without gaps. No one will be likely to assert that in these narratives we possess all the traditions of the age of the Judges. The interest taken in

---

* Besides WELLHAUSEN's pioneer work in the Fourth Edition of Bleek's Einleitung in das Alte Testament (Berlin, 1878), p. 181 ff. (reprinted with additions in "Die Komposition des Hexateuchs und der historischen Bücher des Alten Testaments," Berlin, 1889), as well as the parts treating of this subject in STADE's Geschichte des Volks Israel (Berlin, 1881 ff.) and KITTLEL's Geschichte der Hebräer (Gotha, 1888) [English Translation, Williams and Norgate], use has been especially made of BUDDE's Die Bücher Richter und Samuel, ihre Quellen und ihr Aufbau (Giessen, 1890) in the determination and critical examination of the various strata in the historical books.

the altar of Jehovah-Shalom at Ophrah (vi. 24), and in the worship of the image of Jahweh made out of the gold taken as booty (viii. 24-27a) seems to have been the main reason why the Gideon-narratives were admitted. The following points are especially to be regarded as reliable criteria of the old narratives in contrast with the numerous glosses and expansions. The later redactors (in the " Survey" *Ri* and *R*) took the so-called Judges to be in the strict sense rulers of the *whole* nation: hence the universal concluding formula, not missing even in the case of a Samson, "and he judged (*i.e.*, ruled) Israel . . . years." On the other hand the old narratives know the so-called Judges simply as heroes who in a special calamity were moved by the Spirit of God, and placed themselves at the head of their own tribe (like Jephthah) or of a part thereof (as in the older form of the Gideon-narrative, see below) or, at most, of a few tribes similarly threatened (as Ehud, Deborah and Barak): after performing deeds of deliverance they returned to their former station, like the dukes of German antiquity. Gideon seems to have been the only exception; seeing that the dominion of his seventy sons is mentioned at ix. 2, as a matter of fact, Gideon himself must have set up a kind of tribal kingship. On the other hand the Samson-narratives leave a distinct impression that he always carried on the fight with the Philistines with his own hand. At least the narrative xv. 9 ff. shows that he had absolutely no support from his fellow-countrymen in Judah.

The religious element is by no means absent from the ancient narratives. But in contrast with the so-called theocratic pragmatism of the redactors, which explains every subjugation to the enemy by an immediately preceding idolatry, every deliverance by an immediately preceding repentance on the part of the people, and an express sending of a deliverer by Jahweh, it appears in a peculiarly primitive and sometimes grotesque form. The worship of Jahweh under an image clearly appears to give not the slightest umbrage as yet. In the ancient narrative it is evidently regarded as an honour to Gideon that he made an ephod, *i.e.*, an image of Jahweh, out of the captured gold; it is the redactor (viii. 27b) who adds the condemnatory judgment on this because it occasioned idolatry which became a snare to Gideon and his family. Moreover in the ancient narratives Jahweh does not abandon Israel to their enemies, but these to Israel (iii. 28, iv. 6 ff., 14 ff., &c.). The Spirit of Jahweh not unfrequently appears as a magical something which comes suddenly on the heroes and gives them courage and strength (vi. 34, xi. 29, xiii. 25, xiv. 6, 19, xv. 14). Samson's possession of it and of the gigantic strength which it imparts depends upon his unshorn hair; when this goes Jahweh departs with it. To this peculiar view of the Nazirate the equally mechanical one corresponds of the absolute obligatoriness of a religious vow, which compels Jephthah (xi. 30 f., and 34 ff.) to sacrifice his own daughter to Jahweh. The religious and ethical estimate of events is practically quite in the background. It is only at ix. 56 f. that the fate of Abimelech and the Shechemites is traced to divine retribution following on Jotham's curse. A glance at iii. 20 ff., iv. 18 ff. makes it impossible to deny that the narrators deemed bloody and even murderous revenge on the enemies of the people or the tribe justifiable and even praiseworthy. In accordance with this Samson expressly implores strength from Jahweh for his final deed of vengeance (xvi. 20 ff.).

In *one* narrative alone, the first narrative concerning Gideon (vi. 2, ff., to viii. 3), the religious element, the so-called theocratic pragmatism, comes out more strongly than usual. But in this very instance it can easily be shown that we have to do with a later revision of the ancient tradition. The latter has been preserved in the fragment, viii. 4 ff. (in the " Survey,"*II*[1]). The opening passage of *this* account has been cut out, but can readily be conjectured from v. 18 ff. Midianite chieftains had undertaken a raid against Northern Palestine and killed some of Gideon's brothers. Bound to execute blood-revenge, Gideon summons his clan Abiezer (on which cf. vi. 34, viii. 2) to follow him, falls on the unsuspecting Midianites in the south of the East-Jordan land, and with his own hand executes the blood-revenge on their chieftains, after severely punishing the inhabitants of Succoth and Penuel for their unbrotherly conduct. The campaign which appears in this narrative as a private undertaking of Gideon and his clan, necessitated by circumstances, became in the later narrative an affair of the whole nation. The Midianites are an abiding scourge to the land; for Jahweh has rejected Israel and abandoned them to these enemies. But Jahweh now comes in the form of "the angel of Jahweh" to entrust Gideon with the deliverance of Israel (vi. 13 ff.). But here too the supposition is adhered to that Gideon undertakes the campaign with only three hundred men of the clan of Abiezer. A still later form of the account makes thirty-two thousand men out of all Israel respond to Gideon's summons, but at vii. 2 ff. restores the agreement with the older narrative by dismissing, first twenty-two thousand, then the rest, with the exception of three hundred who lapped water with their tongue instead of conveying it to their mouth by hand.

In Judges vi.-viii. the two narratives *follow one another*, so that at viii. 4 Gideon is suddenly on this side the Jordan again, whereas he had already returned from his campaign at viii. 1 ff. But in the First Appendix (chap. xvii. f.) the parallel accounts (in the "Survey" N and N^1) are closely interwoven. The later revision knows of the exile of 722 (or 734?) whilst the original account knows only of the cessation of the worship in the temple of Shiloh.

At all events the interest taken in the worship of the image of Jahweh at Dan was the primary cause why this narrative was admitted. In the Second Supplement (chaps. xix.-xxi.) the ancient groundwork is not retained unimpaired excepting in the relatively ancient chap. xix. (which itself, however, is probably dependent on Gen. xix.). On the other hand, chaps. xx. and xxi. belong to a quite late revision in the spirit of the Priests' Code, in fact, of the Chronicler, which only here and there allows a glimpse of the phraseology of the original narrative. Amongst other reasons it is clear that the present text of chap. xx. is due to the blending of two parallel accounts from the fact that v. 3a finds its continuation in v. 14 and, yet more clearly, v. 36a in v. 47.

All the old narratives of the Book of Judges hitherto mentioned relate exclusively the deeds and fortunes of the northern tribes, and the whole must therefore have sprung from northern soil. They pass over the tribe of Judah in almost total silence. But this tribe is so much the more thoroughly treated of in that source (Je) which we first meet at 2 Sam. v. 3, 6, 8 ff., then in chap. vi., possibly, too, in the groundwork of chap. vii., certainly in the long series of narratives, chaps. ix.-xx. 22. The scene is almost exclusively Jerusalem: David and his family stand throughout at the centre of events.

As to the superior merits of this source there has long been but one opinion. It is one of the most complete, truthful and finished products of historical writing which have come to us from the Hebrews, and indeed from the whole ancient world. It shows no trace of tendency or adjustment: the succession of events flows from an inner necessity: everything lies before our eyes clear and comprehensible; specially marvellous is the characterization of the king. He is a man, and not beyond the reach of human weakness, nay, of criminal passion. The narrator is far from concealing or even palliating this. Rather does he describe, with searching psychological truthfulness, how David is driven on by the curse of the sin he has committed—first, to low cunning against his injured servant, in order, if possible, to bury his own guilt and shame in the darkness, then to crafty murder and ill-concealed rejoicing at its success, till at last his conduct is shown him in its true light by Nathan. Just as little does the narrator pass over in silence another dark point in the character of David, his weakness towards the sins of his children. This is the very doom of his house, the occasion of a whole series of painful events. He breaks forth into hot displeasure at the wrong done by Amnon to Tamar, but he cannot give his son pain. The result is that Absalom, as his sister's natural protector, takes a kind of blood-revenge on Amnon. The revolutionary plans of Absalom are evidently fostered by the thought that at the worst the father who has forgiven him for murdering his brother will not proceed to the last extremity. And David's conduct after Absalom's death is such that Joab can only bring him to his senses by hard threats. Yet in spite of all this the narrator not only knows how to win our complete sympathy and regard for this same David, but how to augment both continually. We feel ourselves involuntarily touched by the charm which he, like all real leaders, exercises on those around. The obvious contradictions in his character disappear at length in the harmonious total impression. We understand how he could be great and noble, yet at the same time stiff-necked and self-willed, sincerely devout and humble (vi. 21 f., xv. 25 f., xvi. 10 ff.) and yet full of shrewd calculation (xv. 27, 33 ff., xix. 12 ff.). But the most masterly psychological ability is shown in the delineation of his relations to his cousins, Joab and Abishai. A secret dislike of them both, arising from utter dissimilarity of character, is constantly kept down by the politic consideration that he cannot deny their merits or dispense with their services. Occasionally, however, this aversion (as at iii. 39 in another source) finds expression in sharp words (xvi. 10), and after Absalom's murder David braces himself up to the resolve that he will put Amasa in Joab's place. But he is obliged to let things take their course when Amasa is murdered by Joab, and the latter is the only person who can quell the dangerous revolt of the Benjamite Sheba. David is forced to endure to the end the man who is a rough soldier but an embodiment of the monarchical principle. He displays cold-blooded harshness towards David the *man*, when he holds this essential to the welfare of the *king*. With hard words the son's murderer forces the father, who is writhing in deepest grief for his lost one, to sit in the gate and make himself agreeable to the people, and the king, in such an hour, must reluctantly do what his subject bids.

There are, no doubt, many indications that the narrator is separated by a fairly long interval from the events which he relates. For instance, the reference to certain appellations continuing "unto this day" (vi. 8, xviii. 18; cf. also the remark, xvi. 23). It must also be asked whether such a straightforward account of distressing events in the house of David could have been circulated in Judah at a time when those concerned, or at all events a considerable number of their children and nearest relatives, were still alive. This question would at once lose its point if, as some recent critics think, the whole source was originally a part of the so-called Jahwistic history.* But assuming that this could be proved of the present form of the accounts, we should still be obliged to judge that such acquaintance with the details of the events—above all, such certainty in giving the names of almost all the actors—could not have been gained, fully a hundred years after, from popular tradition, but must have been derived from records written by one who drew from the account given by eye-witnesses, or by younger contemporaries of David. This may justify our assigning the *Je* source to the period immediately after Solomon.

The "Hero-Stories" and the "Jerusalem-Source" are followed, in order of time, by the "Histories of Saul" (*S*) in 1 Sam. ix.-xiv., and the "Histories of David" (*Da*) from 1 Sam. xvi. 14 to the conclusion of 2 Kings ii. Both contain a multitude of reliable historical traditions, but are now freely inlaid with passages taken from a quite different source (*SS*) and with redactional additions. Their fatherland can only be determined with some reserve. It is intrinsically probable that the Saul-Source is from a Benjamite, a member, therefore, of the northern kingdom, the David-Source from a Judahite. But the partizanship of the one source for Saul and of the other for David, which used to be so frequently

---

* In opposition to the attempt repeatedly made since 1830, and most recently by Cornill and Budde, to show that the patriarchal sources are prolonged into the older strata of the Books of Judges and Samuel, cf. KITTEL in the Theol. Studien u. Kritiken, 1892, p. 44 ff.

asserted, cannot really be proved. The David-Source can indeed tell of the evil spirit which fell on Saul, and drove him to fierce jealousy and even to acts of revenge. But the account nowhere manifests any hostility to Saul: Jonathan, equally with David, has to suffer through his father's spiritual gloominess (1 Sam. xx. 30 ff.). And the account of Saul's adventure with the Witch of Endor (1 Sam. xxviii.) contents itself with simply stating the facts. The admission of the Elegy, 2 Sam. i. 17 ff., as well as of the accounts in 2 Sam. ii. 4 ff. and iv. 10 ff., proves incontrovertibly that the account of Saul's defeat and suicide, 1 Sam. xxxi., is not at all meant to blacken his memory. After all, it is by no means impossible for both sources to have come from one hand, and also from an age when the verdict on the two first kings had long been purified from party feeling, and was no more disturbed by any tribal jealousy. With this it agrees that 1 Sam. xxvii. 6 (*Da*) obviously knows of several "kings of Judah." But this would not oblige us to date it much later than 900. The marked prominence of the edifying element in such passages as 1 Sam. xxiv. 10 ff. might rather be alleged in proof of the later origin of the David-Stories. Yet it is very debatable how many of these edifying speeches which we find here and at xxvi. 17 ff., are to be ascribed to a subsequent editing. It would have been impossible for the original narrator to continue as he does at 1 Sam. xxvii. 1, if he had written xxiv. 17 ff., shortly before. On the other hand, the relatively high antiquity of the Saul-Narratives is evinced by two tokens. The monarchy is a blessing from Jahweh; He Himself, at His people's cry, appointed Saul to be king and sent him to Samuel, that the Philistine oppression of Israel might be brought to an end (1 Sam. ix. 15 ff.). That is quite a different standpoint from the one occupied at 1 Sam. viii. 10, 17 ff., and in chap. xii., where the people's wish for a king is regarded as treason against Jahweh, and Samuel consequently accedes to it with the utmost reluctance. And further: according to the more recent view Samuel was ruler of the people before the election of the king, and after this was the king's guardian, informing him of Jahweh's commands (1 Sam. xv. 1 ff.), and rebuking him severely when he acted on his own account (v. 14 ff.). In the Saul-Stories, on the contrary, he is a "seer," in high repute amongst the people, and honoured by Jahweh with the duty of anointing the new king, and yet it occasionally belongs to his calling to tell a man where his asses have wandered, in return for a piece of bread, or a quarter of a shekel of silver (1 Sam. ix. 6 ff.).

2. The Beginnings of the Legal Literature: The Book of the Covenant.

All the records hitherto mentioned belonged either to the domain of poetry or to that of historiography, and showed that these departments of literature had reached a high degree of cultivation in early times. On the other hand, we seem to have the oldest record of legal ordinances—probably from the beginning of the ninth century—in the so-called "Book of the Covenant," of which we had to speak previously (p. 7 f.) in another connection. We here leave quite untouched the dispute as to which of the great Pentateuch-Sources, J or E, incorporated this code of law, and as to whether a Decalogue was issued earlier than it, occupying ourselves solely with the contents of Exod. xx. 24—xxiii. 19. It was remarked above that the present text is traversed by many glosses* and redactional additions. None the less evident is it on inspection that the original order of the statutes has been confused in various ways (especially at xxi. 37 ff.). So far, however, as the original text can still be determined it presents, as might be expected, not a legislation embracing the entire life of the people, founded on theoretical principles, but a codification of usage and wont, of customary rights, as these must develop in daily intercourse, especially among neighbours. Hence the greatest amount of space is

---

* The following passages betray themselves by the use of the plural: xxii. 20b, 21, 23, 24b, 30, xxiii. 9b, 13.

taken up by the so-called "Claims for Damages" for manslaughter, kidnapping, murder, corporal injury, theft, negligence with fire, injury to fields or cattle. But alongside this the religious and ethical point of view asserts itself, and not merely in the statutes which especially relate to worship (xx. 24, xxii. 19, 27, 29), or to the rights of male and female Hebrew slaves (xxi. 1-11), but especially in care for slaves in general (xxi. 20 f., 26 f.), strangers (xxii. 20), poor and needy (xxii. 24 ff., xxiii., 10 f.) as well as in the prohibition of witchcraft and incest (xxii. 17 f.). The Sabbath Law is based solely on the duty of humanity (xxiii. 12). But chiefly do we meet with a lofty ethical standpoint in the directions given (xxiii. 4 f.) that if occasion offer a personal enemy must be protected from harm.

We are wholly in the dark as to the circle from which all these statutes proceeded and, above all, as to the public authority by which scrupulous obedience was ensured. Yet such an authority must be assumed, otherwise there would be no meaning in the precise fixing of punishments and amends, from the punishment of death, seven times prescribed, and of the avenging on the body of the guilty person the wrong he had done (xxi. 23 ff.), down to the money-fine. But, emphatically as justice and impartiality in legal cases is insisted on (xxiii. 1 ff.), there is not a single indication as to who is authorized to pronounce sentence or to supervise the execution of the verdict. It is indeed twice ordered that, in case of a law-suit, the man is to be brought "before God," *i.e.*, to a sanctuary, once (xxi. 6), to perform a symbolic act which will have legal effect, the other time (xxii. 8), to obtain an oracle; but even in these cases nothing is said about the agents, priests for example.* With regard to the courts of

* It is a quite untenable opinion, still shared by some moderns, that in these passages the translation should not be "before God" but "before the gods" (grammatically possible, and given by Luther), and that the expression should be understood of the rulers or priests. It should rather be asked whether the expression does not come from a time when God was represented at every sanctuary by an image which was connected with the oracle. In fact, it cannot be pronounced impossible that at xxi. 6 an image is meant, placed in the house itself (at the door?).

justice, the drawing up of the indictment, the procedure, such as the examination of witnesses, and the execution of the sentence, it is evident that long-established customs are taken for granted, so that the codification was simply intended to promote greater uniformity in the decision of cases and in the penalties that were to be imposed. If the statement, 2 Chron. xvii. 9, has been derived from a genuine tradition, the establishment and promulgation of these rules of justice may have been due to Jehoshaphat of Judah. But it is also possible that they sprang from the soil of the northern kingdom.

3. The Jahwistic Historical Work.

Historical composition, as we have seen, had devoted itself in the first place to the events of the earliest period of the Kings, and also, in the northern kingdom, to the heroes of the time of the Judges. The primæval history of the people, as well as the patriarchal age, the Deliverance from Egypt by Moses and the Conquest of the Promised Land, seem to have been left to oral tradition and adaptation until at least the Solomonic period. The oldest *written* presentation of these events accessible to us is found in that splendid historical work which is usually called the Jahwistic (*J*) because of its preponderating use of the divine name Jahweh, which begins even in the history of the Creation.

On the History of Pentateuch Criticism. In this place we must limit ourselves to the following summary of the History of Pentateuch Criticism, or, in so far as the Book of Joshua comes prominently into consideration, Hexateuch Criticism,[*] a criticism which, after manifold aberrations during a space of 140 years, has at last gained a fair number of absolutely fixed results. Isolated doubts concerning the authenticity of the whole Pentateuch had already been expressed in past centuries, when Jean Astruc, of Montpellier, a devout Catholic, made the fundamental discovery that in Genesis the divine names Elohim (*i.e.*, God) and Jahweh

---

[*] But cf. below § 6, 2, last note.

alternate in a striking manner, and founded on this the hypothesis that Moses himself (Pentateuch criticism therefore by no means originated in rejection of the authenticity!) placed side by side two principal documents (*mémoires*), an Elohistic and a Jehovistic, and appended to them, in a third and fourth column, fragments from ten other documents. Our Genesis arose from the blending of these four columns. Astruc published this hypothesis at Brussels in 1753 in an anonymous work (*Conjectures sur les mémoires, dont il parait que Moyse s'est servi pour composer le livre de la Genèse;* German translation, Frankfort, 1789), but no attention was paid to him in France.

In Germany the hypothesis was first published by the *Gött. gel. Anzeigen* of September 19th, 1754: at the end of the year it was warmly opposed by J. D. Michaelis (*Relatio de libris novis*, XI. 162 ff.); but at last it was brought into repute, chiefly through Eichhorn (*Einleitung ins Alte Testament*, first at Leipzig, 1780 ff.). At all events it was in Germany that it first found a deeper scientific foundation and also, before long, a further expansion. Ilgen ("*Die Urkunden des Jerusalemischen Tempelarchivs in ihrer Urgestalt*," first vol., Halle, 1798) discovered that, besides the Jehovistic document, not one, but two independent Elohistic ones must be distinguished. Unfortunately he prejudiced this perfectly correct observation by admitting seventeen distinct documents in Genesis which he thought were to be divided amongst these three writers.

All the divers forms which Astruc's hypothesis passed through before Ilgen are usually grouped together under the title, "*Older Document Hypothesis*." They all recognize a quite external blending of several independent sources. A second stage is formed by the so-called *Fragments Hypothesis*, i.e., the derivation of the Pentateuch from a large number of separate, unconnected fragments which were afterwards united into a whole by a compiler (Vater's view, in his *Kommentar über den Pentateuch*, Halle, 1802-1805, 3 vols.). As the dispute went on, the Older Document Hypothesis underwent a modification to the effect that the Elohistic document at the foundation of the Pentateuch (the so-called "Grundschrift") was supplemented by the redactor with material from another source, the Jehovistic. But as the supplementer was eventually identified with the Jehovist this brings us to the *Supplement Hypothesis*. Prepared for by De Wette, thrown out in 1831 by

Ewald as a conjecture, expressly maintained by Bleek and Peter v. Bohlen, this hypothesis received from F. Tuch, in his "*Kommentar über die Genesis*" (Halle, 1838), a thorough scientific foundation, and, because of its great simplicity, soon obtained almost universal recognition. But after Hupfeld ("*Die Quellen der Genesis und die Art ihrer Zusammensetzung*," Berlin, 1853) had, in the first place, shown the correctness of Ilgen's distinction between two Elohistic documents, and, in the second place, had put the significance of the Jehovistic document as an independent historical work beyond all doubt, there gradually arose, on the ground of these two convictions, *all* the various forms of the "*Later Document Hypothesis.*" The peculiarity of them all is the acceptance of four originally independent main sources (namely, besides the Jehovist [better, Jahwist] and the two Elohists, the Deuteronomic writer [*D*], in the greater part of Deuteronomy). In fact the number four, as well as the special characters of these main sources, has been demonstrated by such incontrovertible reasons, and such a degree of unanimity respecting the detailed analysis of the sources has been reached amongst all competent inquirers, that the rejection of these results now can only be explained by two reasons; either from lack of acquaintance with the facts, or from a resolution, embraced once for all, not to allow any force of facts to bring about the abandonment of prejudices refuted long ago.

On the other hand, the adherents of the Later Document Hypothesis are still at variance on two points. First, as to whether the four main sources existed independently, side by side, till they were united by the redactor (whom all hold to be post-exilic), or whether the Jahwist (*J*) and the Elohist related to him (*E*) had already been blended into a whole when Deuteronomy (*D*) was united with them: in the latter case the final stage of redaction would be the union of *JED* with the other Elohist (*P*, or the Priests' Code). In our Outline, as in the Historical Tables, the second view is accepted as correct.

But, secondly—and this is far more important—the sequence of the four sources is disputed. The older critics were bound hand and foot by the prejudice that the source which stands first (Gen. i.), the Priestly Elohist, must also be the oldest. This seemed to be especially supported by the fact that (at least in Genesis) it actually forms the framework in which the united whole is fitted. Hence there are still distinguished scholars who place this document (P), if not at the head, yet (with Dillmann) after E and before J and D. Others put E and J (or J and E) at the head, but claim for P, or a part of it, priority to D. (The belief that the latter originated in the seventh century is practically unanimous.)

In opposition to all these opinions, the view was next maintained, with ever-growing emphasis, that the Priestly Elohist (P) came last (in and after the Exile), and thus represents the final stage of development within the Hexateuch. Stated first in 1833 by E. Reuss (in theses for his pupils), then propounded in 1835 simultaneously by Vatke (*Die Religion des Alten Testaments*, I., Berlin) and George (*Die älteren judischen Feste, &c.*, Berlin), this hypothesis had practically passed into oblivion when Graf, a pupil of Reuss, revived it in 1866, first with reference to the legal portions of the Priests' Writing, and afterwards including the historical. Hence it has been called the *Grafian Hypothesis*. At first it was only accepted by individual scholars, and that, as in the case of the great Dutch critic Kuenen, after the most exhaustive independent investigation. At last it has won recognition in ever-widening circles, and reached an almost undisputed sway. This is principally due to Wellhausen's brilliant demonstration (in the first vol. of his *Geschichte Israels*, Berlin, 1878 [Eng. Trans., 1885]; the later editions bear the title *Prolegomena zur Geschichte Israels*). The reasons why we concur in thinking it absolutely incontrovertible will be adduced in the further course of our Outline. For all the details on which the analysis depends, we refer to Dillmann's Commentary on the Pentateuch, which is as copious as it is reliable (*Genesis*,[6] 1892 [Eng. Trans., 1898]; *Exodus u. Leviticus*, 1880; *Numeri, Deuter., Josua*, 1886), as well as to Holzinger's *Einleitung in den Hexateuch* (Freiburg und Leipzig, 1893), at the end of which there is an outline in fourteen tables of the results reached by the most distinguished investigators. The history of Pentateuch criticism is given most completely in Westphal's *Les Sources du Pentateuque*, 1888, 1892, Paris [See also Cheyne's *Founders of Old Testament Criticism*, Lond., 1893, *Tr.*]. The reasons on which the analysis rests are more or less thoroughly discussed in all the recent works on the Introduction to the Old Testament. Special mention must be made of CORNILL (Freib. u. Leipz., 1891; 3rd and 4th Editions, 1896); ED. KÖNIG (Bonn, 1893), p. 134 ff.; DRIVER (1st Edition, Edinb., 1891; 6th Edition, 1897; Germ.

Trans. from the 5th Edition by Rothstein, Berlin, 1896). Cf. also the excellent popularly-scientific treatment of the whole problem in W. ROBERTSON SMITH, *The Old Testament in the Jewish Church* (2nd Edition, Lond., 1892), Germ. Trans. by Rothstein (*Das A. Test. Seine Entstehung und Ueberlieferung*, Freib. u. Leipz., 1894). The composite character of Genesis is shown very clearly by differences of type in *Die Genesis mit äusserer Unterscheidung der Quellenschriften übersetzt von Kautzsch und Socin* (2nd Edition, Freiburg, 1891), by differences of colour in Paul Haupt's *Sacred Books of the Old Testament* (Leipzig, beginning in 1893) : up to the present the Hebrew text of Genesis in Eight Colours, by Ball (1896), Leviticus in Two Colours, by Driver and White (1894), and Joshua in Seven Colours, by Bennett (1895), have appeared.

The Jahwist first appears in the present text at Gen. ii. 4b, but the actual beginning of his work seems to have been omitted, possibly owing to its divergence from the immediately preceding cosmogony of the so-called Priests' Code. From Gen. ii. onwards this source flows abundantly through the whole of Genesis and Exodus, and again from Num. x. 29. It is doubtful whether it is represented in Deuteronomy (beginning at chap. xxxi.) : the latest certain trace of it is in the two first chapters of the Book of Judges. It aims, therefore at supplying a history of the Israelite theocracy from the beginning of the world to the settlement of the people in the land west of the Jordan. The only legal portion which can be certainly ascribed to it is the groundwork of Exod. xxxiv. 14-26.

As to the luxuriant freshness and vividness, the charming flow in the narratives of the Jahwist, there has long been but one opinion : passages like Gen. iii. 18 f., xxiv. 44, are true models of classical Hebrew prose. And we cannot value at a lower rate the idea of God and the ethical standpoint of this source. In both respects the powerful influence everywhere betrays itself of those prophetic ideas through which the Jahwistic popular religion was gradually purged from grossly sensuous, and, in part, heathenish ideas and led on to its high destiny as the religion of the world. No doubt Jahweh is at the beginning only the God of Israel, in the primæval and patriarchal periods the God of the chosen families from which the people of Israel is to proceed. To them belongs His special protection and care. But Jahweh is, therefore, at the same time Lord and Judge of all the world. He destroys the degenerate human race of the first age with the Flood; He punishes also with annihilation the unparalleled wickedness of the dwellers in Sodom and Gomorrah. He makes Pharaoh feel His power, and thus compels him to set His people free. If there are traces of a much narrower idea of God, one, in fact, which can only be understood as a remnant of antique mythological views (as Gen. vi. 1 ff., xxxii. 25 ff.), this only shows, first, how far the Jahwist is from mechanical subjection to a carefully elaborated theological system. Further, the boldest ascription of human qualities to God, as in Gen. ii. and iii., and pre-eminently, in chap. xviii., is always so made as to leave unimpaired the impression of divine majesty and dignity. That God becomes visible to man, directly interposing everywhere, serves not merely to give dramatic movement to the description, but chiefly to enhance the impression that Jahweh is a living and therefore a life-giving personality, who demands joyful faith and full surrender. To secure this end genuine religious feeling cannot dispense with the so-called anthropopathisms and anthropomorphisms. It was reserved to a much later age, versed in theological abstractions, to take offence at this ascription of human qualities to God and get rid of it from the old narratives as best it could, but at the same time to destroy the charm which they exercise over an unprejudiced religious mind.

As the idea of God, so also the ethical views of our source are not to be measured by the strictest standard of Christian ethics. It is an utter mistake to charge the Jahwist with taking pleasure in Jacob's deceiving Esau (the Israelite against the hated Aramæan!). On the contrary, he designates Jacob's conduct as guile (Gen. xxvii. 35), and the part which Esau plays in chap. xxxiii. is far more honourable than Jacob's.

The power of the popular customs which still prevailed in the Jahwist's day explains some other points which may seem offensive to us. This especially applies to concubinage and all its consequences. But scandals still remain which cannot be got rid of by the argument that the Jahwist contented himself with an objective narrative and deemed it unnecessary to pronounce an express condemnation. Amongst these we reckon the risk to which Sarah (Gen. xii.) and Rebekah (chap. xxvi.) were exposed by the false statements of their husbands, the out-manœuvring of Laban (type of the hated Aramæan) by the crafty devices of Jacob (Gen. xxx. 37 ff.), and, not less, the robbing of the Egyptians (Exod. xii. 36). The outwitting of foreigners, under certain circumstances, is even counted a clear right. But after all, what are all these details compared with the *general impression* made on us by the unpretentious piety and the moral earnestness of the actors, and therefore of the narrator himself! "I am not worthy of all the benefits and of all the truth which Thou hast shown unto Thy servant." This confession of Jacob (Gen. xxxii. 11) is obviously looked upon as a confession of the people which bears his name. And if the Jahwist thinks of sacrifices and offerings as having been from the beginning of the world the natural expression of a devout disposition, and elsewhere treats the consulting of the divine oracle as a primitive custom (xxv. 22), yet the earliest sacrifice of all teaches that it is the disposition and not the offering which counts, and it is not offerings or other works, but believing reliance on the word of Jahweh which is counted to Abraham for righteousness.

Up to this point we have spoken of the Jahwistic source as a homogeneous work. But a closer examination of its contents showed long ago that here also we have to do with various strata, and therefore with the work of a Jahwistic school. The narrator of Genesis iv. 16-24 knows of no Deluge; for he presupposes that all shepherds, musicians, and smiths are descended in an uninterrupted series from the sons of Lamech. At Gen. ix. 20 ff. the sons of Noah, who still dwell with him in one tent, are called in the original text

Shem, Japhet, and Canaan; and these names here stand in a different, far stricter sense, than Shem, Ham, and Japhet elsewhere. At Gen. xi. 1-9 the dispersion of mankind over the earth is not connected, as in chap. x., with their derivation from the different sons of Noah, but with the confusion of tongues which God decreed. All this warrants our discriminating between an older and a later form of J (J^1 and J^2).* Both relate the primæval history from the standpoint of a history of redemption, but J^1 as the history of Israel and without presupposing the Flood, J^2 as the primæval history of mankind and interweaving the account of the Flood. The latter, although carefully purged from all mythological additions, evinces a closer acquaintance with the Babylonian primæval history and thus shows that J^2 is of later origin than the specifically Hebrew tradition of J^1 (which has a strong mythological colouring at Gen. vi. 1 ff.). By far the greater portion of the remaining matter (from Gen. xii. onwards) must have belonged to J^1. Subsequently, probably in the eighth century, a Judahite hand (J^3) blended the two recensions, so as to form the Jahwist as we now have him in the Pentateuch.

The adoption of this view solves also in the simplest manner the problem as to the Jahwist's native land. In all the patriarchal narratives the utmost care is taken to account for the consecration of the ancient holy places by appearances of Jahweh and special experiences of the patriarchs. But the specifically Israelite sanctuaries also belong to these holy places. How, then, could it be understood that a Judahite, at a time when the temple of Solomon was already in existence, brought the sanctity of Shechem, Bethel, and Peniel into the prominence they have at Gen. xii. 6, xxviii. 13 ff., and xxxii. 31 ff.? But, on the other side, the memory of Abraham and perhaps of Jacob also is almost exclusively associated with Hebron; in the Joseph-Histories it is Judah (not Reuben, as in E) who is spokesman for the brethren; at Exod. xxxii. 1 ff. there is in all probability a Judahite condemnation of the Ephraimite bull-worship. All these apparent contradictions

---

* On this compare the pioneer investigations of Budde, *Die Biblische Urgeschichte* (Gen. i.-xii. 5). Giessen, 1883.

disappear of themselves if we see in J^2 (to say nothing of J^3) a Judahite recension of the *Ephraimite* original which J^1 supplied.

To determine more precisely the time when the Jahwistic source arose we must naturally begin with J^1. The age of Solomon suggests itself as the earlier limit, for the bond-service of the Canaanites, presupposed at Gen. ix. 25 f. (cf. also xii. 6 and xiii. 7), is traced back to that age at 1 Kings ix. 21. Gen. x. 11 ff. has also been adduced as indicating the earlier limit, where the narrator knows Kalchu (Kelach) which Assurnasirhabal has already rebuilt (883 ff.) and made into a royal city, but does not know Sargon's buildings in North Nineveh (722 ff.). But it is questionable whether Gen. x. 8 ff. belongs to J^1. Just as little certainty can be obtained from xxvii. 40. If the whole verse belonged to J^1 it would no doubt testify to his acquaintance with the revolt of the Edomites under Joram (about 845). But the second (prosaic!) half of the verse quite gives the impression of an addition to the poetic utterance which (like xxv. 23) knows only of Edom's *servitude*.

If all this indicates that J^1 belongs to the interval between 950 and 850, certain traces are not lacking of a more recent age than that of Solomon. The existence of the northern kingdom under kings of the tribe of Ephraim is undoubtedly presupposed by the glorification of Joseph in the whole of the Joseph-Stories, and yet more clearly by the preference of the younger Ephraim to Manasseh (Gen. xlviii. 17 ff.). But the influence of prophetic ideas, everywhere traceable and already brought out by us, is the strongest evidence for the ninth century. The time of the religious war which Elijah waged against Baal seems to be left behind, the worship of Jahweh to be unopposed, indeed to be in its prime. Joy in Him resounds everywhere, but not less joy in the blessings which Jahweh has poured on His people, and in the beautiful land which He has given them. The struggles which had to be gone through to win these lie in the far background. Settled conditions, milder manners, have gained the upper hand. Intercourse with neighbouring tribes is almost without exception of a peaceful kind; joyous consciousness of the great position they have won is not spoiled by any misleading national conceit, but is associated with an elevating anticipation that Israel is intended by its God for something greater than an honourable political position in the world of nations. A precise determination of place, time and author is naturally impossible. But if we are to venture on a conjecture there is most to be said for about 855. The commanding position which Omri had won for Israel was then unimpaired. The attack of the Aramæans was victoriously repelled at Samaria and then at Aphek, and the extremely friendly relations with Jehoshaphat of Judah might seem to guarantee a long continuance of these favourable conditions.

4. OTHER RELICS OF THE LITERATURE OF THE 9TH AND 8TH CENTURIES (1 SAM. iv. 1 ff.).—"THE BLESSING OF MOSES."—THE MIRROR OF THE PROPHETS.—1 KINGS xx. 22, &c.

The other, fairly extensive remains of the historiography and poetry of the ninth and eighth centuries, preserved to us in the Pentateuch, and especially in the Books of Samuel and Kings, all seem, like the groundwork of the Jahwistic source, to have sprung from the soil of the northern kingdom. Thus the narrative of the loss and recovery of the holy ark (1 Sam. iv. 1b–vii. 1, designated E in the "Survey"), perhaps a fragment of a history of the sanctuary at Shiloh. The age of the narrative is specially shown by the idea of the holy ark and the magical powers hidden in it which meets us at iv. 6 ff., v. 3 ff., vi. 19 ff. The so-called "Blessing of Moses" (Deut. xxxiii.) is also unquestionably Ephraimite. This is clear from the extraordinarily emphatic glorification of Joseph, v. 13 ff., nothing being left for Judah but the wish that he may be reunited to the rest of the people and freed from his oppressors. The consciousness of might and victory which shines forth from v. 17, and especially from the close, v. 26 ff., is perhaps explained by Joash's victories over Benhadad II. (798 ff.) which put an end to the long oppression of Israel by the Aramaeans of Damascus. The sentences devoted to Levi prove that the Blessing originated in priestly circles. In whatever way we may account for the difficult introductory words a strong consciousness is clearly expressed in v. 10 f. of the importance of the high office and also of the close union and power of the priestly order in spite of all its enemies and haters. It is impossible to determine whether the "Blessing of Moses" has been preserved as a portion of a larger work (the older Elohistic Pentateuch source?) or was first inserted by one of the later redactors.

On the other hand the Prophetical Stories concerning Elijah which we now read in 1 Kings xvii.-xix., xxi. (designated Pr in the "Survey"), usually grouped with the somewhat later Elisha-Stories (Pr^2), in 2 Kings ii.; iv. 1-6, 23; viii. 1-15; xiii. 14-21, under the title "Mirror of the Prophets," must have sprung from a special source. The beginning has not been preserved: Elijah comes on the scene at 1 Kings xvii. without any introduction. Moreover chap. xviii. shows that some account had been previously given of the bloody persecution of Jahweh's prophets by Ahab's consort, Jezebel. But if we have only an excerpt from the whole, and that not free from legendary additions, we have still a right to conclude that our Elijah-Stories are an important monument of that great religious conflict which threatened for a while to end in the victory, or, at least, the strong predominance of Baal-worship in Israel. Not as though a total rejection of Jahweh had been contemplated. Neither can Ahab, whose three children bore names compounded with Jah[weh] (cf. too the rôle which he plays, 1 Kings xxii.), have been a despiser of Jahweh, nor can the people have broken absolutely with their whole past. But the "halting on both sides" (xviii. 21) was itself bad enough. Whilst Jahweh was being worshipped, and yet they would not break with Baal, whom they regarded as the bestower of all the gifts of the fruitful land (cf. Hosea ii. 7), they were dragging Jahweh down into Baal's realm and thus closing the way against the greatest and weightiest of all prophetic ideas, the idea that Jahweh is the sole God, or at all events that His might and glory far surpass all the heathen gods. And the great zealot for this truth, who, amongst all the figures of the Old Covenant, has found his equal only in Moses, hardly in Samuel, who, therefore, according to Mal. iii. 23, was expected by a later age as the forerunner of the Day of Jahweh, has found in the narrator of 1 Kings xvii. ff. an exponent worthy of himself. The mystery of Elijah's person, his lightning-like appearance and disappearance, the magnificent severity of his speeches, and the energy of his action—all this is brought before us with such marvellous plastic force and dramatic vividness as to create at every step the impression of an extraordinary personalty.

Compared with the Elijah-Stories the Elisha ones, which begin at 2 Kings ii., show less descriptive power. The legendary element takes up an almost larger space (cf. especially ii. 8, 24 ; vi. 8 ff. ; xiii. 20 f.), and some sections appear to be due to imitation of the corresponding Elijah-narratives. Yet these portions also give us many a valuable glimpse of the religious and political circumstances of that age, and are therefore a historical source of exceeding value.

This is even truer of the approximately contemporaneous narratives of the time of Ahab, Joram, and Jehu, in 1 Kings xx., xxii., 2 Kings iii. (?), vi. 24-vii. 17, and (with all sorts of additions) chapters ix. and x. All these pieces show a good acquaintance with details of the events which happened about two generations before, and are able to narrate them with great clearness and vividness. In all probability they are portions of a larger historical work: doubtless we owe their admission into the Book of Kings to the fact that some kind of religious interest attaches to them all. Thus 1 Kings xx. (apart from the prophetical sayings subsequently interwoven) is a memorial of the fact that Jahweh, the god of the hills (v. 23), can also conquer with His people in the plains. In chap. xxii., 2 Kings iii. and vi., 24 ff., prophets play a leading part: in chaps. ix. and x. it is told how Jehu, anointed at Elisha's bidding, fulfilled Elijah's threat against the house of Ahab, and at the same time made a complete end of the Baal-worship in Israel.

5. THE HISTORICAL WORK OF THE OLDER ELOHIST.—THE MORE RECENT BIOGRAPHIES OF SAMUEL AND SAUL.

Ephraimite historiography turns once more to the days of grey antiquity. Somewhere about the middle of the eighth century arose the second of the great Pentateuch sources, which is usually called the Elohistic (E), because of its habitual use of the divine name Elohim (*i.e.*, God). In the Survey of the History of Pentateuch Criticism, we have already mentioned (p. 33 f.) that this source, which in our present Pentateuch is only represented by extracts, was but gradually distinguished from the totally unlike priestly Elohist, who also, up to Exod. vi., avoids the divine name Jahweh. The first certain trace of the source *E* is met at Gen. xv. 5, in the history of Abraham. Hence it seems not to have contained a history of primæval times corresponding to the Jahwistic pieces in Gen. i.-xi. On the other hand, it must have run in almost unbroken parallelism with the Jahwist in the patriarchal histories, the history of the Exodus and of the Conquest of Canaan. This is evident from the review given in the words of this source at Joshua xxiv., which takes in the entire period from the immigration of Abraham to the death of Joshua. This work, therefore, also aimed at giving a history of the preparation for and founding of the Israelite theocracy. We have already been obliged (p. 27) to state that it is at least unlikely that its description extended also over the times of the Judges and the earlier Kings.

Its *Ephraimite* origin has long been universally admitted. In fact, every other view is excluded by the striking prominence into which it brings the great Israelite sanctuaries, especially the holy stone of Bethel, by the part Reuben plays as spokesman for the brothers, and by much else. On the other hand, it is disputable whether *E* originated after the Jahwist or was not rather before him. The latter view has been supported by his greater wealth of names and details which have vanished elsewhere. But there are very weighty arguments in favour of the priority of the Jahwist, and the dating *E* not earlier than the middle of the eighth century. Both the idea of God and the ethical standpoint of *E* are far more due to reflection than the Jahwist's. The almost entire avoidance of the name Jahweh is enough to prove this: it forcibly reminds us of the later prohibition of the utterance of this name. And, certainly, it is not by accident that God does not, in this source, as in the Jahwist, hold personal intercourse with men, but calls to them from heaven (Gen. xxi. 17, xxii. 11), or makes use of the mediation of an angel (xxviii. 12). The way in which Abraham is cleared from the reproach of falsehood, xx. 12, and of harshness towards Hagar and Ishmael, xxi. 11 ff., above all that in which at xxxi. 6 ff. Jacob's cheating Laban is transformed into an overreaching of Jacob by Laban, testifies clearly to an endeavour to get rid of the ethical offence taken at the older form of the tradition with which the narrator himself was well acquainted. Nor is it mere fancy that misses from this source not only the flowing, energetic style, but also the patriotic and religious enthusiasm of the Jahwist, and finds, instead of these, a subdued tone and anxious disposition. No doubt this is a *prophetical* historiography, as truly as the Jahwist's is. But, on the whole, it no longer conveys the impression of a triumphant outlook on a glorious future, but rather that of a retrospect on a bygone history, in which were many gloomy experiences. Thus, very especially, all through the concluding chapter, Joshua xxiv., this sentence resounds, " Perhaps there is yet time to avert destruction by sincerely giving up idolatry and turning wholly to Jahweh ": and the people, at Joshua's earnest exhortation, vows to do this. But Joshua himself cannot quite believe it. The gulf between Jahweh's unapproachable holiness and the people's evil disposition is too vast to allow him to hope that the deep wounds will be healed. The people's declaration that they will serve Jahweh alone becomes eventually nothing but a "witness against themselves."

When we remember that this work was evidently transplanted at an early date to Judahite soil, and naturally underwent revision there, till at last it was blended as a whole with the Jahwist, the fact is at once explained that secondary portions were in course of time attached to this source, so that we can speak of an Elohistic as well as a Jahwistic school.

It is to the last decades of the kingdom of Israel that the biography of Samuel and Saul also belongs, which is preserved in 1 Sam. i.-iii., viii., x. 17-24, xv., xvii., and (in many ways inlaid with other elements) chap. xviii. f., xxi. f., then chap. xxvi. last, probably 2 Sam. i. 6 ff. In the "Survey" we call it SS. We have indicated above (p. 28 f.) how sharply the standpoint of this source is distinguished from the older Samuel and Saul-Stories. The kingdom is in no sense a blessing, but a curse to the people, for the longing after it amounts to a rejection of Jahweh, and, notwithstanding his serious warning (1 Sam. viii. 10 ff., x. 17 ff.), it is extorted from the seer who has hitherto ruled the people in God's stead. The very first king fully justified the evil forebodings which might be cherished concerning the kingdom. Alongside this theological pragmatism, such an adherence is elsewhere found to the genuinely popular elaboration and transformation of the older historical tradition (1 Sam. xvii. is a thoroughly classical example!) as to justify the verdict that in this description traditionary elements of manifold kinds are united into a whole, and partly subjected to a criticism from something like Hosea's standpoint. We can only venture, with all possible reserve, on the conjecture that the completion of this source was connected with the redaction of the so-called "Pre-Deuteronomic Book of Judges," which was produced by the blending of the old Ephraimite Hero-Stories (see above, p. 21 f.), and the indubitably far more recent enumeration of the so-called "Minor Judges" (designated ri in the "Survey").

6. General Remarks on Prophetism.

All these historical works, though in divers ways, were chiefly meant to promote the cultivation of the religious life in Israel. But, meanwhile, another champion had come upon the scene, who pursued the same end by a direct road and with far more effectual means—literary prophecy.

It is admitted that there are manifold analogies to Hebrew prophetism in other religions, and that not merely on Semitic soil. The Greeks and Romans also were acquainted with male and female seers, who were taken possession of by their god, spoke in his name, and gave information about the present and the future, things public and private. But the peculiarity of Israelite prophecy is that it completely detached itself from its initial amalgamation with soothsaying, and gave itself entirely to the service of religion—more precisely, the true prophets of God were called and equipped by their God exclusively for this service.

In the older period we find a double form of prophecy. The one is closely connected with the priesthood. For it is their business also, in answer to inquiries on all possible occasions, to give "direction" (tōrāh): but the prophet does not employ external means, as the priests use the image of God (ēphōd) with the Urim and Thummim; he speaks simply by the power of the Spirit who animates him. But this does not exclude the prophet's spontaneously declaring a word of God. When Samuel is asked he can tell that Kish's lost asses have returned, but at the same time he has a word of God in readiness for the inquirer. The same Abijah of Shiloh from whom Jeroboam's consort (1 Kings xiv.) hopes to get an opinion about her sick son for ten loaves and cracknels and a cruse of honey had aforetime, by a symbolical act and words accompanying it, foretold to Jeroboam that he should be king (xi. 29 ff.). At 2 Kings iv. 43 it is taken for granted that on Sabbaths and new moons people were accustomed to inquire about private affairs, even of an Elijah. Hence we must believe that "the prophet" Nathan also, and Gad, David's "seer," from whom we happen only to have divine utterances, given spontaneously, practised as a calling the giving of "directions" in answer to inquiries. Down to Ezekiel's time such inquiries from the prophets are not lacking: the only difference is that in these later times the questions do not relate to private affairs but to the public weal or religious interests.

Alongside that form of prophecy which we have now mentioned, there moves another which in all probability sprang from Canaanite soil but also attained importance in Israel. It is that state of inspiration which seized with supernatural force on single worshippers of Jahweh or, by preference, on crowds of them and so impelled them to ecstatic words and deeds as to drag even the onlookers through their example into similar conduct. The oldest notice of this kind must be that at 1 Sam. x. 5 ff. and 10 ff. Far more powerfully is one of these occurrences depicted at xix. 18 ff., where even Samuel is drawn in. According to Num. xi. 24 ff. (J) something similar happened once, during the journey through the Desert. Echoes from the time of the Kings are found at 2 Kings iii. 15, according to which passage Elisha was usually thrown into a state of inspiration by the playing of a harp, and ix. 11, where Jehu's officers laconically designate the disciple of the prophets whom Elisha had sent as a "mad fellow." We may remark, in passing, that the "sons of the prophets" (see below!) who were gathered round Elijah and Elisha are, however, not to be put in parallelism with those "Jahweh-excited" crowds of the time of Samuel.

The designation of the prophets as *nābī* (pl. *nebīīm*), which afterwards became the usual one, evidently belonged at first to these enthusiasts. The word strictly signifies a caller, more precisely one who in holy ecstasy utters cries, perhaps even inarticulate sounds. The verb derived from the noun (*hithnabbēh*) afterwards meant simply "to predict," but at 1 Sam. x. 5 ff. it evidently continues to import "acting ecstatically." As was originally the case with the Greek word *prophētēs*, the idea of foretelling had at first nothing to do with it.

At 1 Sam. ix. 9 we are expressly told that in earlier times prophets of the class we first mentioned were not called *nebīīm* but "seers." With this it agrees that Amos (vii. 14) deprecates being looked on as a prophet (*nābī*) or a "son of the prophets," i.e., according to Hebrew usage, a member of the prophetic guild. The word obviously retains a bad connotation: it reminds men of the days when prophecy was in many ways associated with soothsaying, and prediction with divination. The common people certainly never distinguished between the two. It is thus clear how *nabi* at last could make its way into universal use as the name, nay the name of honour, of God's true prophets. The original meaning passed away. The *nabi* is "the speaker," who *speaks* at God's bidding, but solemnly, not ecstatically. Thus the word can finally denote also the spokesman for another man (Exod. vii. 1; cf. iv. 16, where, for *nabi*, is simply "mouth"), or, quite generally, God's instruments chosen for the good of the theocracy (Deut. xxxiv. 10; cf. xviii. 18), and, still more generally, God's confidants and favourites (Gen. xx. 7; Ps. cv. 15).

Where Jahweh-prophetism reaches its highest point it always presupposes that the prophet has been directly and expressly called, although this may not have been expressly stated concerning each one. This calling is not confined to a special rank or a special culture or a fixed age or even to the male sex. Beside the priests Jeremiah and Ezekiel stands Amos, the shepherd of Tekoa; beside the long series of prophets the prophetesses Huldah and Noadiah. The Spirit of God, in whose might the prophet speaks, sometimes appears to be given for a special occasion and end, perhaps when the prophet has at first had no counsel to give and has been waiting awhile (cf. the remarkable cases Jer. xxviii. and xlii. 4 ff.), sometimes as the result of that gift of the Spirit which was bestowed when God called the prophet, which made him a "man of the Spirit [of God]" (Hosea ix. 5). But as the possession of the Spirit does not depend on the prophet's will so is His operation on the prophet absolutely irresistible. As the lion's roar makes the bravest shudder involuntarily so does the voice of Jahweh compel him to prophesy whom He has called (Amos iii. 8). And if he would attempt to keep to himself the word of Jahweh it would become "a burning fire within him" which he could never endure (Jer. xx. 9). These and other testimonies of the prophets allow of no twisting and distorting, although the manner in which the Spirit is imparted, the process of the prophetic "vision" may even remain a mystery. The inspiration of the prophets is the heart of the Old Testament Revelation; their whole appearance is the strongest guarantee of the choice and training of Israel as a special arrangement of God's, as the beginning of His saving ways towards mankind.

When we consider it carefully there is but a relative justification for the common distinction between prophets of deed (as Elijah and Elisha) and prophets of word (*i.e.*, especially of the written word). The manner in which Isaiah (vii. 3 ff.) confronts King Ahaz or even a Shebna (xxii. 15 ff.) or that in which Jeremiah faces the kings, princes, priests and the whole people of his day, also deserves to be called "deed." Moreover the literary prophets do not dispense with symbolical actions, although in the earlier period they occur but rarely (in Isaiah only in chap. xx.) and in a very simple and easily understood form, whereas subsequently (especially in Ezek. iv. f.) they are found, in part, in such a complicated form that they can only be understood as the literary expression of didactic thoughts. Yet, with all this, the main form of prophetic activity, at least in the pre-exilic period, is the spoken word, whether in the shape of direct exhortation and threatening (as, *e.g.*, Isa. i.) or of parable (as Isa. v., xxviii. 23 ff.). In the latter case a more or less complete interpretation is not excluded. But, for the rest, it may be confidently believed that our extant oracles of the pre-exilic time rest mainly on a later, though very free, record of speeches which were actually delivered. As we learn from Jer. xxxvi. 1 ff., Jeremiah did not get Baruch to write out all the words of God which had come to him since the days of Josiah till after thirty-three years of activity. On the other hand the prophets of the Exile were naturally led to do their work rather by writing. It is characteristic of this that Vision, the form of God's Revelation which is found but rarely in the older prophets (in Isaiah, *e.g.*, only chap. vi.), and then in lofty simplicity, is now a matter of complicated artistic elaboration (especially Ezek. i.). In Zechariah's Night Visions (i. 7–v. 9) it appears indeed as the only form of representation.

7. THE MOST ANCIENT LITERARY PROPHETS.—ISA. XV. f., AMOS, HOSEA.

Our oldest example of literary prophecy must be Isa. xv.-xvi. 12, a piece from an unknown hand which the prophet Isaiah designates as spoken "once" (or "long ago") and now (xvi. 14) supplies with the renewed announcement that it shall speedily be fulfilled. The original situation is obviously this: The Moabites, reduced to severe distress by the irruption of an enemy from the North (probably Jeroboam II. of Israel), resort to Judah for protection in their extreme need, but are repulsed by the latter. The way in which they sue for Judah's favour at xvi. 5, as well as the answer in v. 6, betrays the authorship of a Judahite prophet, and with this the evident fact would very well agree that Moab is deeply commiserated on account of devastation inflicted *by the Israelites*. If the prophecy in these chapters struggles in a striking fashion with the form in which it is clad, this cannot be explained by saying that we have it here in the very moment of its endeavours after a suitable form. Poetry had long before reached a height which would have enabled it to provide suitable forms for such material. We must consequently ascribe it rather to a peculiarity of this individual prophet (to say nothing of the great corruption of the text).

The first literary prophet whose date we can fix with some

certainty is Amos. True, we know nothing more about his person than what we are told in the title of his book, and in the historical episode, vii. 10 ff., viz., that he was a cowherd and sycomore-fig grower at Tekoa, which doubtless is identical with the present *Taqûa'*, two hours south of Bethlehem; that Jahweh sent him from the herd as a prophet against His people Israel, and that he accordingly appeared in the chief sanctuary of Israel at Bethel, preaching repentance, till Amaziah, the chief priest of Bethel, accused him to Jeroboam of threatening Israel with exile and Jeroboam with death by the sword. The King's reply is not reported, but is probably contained in Amaziah's words to the seer, bidding him fly at once to Judah. Obviously they wanted to get rid as soon as possible of the unwelcome preacher of repentance, but shrank from violence or bloodshed. Amos answers fearlessly by pointing to his Divine commission. Yet there can be no doubt that he was obliged to comply with Amaziah's strict order, and, returning to Judah, drew up there the book which has been preserved to us. The date given in the title, "Two Years before the Earthquake," shows that several years elapsed before he did this. Zech. xiv. 5 proves that this earthquake happened in the time of Uzziah, the contemporary of Jeroboam II. From vi. 14 it appears that Israel was once more in possession of the entire East-Jordan land, and therefore that Jeroboam II. had already waged his successful wars. According to all this we must place the appearance of Amos about 760.

Jerome's description of the seer of Tekoa as *imperitus sermone* (unskilful in speech) is evidently a hasty conclusion from his rural occupation, perhaps also from five or six examples of unusual orthography. Far more correctly have the oracles of Amos been recently designated as a model of good style and vivid language, and admiration been felt at the abundant imagery which he had at command, as well as at his breadth of view. But the epoch-making thoughts which Amos uttered are more important than these external features. Not as though he had been the first to demand justice and righteousness as the most pleasing manifestation of the religious disposition in the sight of God. It would have been impossible for him to put this with such earnestness and emphasis if it had been an entirely new thing for the people. But it was a new thought that the terrible severity of the "Day of Jahweh," which the people impatiently longed for as a day of judgment on its foreign foes, would be turned mainly against the sinners amongst themselves. It was a new thought that the holiness of God, everywhere and under all circumstances, must triumph over injustice and wickedness, as amongst foreign nations (i. 3 ff.), so especially in Israel itself. Indeed, that holiness of God which they had presumptuously provoked does not shrink from the extremest measures conceivable. In opposition to the popular idea that the national God must needs interpose at the decisive moment for His people and land, in order to vindicate His own honour, the prophet announces that Jahweh will make use of the enemies of the people for its destruction. Though it perish Jahweh will remain and His will be executed. Thus is the way prepared for an altogether new, infinitely higher, view of Jahweh and of His relation to Israel and the other nations as well.

Both in time and in contents the prophecy of Hosea attaches itself to Amos. As to his person we know positively nothing. According to the statement at i. 1, which is due to some redactor, he prophesied under Jeroboam II., and it is a fact that at i. 4 the continued existence of the dynasty of Jehu is assumed. This ended with Zechariah's half-year's reign about 743. But according to vii. 7, viii. 4, x. 3, xiii. 10, Hosea is also aware of the swift changes of kings after Jeroboam's death and Menahem's introduction of the Assyrians (v. 13, vii. 11, viii. 9, xiv. 4). There is no trace of anything later: in particular, Hosea knows nothing about the league of the Aramæans and Israelites against Judah. Hence the other statement of i. 1, that he worked under Hezekiah, cannot be maintained. On the contrary, chaps. i.-iii. belong to the time before 743, chaps. iv.-xiv. to the time before 736.

All the contents of his predictions, to say nothing of vii. 5, when he speaks of the kings of Israel as "our kings," show that he belonged to the northern kingdom. It is for *his* people that he must feel deepest anxiety of soul, whose sins stir him to holy wrath, on behalf of whom, in spite of everything, he hopes God's mercy even in the latest hour (xi. 8 ff., xiv. 2 ff.). And thus his speech continually alternates between fear and hope, reproach and consolation, with no strict consecution of thoughts, frequently a sob rather than a speech, and in many points (partly owing to textual corruptions) hard to explain. The old dispute as to whether we are to recognize actual experiences of the prophet in the events of chaps. i.-iii., or a mere literary clothing of prophetic thoughts, must doubtless be answered in favour of the first view. Light came afterwards to Hosea, as to Jeremiah (xxxii. 8), showing him that certain events of his life were due to a special appointment of God. The unfaithfulness of his wife, and his receiving her back again by God's direction, was to serve as a picture of the people's great guilt and of that pitying love of God which in spite of all endured to the end.

8. Isaiah.—Micah.

If we have become acquainted in the Book of Amos with a monument of Judahite prophetic activity on foreign soil it meets us now in Isaiah on its own ground and in such surprising greatness, that neither before nor after can we name its equal in the realm of the Old Testament. Nor is it merely those famous predictions in chaps. ix. and xi., those pillars of the Messianic hope during more than seven centuries, that justify Isaiah's being called the Evangelist or even the king of the Prophets. The time in which he was placed was one of endless struggles and severest dangers. But at all times he knows only of one standard by which to interpret the signs of the times, of one way leading to deliverance and peace, trust in his God, firm as a rock, and inviolable obedience to His holy will. He sees Aram and Israel advance, leagued against the far weaker Judah; this excites in him no fear, Little-Faith alone would despair "because of these two smoking stumps of fire-brands." He sees them rendered innocuous by the Assyrians' approach, but in this he beholds no deliverance for Judah. For the unbelief of Ahaz had summoned the Assyrians, to his own condemnation. He sees Samaria, "the proud crown of the drunkards of Ephraim," fall, but her fate is to him nothing but a sign of the judgment which Judah also will not be able to escape. Yet with all this the prophet is immovably certain that Assyria is simply "a rod of anger and staff of indignation in the hand" of Jahweh. If it imagines that it can act out of the fullness of its own might—can destroy at its pleasure when Jahweh meant it only to chastise—this is as foolish as if "the axe were to boast itself against him that heweth therewith, or the saw to magnify itself against him that worketh it" (x. 15). And the foolishness of those who would thwart God's world-plan by the cleverest carnal means, especially by leagues with Egypt and other nations, seems to the prophet just as great. As Jahweh Himself awaits His hour and lets things proceed to an extreme, till He "lops the boughs with terror, cuts down the thickest of the forest with iron and brings Lebanon (the Assyrian army) low" (x. 33 f.), so is it Judah's part to wait patiently till the yoke of its burden is removed and the staff of the oppressor broken. Even when the ferment began in the whole of Western Asia, after the death of Sargon (705), and everyone believed the hour of freedom had come, and even a Hezekiah allowed himself to be hurried into premature action, Isaiah adhered immovably to his word: not from Pharaoh, not from Egypt, can help come, but "in returning and rest shall ye be saved, in quietness and confidence shall be your strength" (xxx. 15). And *he* held fast to this confidence even when Sennacherib was close to Jerusalem and the surrounding country was terribly laid waste, and Hezekiah had vainly hoped at least to avert the surrender of the capital by paying an immense tribute. Whilst the king rends his clothes and deems everything lost, Isaiah has naught but contempt and scorn for the Assyrians' onset. And his faith wins the day. The Assyrian host is wasted by the pestilence; prophecy celebrates its greatest triumph.

But the relation of Judah to Assyria is only a fragment of that world of thoughts in which the prophet moves. Along with it his eagle glance takes in the present circumstances of the people, the relaxation of justice under the rule of women and boys, the far future, too, where "Jahweh has removed men far away and the desolation has been great in the midst of the land," where the rescued tenth is again given up to destruction, till at last nothing remains of the fallen oak except its stump—the holy seed of the new Israel (vi. 11 ff.).

How eloquent, too, are the words in which his lofty thoughts are everywhere expressed! How impressively the prophet can utter his anger in the very first speech, how touchingly he can mourn over the city which had formerly been so faithful, with what terrible earnestness can he threaten with a fire which none can extinguish! Again, how sweetly can he sing (v. 1 ff.) of Jahweh's vineyard, how warmly can he comfort and strengthen wavering faith! And the most wonderful thing of all, recurring nowhere else to the same degree, is that in all the vehement storms and waves, the manifold varying forms of Isaiah's language, we never for a moment lose the feeling that there is a spirit behind all this which deeply sympathizes and commiserates, yet is subject to no weakness and no disquiet, because it is sure of its God and blessed in Him.

Here again we must profoundly regret that so little has come down to us concerning the person and the outer life of this mighty witness. *Jesha'jāhu* (*i.e.*, Jahweh helps), the son of Amoz, according to all the indications, lived and worked exclusively in Jerusalem. Like himself, his two sons, whom he mentions (vii. 3 and viii. 3), bore significant names. He mentions (vi. 1) the year of Uzziah's death (*ca.* 740 B.C.) as that of his own calling. We have the latest trace of his activity in the oracles belonging to the time of Sennacherib's invasion (chaps. xxx. f. and xxxvii. 22 ff.), in the year 701. Chronology therefore would interpose no obstacle to the credibility of the legend of his martyrdom under Manasseh (and that by sawing asunder, referred to perhaps at Heb. xi. 37). But this was probably evolved from 2 Kings xxi. 16. For it would be difficult to believe that no historical statement has survived concerning such an end to Isaiah's life.

The Book of Isaiah (chaps. i.-xxxix. ; we shall have to speak of chaps. xl.-lxvi., the so-called Deutero-Isaiah [and Trite-Isaiah] much later) has come down to us in a form which betrays manifold redactional activity in times far apart from each other. All the attempts to prove a continuous arrangement in the order of time or events are to be regarded as failures. In the first place it is possible to distinguish a series of sections which are either founded on a later enlargement of genuine oracles (xi. 10—xii. 5, chap. xxxii. f.), or on the expansion of an Isaianic nucleus (chap. xxiii), or finally, on the erroneous intermingling of exilic and post-exilic oracles (xiii.-xiv., xxiii. 21 ? xxxiv. f.; the peculiar apocalyptic passage, chaps. xxiv.-xxvii., cannot have originated till a later, post-exilic time). The historical appendix, chaps. xxxvi.-xxxix., was added by some redactor, who took it from 2 Kings xviii. 13—xx. 21, partly on account of the Isaianic oracles which are given there, and partly as a key to the historical comprehension of those utterances of Isaiah which refers to Sennacherib's invasion.

When all this has been removed the remainder falls easily into three groups. I.: Chaps. i.-xi. 9, oracles concerning Judah and Jerusalem alone. Within this group chaps. ii. to iv. or v. evidently form a distinct collection, with a special title from Isaiah's own hand; it retained its place when the incomparable Prologue, chap. i., was placed at the head and provided with a special title. After the oldest collection in chaps. ii.-v. it seems that Isaiah placed a second, which opened with the account of his call (the so-called Inaugural Vision, chap. vi.). This explains in the simplest way how chap. vi., which we should quite expect to be at the head of the whole, came to stand in the middle of the first group. II.: Chaps. xiv. 24—xxii. 25 exclusively directed, with the exception of the two oracles in chap. xxii., against foreign nations (like the oracle xiii. f., xxi., xxiii., which we have distinguished above), and provided by a redactor with the special designation *massā*, i.e., [solemn] utterance. III.: Chaps. xxviii.-xxxi., the so-called Assyrian Cycle. Chap. xxviii. 1-6 implies the existence of Samaria; but the prophet has probably put this older section in the forefront as an introduction in order to follow it by a declaration that Judah is in the same condemnation. Hence all that follows xxviii. 7 may belong to the time after Sargon's death. Chaps. xxx., xxxi. are obviously not far distant from the catastrophe (701 B.C.).

Isaiah's contemporary, Micah (precisely, *Mīkhāyāh*, i.e., Who[is]like Yah[weh]?), of Moresheth, near Gath, in the Judæan lowland, worked in the same spirit and the same certainty that God had sent him, though inferior to Isaiah in majesty of diction. The title, i. 1, states that he was also active under Jotham and Ahaz; but according to the weighty testimony of Jer. xxvi. 18, where Micah iii. 12 is verbally quoted, his work did not begin till the reign of Hezekiah. But a distinction must no doubt be drawn between an earlier and a later period. Chaps. i.-iii. form a connected utterance, and, so far as the very corrupt text allows us to judge, an extremely vigorous one, in which Samaria first (consequently prior to 722) and then Judah and Jerusalem are threatened with destruction because of the utter failure of law and discipline, but, above all, because of the deep corruption of all the leaders of the people, and the carnal reliance placed on Jahweh's presence.

No kind of critical suspicion prevails respecting these three chapters (excepting as to ii. 12 f., verses which are perhaps only in the wrong place). But it is very questionable how much of chaps. iv.-vii. should be denied to Micah. The only point on which there is practical unanimity is that chap. vii. 7-20, with its totally different pre-suppositions, cannot have been composed earlier than the Exile (or possibly even in late post-exilic times). Chap. vi., with its impressive summary in v. 8 of all prophetic teaching, and chap. vii. 1-6 are universally ascribed to the time of Manasseh, but some scholars do not deny that they are Micah's. All recognize that in the present text of chaps. iv. and v. thoroughly heterogeneous elements have been worked up—cf. especially iv. 10, where the taking of the city is expected, with v. 11, 13, where its deliverance is foretold. Since Micah himself confidently looks forward to the destruction of the city, iv. 9 f., 14, and v. 1-8, as well as the original form of 9-14, might easily belong to him. On the other hand, the section iv. 1-4, which is almost identical with Isa. ii. 2-4, seems to have been subsequently appended to chaps. i.-iii., so as not to leave off with the comfortless prospect of iii. 12. At iv. 6-8, on the contrary, a state of deep humiliation for Jerusalem, and the loss of the "former dominion" seem to be implied.

§ 4. FROM THE DESTRUCTION OF SAMARIA TO THE EXILE.

1. NAHUM.—ZEPHANIAH.

Our reference to the later activity of Isaiah and Micah has already carried us beyond the great catastrophe of the year 722, which brought on Samaria the long-threatened destruction and left Judah alone on the scene. The new position thus created, the restriction thenceforward to Judah alone of all the memories of a great past, and all the hopes of the future too, was evidently realized by but few in the anxious time from 722 to 701, when men were in constant dread that the now-gigantic power of Assyria might suddenly crush them. When the God who was enthroned on Zion vindicated the irrefragable promise of His prophet, and in one night triumphed over the myriads of Assyria, we should have thought that a profound movement, the consciousness of an immense debt of gratitude, would necessarily have taken hold of the whole nation, and made it willingly obedient to the true prophets of God. But according to all that we can gather from the scanty traditions of the time of Manasseh; mingled as they also are with all sorts of later additions, something quite different happened. The deliverance was ascribed, not to the God of Isaiah, who was able to control all nations according to His holy will, but to the national god of Israel, who would not allow his habitation to be violated, or the heaps of sacrifices and offerings brought to him to remain unrewarded. All the aberrations of Manasseh, including the sacrifice of children, which were afterwards summarily set down as idolatry, in all probability arose from a reaction against Hezekiah's attempt to purify the service of Jahweh from all the remnants of the former naturalistic and sensuous cultus. The much innocent blood which Manasseh, according to 2 Kings xxi. 16, shed in Jerusalem, must have been chiefly that of the people who followed Isaiah and Micah, and would not adapt themselves to *this* turn of affairs.

The above-named sections, Micah vi. and vii. 1-6, enable us to see a long way into the circumstances of Manasseh's reign. But besides them only one monument of prophecy has been preserved to us from the whole interval between Isaiah and Zephaniah, the extremely sublime prophecy of the destruction of Nineveh by Nahum the Elkoshite. According to Jerome, Elkosh was in Galilee. But this does not imply that Nahum was an Israelite: on the contrary, passages like i. 11 (obviously an allusion to Sennacherib's invasion), i. 13, ii. 1, will not permit us to think of any but a Judahite. The precise date of the oracle is doubtful. On the one side we get the impression that the prophet retained a vivid recollection of the Assyrian invasion (i. 11, ii. 3): and earlier critics wished on this account to put Nahum back into the eighth century. On the other side, the whole tone of the oracle points to an imminently threatening danger to Nineveh: hence the more recent critics think mostly of the siege by Cyaxares and Nabopalassar. But it may still be questioned whether such passages as ii. 2 and iii. 14, on which the chief reliance has been placed, are not rather to be put down to poetic art which can make the future most vividly present. If we add that the devastation of the Egyptian Thebes, mentioned iii. 8 ff., is obviously remembered very vividly and in all probability is the conquest of Thebes by Esarhaddon or Assurbanipal, we shall be rather inclined to come down to the time between 670 and 660 as the date of Nahum. For the rest, Nahum is rightly regarded as one of the most difficult of the prophets: this difficulty comes both from the poetically bold, nay fiery phraseology, and from the manifold corruptions of the text.*

---

* "Der Untergang Ninevehs und die Weissagungschrift des Nahum von Elkosch," by Col. A. Billerbeck and Dr. A. Jeremias (in Delitzsch and Haupt's "Beiträgen zur semit. Sprachwissenschaft," III. [1895], 1) gives a thorough discussion of the text (also with reference to military technical terms).

Zephaniah's date can be determined with more certainty than Nahum's. When his genealogy is traced back at i. 1, to Hezekiah as his great-great-grandfather, it would be difficult to think of any other than King Hezekiah. If Amariah, his great-grandfather, was born before Hezekiah's accession, Zephaniah may have been born about 655. Of his oracles chap. i. at least, with its sharp denunciations of the idolatry and the outrages practised in Judah, must be assigned to the time previous to Josiah's purification of the cultus (622). According to an opinion which is shared by many moderns, the Scythian invasion (*ca.* 628) occasioned Zephaniah's preaching of repentance, and supplied him with the colours for depicting the terrible judgment-day of Jahweh. Yet it may be questioned whether iii. 6, which is specially adduced in favour of this, has not the victories of the Medes and Chaldæans in view; besides which there are other grounds for placing chaps. ii.-iii. 13 later than Josiah's reform of the cultus. BUDDE (Theol. Studien u. Kritiken, 1893, p. 393 ff.) has at all events made it very possible that ii. 4-15 is a later interpolation. But it is almost universally agreed that the conclusion (iii. 14-20) cannot have originated earlier than the Exile or the immediately succeeding period.

2. THE HISTORICAL WORK OF THE JEHOVIST.—DEUTERONOMY.

We have no means of knowing to what extent historical writing was practised in the whole of this interval, perhaps in the shape of a renewed recasting and supplementing of older works, as is natural in a literature propagated by manuscripts and devoted almost exclusively to the interests of religion. But we have a proof that the older monuments of this class already enjoyed a sort of canonical dignity. Otherwise it would be difficult to understand how men came to think of so careful a blending of two ancient historical works as we have in the union of the Jahwist (*J*) and the older Elohist (*E*), which probably was effected in the second half of the seventh century. The fundamental principle of the redactor (who is usually designated JE^r or Rje, *i.e.*, the "Jehovistic" redactor) doubtless was to sacrifice nothing that bore the marks of an independent notice. Occasionally he allows only *one* source to speak for a while: the narrative of the other is then brought in incidentally (*e.g.* E, Gen. xxxi. 4 ff., as parallel to J, xxx, 31 ff.), or, if the discrepancy seemed too great, is left out entirely. But if the parallel accounts substantially agree, the phraseology of both sources (especially with retention of both divine names) is adduced in such close and apt combination that the successful analysis of the sources demands most careful observation of the vocabulary and linguistic usage of each source. Not unfrequently these indications fail and we have to be content to speak of *JE*. A translation corresponding to the original phraseology enables the observant reader to detect the manifold joints and seams which were necessarily evolved when narratives almost identical in language were placed side by side. Thus at Gen. xxvii. 4 (*J*) there is a fresh beginning of what had been begun at v. 21 (*E*). At xxxvii. 28 *Midianite* merchants came up to Joseph's brethren: these then drew him out of the well and sold him to the *Ishmaelites* (cf. the analysis in the "Survey")—a striking instance of the manner in which the redactor sometimes despaired of reconciling differences which might have been got rid of with the utmost ease. The redactor's own additions must have been few: we regard Gen. xx. 18 as an indisputable example.

About the same time as a canonical history of the primæval age was thus produced another task of extreme importance was undertaken in the circle of the disciples of the prophets: —the formation of a comprehensive corpus of ritual and civil laws which should re-model the prevalent practice in the commonwealth and in the cultus. The relapse under Manasseh to the naturalistically inclined popular religion had shown that no improvement of circumstances was conceivable so long as the service of Jahweh was abandoned to all the arbitrariness and all the superstition, the intermixture even of all sorts of ancestral heathen customs, which prevailed up and down the country at the local sanctuaries, and especially at the high-places (*bāmōth*), some of which were primaeval. There was only one remedy: the strict limitation of the sacrifices and festivals to *one* legitimate sanctuary, *i.e.*, self-evidently, to the temple in Jerusalem. The issue of these considerations was the original form of our Deuteronomy, the so-called Ur-Deuteronomy.

It has long been recognized that the Book of the Law which the chief priest Hilkiah found in the temple in the eighteenth year of Josiah, cannot have been the whole Pentateuch, but only the original form of Deuteronomy. This is confirmed step by step by the detailed account in 2 Kings xxii. 3 ff. Shaphan, the scribe, happening to visit the temple, Hilkiah acquaints him with the finding of the law-book, and hands it over to Shaphan, who reads it. For a merely cursory perusal of the Pentateuch at least five or six hours would be requisite: for that of the original Deuteronomy half an hour would be ample. Then Shaphan repairs to the King, gives him a short account of the execution of his commission, and continues: "Hilkiah the priest hath given me a book." And Shaphan read it to the King. The King is quite horrified at its contents. He rends his clothes, and sends the priest and others to the prophetess Huldah to obtain through her a pronouncement from Jahweh concerning this book. Next he assembles at the temple all the notables, together with all the priests and prophets and the whole people; reads to them all the contents of the newly-found law, and solemnly binds himself, with the whole people, to observe it most strictly. The ensuing narrative of the ritual reform in the temple, in Jerusalem, and all the rest of the land, brings positively incredible facts to light. We see from it (even from the original narrative, apart from the many intensifying additions of later date), that not only the open country but the capital and the temple were practically crammed with the signs of a naturalistic Jahweh-worship and absolutely heathen idolatry, and all this under the eyes of so pious a king as Josiah, and under the eyes of the temple priesthood.

The strong emotion, the deep grief of the King, can obviously be explained only by the fact that when the law-book was read he perceived something entirely new, opposed outright to the prevailing custom. This new thing is the demand for the concentration of the worship at *one* place, and the thorough abolition of all remains of the previous Nature-worship. Both are enjoined most emphatically at the very outset of the Code proper (chap. xii.). In accordance with this it is brought out prominently at 2 Kings xxiii. 21 ff., that a strictly legal celebration of the Passover (*i.e.*, by the whole of the people at the central sanctuary) was held under Josiah for the first time since the Judges. The more ancient festival-laws know nothing about such a demand: it is advanced for the first time at Deut. xvi., and evidently as an innovation.

The fact that the law-book was found by the chief priest Hilkiah, and handed by him to the scribe—naturally to be given in turn to the King—has given rise to the conjecture that the priest had a hand in its composition, and that the whole affair was a "pious fraud." All things considered, we must rather conclude that Hilkiah himself was surprised at the discovery. The position of the priests in Deuteronomy is not at all such as to explain any special zeal on their part for its composition and introduction. No doubt the centralization of the worship assured to the priests at Jerusalem a consider-able increase of influence and revenue, although the payments to the priests were in themselves very modest (Deut. xviii. 3 ff.). But then every privilege was nullified by the express direction (xviii. 6 ff.) that the rural priests should thence-forward have a right to officiate in the temple and share in the priests' dues. We shall, indeed, see that this direction was not permanently carried out: 2 Kings xxiii. 9 knows only of the rural priests participating in the meal offerings, not of their right to officiate. But the Deuteronomic writer obviously meant the direction at xviii. 6 ff. to be understood seriously, and this is a proof that he must be sought, not in the priestly, but in the prophetic circles. That the book came to light during building alterations in the temple is the first evidence of its having been actually deposited there by an unknown hand, in the sure hope that it would be found sooner or later and then would attain its end. But secondly, one cannot see why, amidst the most favourable conditions imaginable for a reform of worship, they should have waited till the eighteenth year of Josiah to bring out in such a way a work which must long have been urgently required. This question answers itself if we admit that the book was composed in a time of distress, possibly under Manasseh, and deposited in the hope of a better time, but that the author had died meanwhile.

It must, no doubt, be admitted that even in its original form the law-book claimed to be founded on an address delivered by Moses to the people immediately before his decease. Thus the statement at xxxi. 9 ff., that Moses wrote down "this law" and delivered it to the priests to be read at every Feast of Tabernacles in the Year of Release, can only refer to the original Deuteronomy. But the further conclusion that this is a work of fraud overlooks a fact which has long been recognized. As regards *speeches*, put into the mouths of older authorities, the idea of literary property is altogether unknown, both to the Old Testament writers and to antiquity in general. The moment the conviction seems justified that a certain statement is in the mind and spirit of that higher authority and must contribute to the welfare of the people, its ascription to that authority is justified. This applies as forcibly to the original Deuteronomy as to the so-called Priests' Code, which in innumerable passages introduces Moses as the speaker, or to "Ecclesiastes," which makes a Solomon testify to the vanity of all things. We do not here touch on the frequency with which the Deuteronomic writer drops the veil and lets it be seen that he is really addressing a people which has long been settled and is living in the midst of a fairly advanced civilization—thus, as early as xii. 2, in the perfect tense, "have worshipped" [Luther and E. V. "served"].

The question as to what portions of the present Deuteronomy belonged to the original Deuteronomy is an extremely complicated one, and has become more and more a matter of controversy. The comparison of ii. 15, on the one hand, with v. 3 ff., ix. 7 ff., 22 ff., xi. 2 ff., on the other, shows that the Prologue, up to iv. 40, or at any rate chaps. i.-iii., can only be regarded as a revision of the original Prologue. The yet further-going assertion that the original Deuteronomy did not begin with chap. v., but with chap. xii. (as the commencement of the legislation) has been met by distinguished investigators with another assertion, viz., that the "Exhortations" in chaps. v.-xii. were indeed composed later than the laws, but by the same hand. On the other hand, it is pretty generally recognized that chap. xxvii. and the Epilogue, beginning at chap. xxviii. 69, with the possible exception of xxxi. 9 ff., cannot have been part of the original Deuteronomy. But we must go a step further. Closer observation of the legal part has discovered that we there have to do with all sorts of repetitions which can be satisfactorily explained only in *one* way. The original Deuteronomy must have passed through at least two revisions, in many respects harmonious but in others diverse. Our present Deuteronomy is the result of an amalgamation of these, thought by most to have been effected in the course of the Babylonian Exile and not to have been accomplished without all kinds of final additions.*

---

* W. STAERK, in "Das Deuteronomium, sein Inhalt u. seine literarische Form" (Lpzg., 1894), attempted a restoration of the law-book presented to King Josiah, based mainly on the observation that the people are addressed partly in the singular, partly in the plural. Independently of Staerk, C. STEUERNAGEL ("Die Entstehung des deuteronomischen Gesetzes, kritisch u. biblischtheologisch untersucht") has subjected it to an exceedingly acute analysis, founded on the same observation. The result is that neither the *Thou*-source nor the *Ye*-source is a strictly homogeneous and original work. On the contrary, the Deuteronomic fundamental law (relating to the concentration of the worship at Jerusalem) forms the starting point. From the union of this fundamental law

This does not render it impossible for the present form of the nucleus of Deuteronomy (designated *D* in the Survey) to bear an almost entirely homogeneous stamp. And if we leave out the section xiv. 1-21, which strongly reminds us of the so-called Law of Holiness (see below), and can scarcely have belonged to the original Deuteronomy, it is the spirit of prophetism which everywhere meets us in these laws. It reveals itself on the one side in its insistence on the main thing, *i.e.*, undivided, obedient devotion to the God of the fathers. Immediately on the inculcation of the fundamental truth, "Jahweh is our God, Jahweh alone,"* (vi. 4) follows the demand that they shall love Him with all their heart, all their mind, and all their strength. This love is founded on the hearty gratitude of the people for God's having first loved them, notwithstanding all their unworthiness, chosen them for His possession, redeemed them from bondage, and richly blessed them (viii. 10 ff.; ix. 5). And God demands no return for all this, save that the people will love Him again, walk in His ways, and be of circumcised heart (x. 12 ff.; xi. 1, xiii., &c.).

On the other side, the spirit of prophetism is revealed in the numerous directions which betray so noble and true a humanity, nay, such ethical delicacy, that an evangelical strain in this legislation has been quite justifiably spoken

---

with the legal enactments arises the fundamental Deuteronomic collection. The latter underwent a double revision in the "Sources of the Elders" and the "*Thou*-source," other sources of laws being utilized both times. From the uniting the "Sources of the Elders" with utterances of another kind the *Ye*-source arose; by the blending of the latter with the *Thou*-source and a few additions a redactor (D^r) produced the law-book which was presented to King Josiah, and this—apart from a few exilic and post-exilic additions—is in the main identical with our Deuteronomy. Steuernagel thus, in opposition to the view which formerly prevailed, puts the origin of Deuteronomy in the time previous to Josiah's ritual reform. According to him the fundamental collection may belong to the eighth century: the chief redactor (D^r) would have to be placed about 650 at the latest.

* According to another explanation, "Jahweh our God, Jahweh is one" (or "is one Jahweh"), that is, in contrast to the distinction of divers Jahwehs as the special divinities of certain sanctuaries.

of. From the time of Amos, it was the Alpha and Omega of prophetic preaching to insist on the practice of justice and righteousness, to warn against the oppression of the poor and helpless; and, in like manner, the Deuteronomic writer unweariedly pleads for the poor, the widows and orphans, even for the strangers and slaves. What a glimpse we get of the legislator's heart through such prescriptions as xxiv. 10 ff. and xxiv. 19 ff., compared with the customs which prevailed in the rest of the ancient world.

3. THE BOOK OF KINGS.

The natural consequence of the great innovation, the abolition of worship at the high-places, was that an entirely new view was taken of all the preceding history. The Deuteronomic demand for unity of worship did not, indeed, extend to the time before Solomon's building of the temple. It came into force when Jahweh had made peace for His people before all surrounding enemies, and had chosen for Himself a place where He would have His name dwell. But after the building of the temple, all worship away from the temple was sin; and this applied particularly to the worship in the northern kingdom, especially because this was connected with bull-worship (the "sin of Jeroboam"). The work in which this new view of things found appropriate expression is "The Book of Kings." Originally *one* book, it was divided into two in the Greek and Latin Bible,* thereafter in the German and (since 1518) in the Hebrew Bible. The Book of Kings includes three great groups: I.—The History of Solomon (1 Kings i.-xi.). II.—The History of the Divided Kingdoms up to the destruction of Samaria (1 Kings xii. to 2 Kings xvii.), concluding with

---

* The Greek and Latin Bible reckon our two Books of Samuel and Kings as four "Books of the Kingdoms." Our Books of Kings are, therefore, the third and fourth Books of the Kingdoms (or briefly, "of the Kings").

a lengthy consideration of the reasons of its fall, and notices about its re-colonization. III.—The History of Judah, down to the kindness shown to Jehoiachin, 561 B.C. (2 Kings xviii.-xxv.). The kings are all arranged in the exact order of their accession. Thus Jeroboam I. is followed by the three kings of Judah who were contemporary with him, then by the six kings of Israel, who ascended the throne during Asa's lifetime, &c.

A superficial glance is enough to show that the book is not intended to be a compendium of the external history of Israel. The author could point to other sources for this. He aims at giving a sort of Church History, above all, a history of prophetic action in both kingdoms. For this purpose he has extracted the material from more comprehensive works, and at the same time pronounced his judgment on all the kings, and often on their individual acts. Deuteronomy is the standard by which he judges everywhere. The spirit and the linguistic usage of that book asserts itself in such a way that the analysis of the passages due to the author of the Book of Kings himself can in almost every case be carried out with certainty. Hence the designation of the author and of the writers related to him as "Deuteronomists" is thoroughly justified.

When each king of Judah and Israel is introduced in turn, one and the same scheme is used with painful uniformity. The date of accession is given, according to the regnal year of the contemporary king of the other kingdom; the length of reign; for the kings of Judah, the age at accession and the mother's name; for all alike the verdict on their religious character. For the kings of Israel this regularly runs: "He did that which displeased Jahweh," or "he walked in the ways of Jeroboam, and in his sins, wherewith he made Israel to sin." The kings of Judah are judged diversely, sometimes being compared with their predecessors, or, as in Hezekiah's case, with David. To all of them, however, even the best, down to Josiah, it is imputed as a fault that they tolerated the worship at the high-places (1 K. xv. 14; xxii. 44). The author assumes that *all* the kings ought to have known and observed the Deuteronomic law.

If we inquire whence the author took the historical material which he records, sometimes more fully, but usually, where histories of prophets are not in question, in the briefest manner conceivable, the reply must be: From the works which he quotes for almost all the kings for everything "else which remains to be said about each," *i.e.*, from the "Book of the History of the Kings of Judah," and the "Book of the History of the Kings of Israel." For, in all probability, the "Book of the History of Solomon" (*Sa* in the Survey), quoted at 1 xi. 41, as well as the Ephraimite histories of prophets, and other narratives (P, E, P^2), already mentioned by us at p. 41 f., were known to our author merely as portions of those history-books about the kings of Israel and Judah. It must even be asked whether we actually have to think of two separate works or of *one* Book of Kings cited under diverse names, according as it treated of kings of Israel or Judah. This seems to us a very probable idea, and we shall therefore henceforward designate the book simply as "the great King's Book."

From several additions made to the quotations of this work in our Books of Kings, it is clear that it must have treated both of martial deeds abroad (*e.g.*, 1 K. xiv. 19; 2 K. xiv. 15, 28), and of conspiracies (1 K. xvi. 20; 2 K. xv. 15), and Government measures (especially buildings, 1 K. xv. 23, xxii. 39; 2 K. xx. 20) at home. Once only (2 K. xxi. 17) are the "sins" of a king mentioned, and there, doubtless, transgressions of the legitimate ritual are meant. Yet it is questionable whether this religious pronouncement was found in the great King's Book, or was made by the Deuteronomist himself.

We have, for the most part, no means of determining the sources on which the great King's Book drew. Leaving aside the above-named extracts which its author probably made from larger independent works, there remain a fair number of isolated notices which bear the stamp of great simplicity, and therefore of reliableness. Where we seem to have their very phraseology they are designated *K* in the Survey. But all kinds of statements which the Deuteronomist has interwoven in his introductory formulas belong to this class, especially the length of the reigns and, for the kings of Judah, the mother's name. All this material, which we designate *K*, was probably taken from a kind of Chronicles, begun early in both kingdoms, and afterwards continued down to a late period, the work of continuation being taken up by one writer after another, as was in part the case with our mediæval Chronicles. For instance, the note at 2 K. viii. 22, "unto this day," cannot have been written by a person who was aware of Amaziah's victory (xiv. 7; cf. xvi. 6). Yet we must undoubtedly abandon the still prevalent opinion that those chronicles are identical with the official annals of the two kingdoms. In proof of that opinion, appeal has been made to the supposed mention of a royal annalist under David (2 Sam. viii. 16, xx. 24), Solomon (1 Kings iv. 3), and Hezekiah (2 Kings xviii. 18, 37). But the expression in question (*mazkir*) cannot really mean anything but an official who "brings to remembrance" the events of the reign before the king, and is therefore a reporting counsellor, corresponding to the vizier of the Mohammedan rulers, or to our "chancellor." With this it agrees that the mazkir is reckoned amongst the highest officials, being placed before the high priest in the Second Book of Samuel. But, considering the repeated changes of dynasty, which were often effected by assassination, it is very improbable that there were official annals in Israel. There are also notices concerning the kings of Judah, in all probability taken from the great King's Book, which it is difficult to believe that the son of the king in question took care to have inserted in the official annals. This does not necessarily imply that the author of the great King's Book did not frequently make use of very ancient documents and notes (amongst other examples, cf. 1 iv. 1 ff., iv. 7 ff., v. 2 f., and the dating of the building of the temple by pre-exilic names of months at vi. 37 f., taken, perhaps, from an inscription in the temple). In some cases we come across parallel accounts, concerning which it is difficult to say what is their historical worth, and whether they were admitted by the author of the great King's Book or were first adopted by the Deuteronomist (1 K. ix. 23, xi. 13 ff.; 2 K. xviii. 14 ff., xxiii. 8b and 19 f.; much else of this kind is assigned to definite sources in the Survey, but with a ?). It is universally recognized that in 2 K. xix. 10 ff. (K^2 in the Survey) there is a parallel to xviii. 17 ff., which 9b has turned into an independent account.

The reference to the great King's Book is found with all the kings of Israel except Joram (obviously because in the present arrangement of the material there is no room for it) and the last king, Hoshea. On the other hand, it is not wanting with Zimri, who reigned a week, and Shallum, who reigned a month. Nor is it lacking with any of the kings of Judah, down to Jehoiakim, except Ahaziah (for the same reason as with Joram of Israel) and Jehoahaz, who did not really reign. The latest reference being to Jehoiakim, we must hold that the great King's Book extended as far as his reign, and the only remaining question is as to when the Deuteronomist prepared his excerpt.

The answer seems easy. At 2 K. xxv. 27 ff. the favour shown to Jehoiakim in the thirty-seventh year after his captivity (561 B.C.) is mentioned, and his death implied. The Deuteronomist, therefore, wrote at the earliest date about 560, in the Exile. With this it agrees that at 1 K. v. 4 all the kings west of the Euphrates are spoken of as on *that* side the river, and that in various passages (1 K. viii. 44 ff., ix. 1 ff.; 2 K. xvii. 19 f., xxi. 7 ff., xxii. 15 ff., xxiii. 26 f.) the exile of the people and the destruction of Jerusalem is presupposed. Yet it has long been recognized that many other passages witness quite as certainly to the pre-exilic standpoint of the Deuteronomist (thus 1 K. viii. 15 ff., xi. 29 ff.; 2 K. xvii. 21 ff. and 41), and the remark has justly been made that the cultus-reform under Josiah could not have been so narrated by any one who did not continue to attach to it the hope of the salvation of the commonwealth.

Two redactions of our present Books of Kings must therefore

be distinguished. The first (somewhere about 600, in the Survey Dt) reached at least to 2 K. xxiii. 30, probably to xxiv. 1. The second (designated Dt^2 in the Survey) added the conclusion, down to xxv. 30, and all kinds of notices elsewhere (see above). Its religious standpoint is, in one particular, stricter even than that of the first redactor. The latter (1 K. iii. 2) looked on the worship at the high places *prior* to the building of the temple as not blameworthy; but the second redactor (v. 3) regarded it as a fault in Solomon that he sacrificed at the great high-place in Gibeon, and made him bring at least a supplementary burnt-offering and peace-offering before the ark of the covenant.

Finally, we must attribute to the second redactor a portion of the Books of Kings which has given rise to much dispute and thought. This is the so-called synchronisms, *i.e.*, the dating of the kings of Judah according to the regnal years of the kings of Israel, and conversely. The lack of an era was, no doubt, supplied in this way: but the result shows how difficult it was to carry it out. From the death of Solomon to the destruction of Samaria 260 years are allotted to the kings of Judah; to the kings of Israel 241 years, 7 months, 7 days. There is, therefore, an error of reckoning. We come to the same result by comparing the astronomically certified chronology of the Assyrian Cuneiform Inscriptions. According to these Ahab of Israel took part in the Battle of Karkar (854 B.C.): from that date to the destruction of Samaria 132 years elapsed. But in the Books of Kings 157 years, 7 months, are assigned to the kings from Ahab's son Ahaziah to Hoshea. When we add that the numbers for the first eight kings of Israel, leaving out Zimri, are 22, 2, 24 (probably 22 originally), 2, 12, 22, 2, 12, the suspicion arises that 12, as an average number, has been taken for the foundation. It occurs twice, and the 22 seems to be thrice increased to 2 × 12 by the addition of 2. All this makes it impossible to deny that the chronology, and especially the synchronisms, have in several instances been artificially corrected. This was necessitated, partly by the lack of traditional numbers (especially for the Israelite kings), partly by the corruption or the contradictions in the actual tradition. And, in conclusion, the influence has been felt of a system which is both late and artificial, the traces of which appear at 1 Kings vi. 1, as well as in the numbers of the kings. According to 1 Kings vi. 1, 480 years (*i.e.*, 12 generations of 40 years each) elapsed between the Exodus and the building of the temple. From then to the end of Zedekiah 430 years are given to the kings of Judah, 50 to the Exile, and the total again is 480 years. It may still be questioned whether the second redactor himself contemplated this extension of the system of 12 years each to the time from the building of the temple to the re-founding of the commonwealth. If he did we must assign his activity to the post-exilic age. But there can be no doubt that this system affected the final determination of the numbers of the kings. This is all the less difficult to believe since, without it, a considerable number of additions (designated Z in the Survey) to the original text of the Book of Kings must be registered. Nor are these merely such as the second redactor might find extant and receive into the text, but others, indubitably post-exilic, which show themselves to be later additions, either by their dependence on the Priests' Code in the Pentateuch (thus 1 K. viii. 4b), or by their divergence from the Deuteronomist's own utterances, or, finally, by their being Midrashic in character (1 K. xii. 21 ff. and 33 ff.; 2 K. i. 9 ff.).

4. Habakkuk.—Jeremiah.

It was a prophet's voice which sounded in the ears of the deluded multitude from all the prophetic histories and from the whole of the view given by the Book of Kings, a moving sermon on the infinite guilt of the people and its kings, on the long-suffering of God which, on one occasion, by the judgment on Israel, had shown itself exhausted. But no prophetic voices could any longer avert that increased hardening, followed by judgment, which Isaiah himself (vi. 9 ff.) had designated as the true result of the preaching of repentance, willed by God Himself. Nor did *those* prophetic voices accomplish anything different which we have now to think of as belonging to the time between 623 and 586, that of Habakkuk, and that of one of the greatest of all, Jeremiah.

Formerly there was almost complete unanimity respecting the interpretation and position of Habakkuk's prophecy. The allusion to the terrible power and the mighty deeds of the Chaldæans (i. 6) seemed to admit of no other date than after the battle of Carchemish, through which Nebuchadnezzar may be said to have entered on the rule over all Hither Asia, that is about 604. For chaps. i.-ii. 8 this view was still held when Stade (Zeitschrift für die Alttest. Wissenschaft, 1884, p. 154) assigned ii. 9-20 to a post-exilic reviser, and also explained chap. iii., the so-called Psalm of Habakkuk, as a post-exilic congregational hymn. The second of these ideas met with almost universal assent (especially because the musical marks in the title and subscription point to its having been subsequently appropriated from a collection of songs): but Budde (see below) claims respecting ii. 9 ff. that at least vv. 9-12 and 15-17 belong to the original oracle. And since Giesebrecht ("Beiträge zur Jesaiakritik," Gött., 1890, p. 197 f.) and, independently of him, Budde and Rothstein, have proved that i. 5-11 breaks the connection between v. 4 and 12, other hypotheses have been built on this, which also seem worth mentioning. Giesebrecht himself was of opinion that the prediction, i. 5-11 (an oracle complete in itself, the first announcement of the Chaldæans) should be placed before v. 1, and that the rest formed an independent piece, composed under the stress of the Chaldæan rule, probably in the Exile. Budde, on the contrary (Theolog. Studien und Kritiken, 1893, p. 383 ff.), saw in the oppressor of the pious, not the Chaldæan, but the Assyrian, who was threatened with destruction by the rising might of the Chaldæans. The original position of the threat (i. 5-11) would be after ii. 4: the whole oracle, apart from the later additions, ii. 13 f. and 18-20, would belong to about 615. Rothstein, finally (Theol. Stud. und Krit., 1894, p. 51 ff.), comes to the conclusion that Habakkuk's original oracle (about 605) was chiefly directed against the prevailing ungodliness and violence in the midst of Judah which Jehoiakim's rule had furthered, and announced the punishment of the apostate land and people which should be accomplished by the Chaldæans. This oracle (the original order of which was i. 2-4, 12a, 13, ii. 1-5a, i. 6-10, 14, 15a) would then be so revised and expanded by a later writer (in the Exile) that, at least in its greater part, it became an oracle against Babylon. Apposite reasons have been advanced for both the last-named hypotheses. On the other hand they both lie open to the objection that they displace at least five verses within the original oracle. Hence it is difficult to decide.

The mention of Habakkuk has brought us at any rate far beyond the beginning of Jeremiah's activity. But it is with good reason that we now for the first time mention him as the great witness to the righteousness and unapproachable holiness of his God at the close of the pre-exilic age. On him had fallen the unspeakably heavy lot to be obliged to behold, whole decades long, the death-struggles of his fatherland, assured that even the intercession of a Moses and a Samuel could no longer save it. Isaiah and Micah had descried the destruction of Judah a considerable distance off: Jeremiah personally experienced it, with all its horrors. His language accordingly, from beginning to end, is full of reproaches, threats, care and woe. Yirmejahu (*i.e.*, according to the usual interpretation, "Jahweh establishes") was descended, according to i. 1 (cf. also xxxii. 6 ff.) from Hilkiah, one of the priests who lived at Anathoth in Benjamin (now '*Anâta*, an hour N.E. of Jerusalem). Called to be a prophet whilst still a young man (i. 6), in the thirteenth year of Josiah (628 B.C.), he afterwards laboured constantly at Jerusalem (ii. 1, vii. 2, &c.). Chap. iii. 6 ff. is the only oracle dated in Josiah's time: yet Jeremiah himself says (xxv. 3) that he spoke unweariedly to the people for twenty-three years, from the thirteenth year of Josiah. At least chaps. ii.-vi. must therefore be regarded as an echo of speeches belonging to Josiah's time. We read a eulogistic judgment on Josiah by the prophet at xxii. 15; according to 2 Chron. xxxv. 25 he also composed a dirge over the greatly lamented king after the battle of Megiddo. Chap. xxii. 10 ff. is the only utterance which deals with Jehoahaz (under the name Shallum).

The state of the commonwealth, and with it that of the prophet, waxed ever gloomier under the reign of Jehoiakim, the unworthy eldest son of the noble Josiah (xxii. 13 ff.). Probably in the beginning of this reign the symbolic action with the linen girdle (xiii. 1 ff.) was performed, certainly another was, the breaking of an earthen pitcher in the valley of Hinnom, and the threatenings connected therewith (xix. 1 ff.). The sequel of the repetition of this in the forecourt of the temple is that Pashur, chief overseer of the temple, smites Jeremiah and puts him in the stocks for a night (xx. 1 ff.). For this the prophet predicts to him that he shall go through all the horrors of the taking of Jerusalem, and afterwards, together with his family, die in Babylon. No doubt it was during that night of imprisonment that the two striking passages, xx. 7 ff. and 14 ff., originated; the first of which is almost an indictment of Jahweh, who had deceived him and given him up to be a common laughing-stock. This is an outburst of despair, from which the prophet struggles back to renewed trust, yea even to praising God. The other is a cursing of the day of his birth, and of the man who brought tidings of it to his father.

Chap. xxvi., which also belongs to the beginning of Jehoiakim's reign, records an almost greater danger to Jeremiah than that of chap. xx. Embittered by the threats which he has uttered against the temple and the commonwealth in the forecourt of the temple, which was filled with visitors to the feast, the priests and prophets seize him, crying, "Thou must die!" The chiefs of Judah, whom we elsewhere see favourably disposed to him, when they hear this, hasten to the rescue and institute a regular trial. Then Jeremiah shows himself in all his greatness. In answer to the accusations of the priests and prophets he appeals stedfastly to Jahweh's commands, who bade him prophesy thus: Oh, that they therefore would not let the call to repentance sound unheard! But as to himself he is in their power, and whatever they please may happen to him: only let them remember the guilt which his death will bring on them.

Such words and such dignity conquer the people. Along with the chiefs they take the prophet's side. A few of the leading men also remember what happened in Hezekiah's reign, Micah's menacing prophecy, which did not bring about the death of the prophet but the repentance of the people. Jeremiah thus escaped the threatened death, chiefly through the protection of Ahikam, son of Shaphan.

After the battle of Carchemish (605) Jeremiah indefatigably proclaims that the judgment on Judah will come through the Chaldæans. The land must become desolate, the people an object of astonishment and scorn, and must serve the king of Babylon seventy years, till God's judgment come upon him also and *his* land in turn become desolate (chap. xxv.).

In the same year, 605, Jeremiah's oracles were first written out. The fate of the roll which Baruch wrote at Jeremiah's dictation is vividly and impressively depicted in chap. xxxvi. The only result of Jehoiakim's destruction of the roll was that Jeremiah caused Baruch to prepare another, and added to the contents of the first many sayings of like import.

Jehoiakim's revolt in the year 602 could not be immediately punished by Nebuchadnezzar. And it is questionable whether Jehoiakim lived to see the beginning of the siege of Jerusalem. A shameful death is indeed foretold him, Jer. xxii. 18 ff. and xxxvi. 30, and this could not have come about earlier than in a sally against the Chaldæans. The siege does not seem to have been vigorously prosecuted till Nebuchadnezzar himself interposed. It was brought to a close by Jehoiachin's voluntary submission, which was probably made by Jeremiah's advice, certainly in harmony with his views (cf. xxii. 20 ff.).

The vision of the good and bad figs (chap. xxiv.) in the beginning of Zedekiah's reign enables us to see what Jeremiah thought of the situation, viz., that this first deportation was the seal put on the destruction of the people. He expects that the deported will obtain by their repentance grace and restoration: for the remainder in Judea and Egypt all the earlier threatenings remain in force.

In the fourth year of Zedekiah (*i.e.*, 594) the ambassadors of the surrounding smaller nations were gathered together at Jerusalem, evidently for the purpose of conspiring against the Chaldæans. Jeremiah was then directed by Jahweh (chap. xxvii.) to put bands and yokes on his neck, and send a message to the kings of those nations that the only way of escaping utter destruction was by willingly submitting to the Chaldæans. Jeremiah gave the same directions to Zedekiah, the priests, and all the people, accompanying it with impressive warnings against the false prophets who flattered their foolish hopes and promised the speedy restoration of the holy vessels which had been carried off, whereas in truth the remainder, hitherto spared, would have to go to Babylon. Shortly afterwards (xxviii. 1 ff.) Hananiah, a prophet of Gibeon, prophesied anew in the temple that within two years Jehoiachin and the vessels of the temple would return. Although Jeremiah felt some suspicion he supported this with an "Amen," and even suffered Hananiah to take the yoke off his neck and break it in pieces as a sign that before the lapse of two years Nebuchadnezzar's yoke on the neck of the nations should be broken in pieces. But Jeremiah had scarcely turned his back ere the word of Jahweh came to him: in place of the broken wooden yoke an iron one shall be imposed, and Hananiah, as a false prophet, is to die in the same year. And Hananiah died in the same year, in the seventh month.

Jeremiah also utters his warning against false prophets in a letter to the exiles in Babylon at about the same time (xxix. 1 ff.). On this account he is accused before the priests in Jerusalem by the prophet Shemaiah, but replies only by a minatory prediction against Shemaiah.

The advance of the Chaldæans about 588 causes Zedekiah (xxi. 1 ff.) to send two messengers to ask for an oracle from Jeremiah. They receive a most unfavourable answer. But the prophet counsels the people to flee to the Chaldæans: for none but the fugitives shall save their life. And when, in the second year of the siege, a gleam of hope appears through Nebuchadnezzar's raising the siege because of the advance of Pharaoh Hophra, Jeremiah still adhered immovably to his declaration. To Zedekiah's messengers, sent to solicit his intercession, he declares that the Chaldæans will return, take the city, and burn it. Yea, if the whole army of the Chaldæans were beaten, so that only a few wounded survived, *these* would rise up in their tent and burn the city.

Shortly afterwards (xxxvii. 11 ff.) Jeremiah was seized by a warder as he was going out of the city, and, in spite of his denial, brought to the princes as a deserter. They had him scourged and put him in prison in the house of Jonathan the scribe, in a subterranean vault. It was not till some time after, when the siege had been resumed, that Zedekiah had him secretly brought to the palace to hear a word of Jahweh from him. The answer sounds as ever: Thou wilt be delivered into the power of the King of Babylon. But Jeremiah wants to know from the king how he has merited imprisonment, and finally entreats that at least he will not have him taken back to prison in the house of Jonathan. Zedekiah has him kept thenceforward in the court of the guard, and a loaf of bread given to him daily until all the bread in the city was consumed. But during his stay in the court of the guard, Jeremiah is taught by a remarkable event (chap. xxxii.) that behind all these afflictions which await the state and the people, the comfortable hope of the return of the banished and the restoration of the state holds good—a promise which is further developed in the sayings that follow in chap. xxxiii.

Chap. xxxviii. brings us into the last days of the siege. Even in the court of the guard Jeremiah is not weary of repeating his prediction of disaster. The princes at last become tired of this, and demand of the king that he shall die, because he only makes the people despondent. Zedekiah faint-heartedly gives Jeremiah up to them. But even then they have not the courage to outrage his hallowed person. To make him at all events innocuous, however, they let him down by cords into a cistern in the court of the guard which was so full of mud that the prophet sank in it. It is a testimony of the strongest kind to the righteousness of the Divine judgment on Judah that in this hour no one took pity on the martyr save a stranger, Ebed-Melech, the Ethiopian, one of the king's chamberlains. He obtained from Zedekiah Jeremiah's deliverance: for this the prophet promised him (xxxix. 15 ff.) escape from the sword of the Chaldæans.

But the same Zedekiah who had so readily abandoned him has him secretly fetched once more (xxxviii. 14 ff.) to inquire of him, and swears that in any case he shall be safe. Again he receives nothing but the counsel to save his life and the existence of the city by voluntary submission. Zedekiah, however, is incapable of any manly resolution. He is afraid of being given up to the Judahite deserters in the Chaldæan camp. All Jeremiah's exhortations effect nothing. Instead of replying, Zedekiah merely enjoins strict silence as to their conversation, and in case of the princes asking about it, suggests an evasion. Jeremiah obeys, and the affair is thus kept secret.

We have a twofold account of what befel the prophet after the taking of the city: the one (much interrupted by later interpolations) in xxxviii. 28b, xxxix. 3 and 14; the other in chap. xl. 1 ff. The two can be so combined as to bring out the fact, that after the city was taken, Jeremiah was saved by the Chaldæan officers (perhaps on the intercession of Gedaliah; according to xxxix. 11 f. by Nebuchadnezzar's order), but afterwards was carried to Ramah with the other prisoners. It was here that Nebuzar-Adan, who had been occupied meanwhile with the destruction of the city, discovered him, and gave him the choice whether he would go under his protection to Babylon, or betake himself to Gedaliah at Mizpah.

Jeremiah chooses the latter, and Nebuzar-Adan dismisses him with a present.

After the murder of Gedaliah and all the sad events narrated in chaps. xl. 7—xli. 18, Jeremiah and Baruch fled with the remainder of the people from Mizpah to the South. During a rest near Bethlehem the people desire (xlii. 1 ff.) that Jeremiah will intercede with Jahweh for them, and inquire of Him. The prophet promises to keep back nothing of God's answer from them, and they bind themselves by an oath to obey the Divine word. After ten days the word of Jahweh comes to the prophet; the only way of saving their life would be by remaining in the land, not by their proposed flight to Egypt. But the prophet had hardly made this word known when insolent voices are raised; "that is a falsehood and not God's command, Baruch has set the prophet on, that they may all fall into the hands of the Chaldæans." In short, they do not obey, but set off, and compel Jeremiah and Baruch to accompany them to Egypt. They settle at Tahpanhes, *i.e.*, according to the Greek Bible, Daphne, near Pelusium, close to the border. The prophet is here directed (xliii. 8 ff.) to foretell to his countrymen, by a symbolic action and its interpretation, the devastation of Egypt by Nebuchadnezzar. This prediction was first fulfilled in 525 by Cambyses.

The last trace of Jeremiah's activity lies before us in chap. xliv. in the reprimand of the Egyptian Jews because of their idolatry, practised especially by the women, according to v. 15, and, according to v. 17 and 25, vowed even before the immigration. Seeing that all the misery of the people has not served for a warning to them the last remnant must also perish. The people answer impudently that things are just the reverse. So long as they offered to the Queen of Heaven they had had bread enough and saw no evil. But since their offerings ceased (*i.e.*, since the purification of the cultus by Josiah) they have lacked all things and been consumed by the sword and famine.

Jeremiah's reply is for us the swan-song of the prophet.

Once more he bears testimony against the despisers of God. Let them keep their wicked vow, but no one shall again take the name of Jahweh in his mouth. Only a scanty remnant shall one day return to Judah whilst the rest perish in Egypt. Then will it appear whose word is true, his or theirs.

An approximate calculation of Jeremiah's age shows that he cannot have long survived this event. If he was about thirty years old in 628, when he was called, he must have been at least seventy at the destruction of Jerusalem. And what anxiety, privation and ill-treatment he endured in these closing years! According to a Jewish tradition he was finally carried to Babylon. The other tradition is much more probable which says that he was stoned by his own people at Tahpanhes. In 2 Macc. ii. 1 ff., xv. 14 ff., and again in Matt. xvi. 14, we have eloquent testimony to the vividness with which the people's memory occupied itself with the figure of the great sufferer. There are diverse reasons which explain why he was the prophet whose significance was estimated more and more highly as time went on. Not least of these is the fact that no other prophet is personally so near to us, so humanly comprehensible. True we meet with slight traces in Hosea also of the gulf between what he might hope and wish for as a mere man, and what the Spirit of God compelled him to expect and threaten. But in Jeremiah this gulf runs in striking fashion through almost his entire activity. Not as though the prophet were ever unfaithful to the Divine command (i. 18) to show himself "a defenced city, and an iron pillar, and brazen walls, against the whole land, against the kings of Judah, its princes and priests." But what a glimpse we there get into his own distressful heart, which almost gives way under the holy wrath he feels at his people's sins, and at the same time under the deepest pain at his people's destruction! This incessant struggle between the divided forces within him imprints itself to a certain extent on his speech. Although it is very unlike the mighty waves of Isaiah's language it also is able in a peculiar manner to seize and touch the heart by its elegiac tone. Jeremiah has with reason been called "the first poet of feeling amongst the prophets."

The origin of our present *Book of Jeremiah* can be traced in the main to five stages of redaction: the book itself testifies to the four first.

According to xxxvi. 2, Jeremiah commenced his literary activity in the fourth year of Jehoiakim, when he dictated to Baruch all the oracles of the years 628-606. This roll is read to the people by Baruch, and burnt piecemeal in the brazier by Jehoiakim. We can only surmise how much it embraced of the present contents of the Book of Jeremiah. Besides an account of the prophet's calling, the greater part of chaps. ii.-xx., xxi. 11—xxii. 19, xxv. 1-14 probably belonged to it. From the phraseology of xxxvi. 2, it is clear that oracles against external nations were also attached to it. And this is confirmed by the fact that the oracles against foreign nations which are to be read in the Hebrew Jeremiah in chaps. xlvi.-xlix. are arranged in the Greek Bible next after xxv. 13, the only indication in the Hebrew text of their original position being xxv. 15-38. Still it must remain an open question how much of the present contents of xlvi-xlix. can have belonged to Jeremiah's first collection. According to xxxvi. 32, when the roll burnt by Jehoiakim was reproduced, "many like words" were added (amongst them probably the saying to Baruch, chap. xlv.). Hence this is to be regarded as a second stage in the redaction of the book. A third stage is evidenced by the present prologue to the whole (i. 1-3). It dates the ensuing collection from the days of Josiah and Jehoiakim (thus far the title of the first and second roll perhaps extended), but then comes down to the fifth month of the eleventh year of Zedekiah. The redaction of this collection therefore falls in the time after the destruction of Jerusalem: it cannot be determined whether Jeremiah completed it during his two months' stay with Gedaliah, or afterwards in Egypt. But since it says nothing about the oracles in chaps. xlii.-xliv., or the events after the fifth month, it is easily to be distinguished from the fourth step of the redaction, which added chaps. xl.-xliv. and various other accounts of events in Jeremiah's life. This redaction possibly belongs to the first half of the Exile, and may have come from Baruch's hand (but cf. the note). In any case these narratives are founded almost everywhere on excellent information which could only have been obtained from records made by Jeremiah or Baruch themselves, or from the statements of eye-witnesses.* We are finally led to a fifth and last stage by the manifold additions (designated Z in the Survey), parts of which can only have originated in post-exilic times. The interpolations in chap. xxxix., arising from a mistaken idea of the context, certainly belong to this class (v. 1-2 came almost verbally from 2 Kings xxv. 1-4 [Jer. lii. 4-7]; v. 4-13 from 2 Kings xxv. 4-12 [Jer. lii. 7-16]), as also chap lii. (from 2 Kings xxiv. 18—xxv. 21), and the oracle against Babylon in chap. l.-li. 58. The latter was composed in Judea about 400, and founded on the older oracles against Babylon (Isaiah xiii. f., xxi., xxxiv. f., &c.), which in many points it reproduces almost verbally.†

---

* In the Chronological Table, the chapters in question, belonging to 608, are enclosed in square brackets. The reasons for this belief in an exilic stage of the redaction are set forth in a peculiarly convincing manner by Kuenen (in the second edition of his "historisch-kritischen Untersuchung der Bücher des alten Bunds," ii. 255 ff.). It would be especially difficult to understand the very surprising arrangement of many of the oracles, and the use of the name Nebuchadnezzar (instead of the correct form Nebuchadrezzar which Jeremiah himself used) on the assumption that it was due to Jeremiah, or, indeed, to Baruch. According to Kuenen, chaps. xviii.-xx., xxvi.-xxix. and xxxiv.-xliv. are also to be ascribed to this redactor. Stade, too (ZAW, 1892, p. 276 ff.), believes that this redactor's activity was far-reaching, and shows his secondary character in chaps. xxi. and xxiv. f. which he derives (together with xxvi. and xxviii. f.) from a book containing narratives about Jeremiah. Giesebrecht ("Kommentar über das Buch Jeremia," Göttingen, 1894), in a very instructive way, has recently distributed the material under the three categories, "Jeremiah, Baruch, Reviser."

† Cf. the more detailed demonstration of the composition of this oracle (published, doubtless, in Jeremiah's name, and therefore inserted, probably on purpose, before the genuine passage, li. 59 ff.) by Budde, in the "Jahrbücher für deutsche Theologie," Vol. 23, p. 428 ff.

§ 5. THE PERIOD OF THE EXILE.

1. EZEKIEL.

THE period of the Exile—apart from Ezekiel, Lamentations, and a number of elegiac psalms—was formerly considered a time of deathly sleep as regards literature. But in reality a great literary movement went on at this very time, an obvious eagerness to arrange the inheritance of the pre-exilic past, to revise it from a definite view-point and to unite into a great whole the related parts. Along with this there were not lacking fundamental new creations, and this in two apparently quite diverse realms, that of legislation and that of prophecy. Indeed in Ezekiel, the connecting link between the pre-exilic and the exilic time, we have the noteworthy phenomenon of a prophetism which comes forward to legislate and thus becomes of immeasurable significance for the re-founding of the Jewish state as a "theocracy." *Jechāzeqēl*, *i.e.*, God strengthens, son of Buzi, and a member of the priestly order, had been carried captive with Jehoiachin in 597. According to i. 2,* he was called to be a prophet in the fifth year after the captivity of Jehoiachin, *i.e.*, 593 B.C. Ezekiel was then amongst the exiles at Tel Abib (iii. 15), by the river Chebar, in the land of the Chaldæans (i. 3), and thus, without doubt, in Babylonia proper. According to iii. 24, viii. 1, he dwelt there in his own house. Chap. xxiv. 15 ff. shows that he was married: in the ninth year after his captivity his wife, "the desire of his eyes," was taken from him by disease. It is usually concluded from viii. 1, xiv. 1,

---

* The date which precedes this in i. 1, "in the thirtieth year," is usually traced to some Babylonian era, such as that of Nabopolassar as king of Babylon (625). But the original position of the verse was probably at the beginning of an oracle, now lost, belonging to the thirtieth year after Jehoiachin's captivity. Otherwise it is altogether incomprehensible.

where the elders of the people sit before him, that he was held in special honour by the exiles. But the words simply mean that they wished to inquire of him as a prophet (so expressly at xx. 1), as members of the nation elsewhere inquire of him (xxiv. 19, xxxvii. 18). xi. 25, tells of his appearance in a larger circle.

Ezekiel's age at the time he was called is nowhere indicated. But his evidently very exact knowledge of the temple allows us to conjecture that he did not leave Jerusalem as a mere youth, but had probably officiated there as priest. The latest date in his book (xxix. 17) is the twenth-seventh year [after the Captivity], *i.e.*, 571. Hence his prophetic activity lasted twenty-two years. In spite of the favourable judgment which Jer. xxiv. pronounces on the exiles compared with those who had remained behind, Ezekiel (xiv. 3 ff., &c.) has grave complaints to make against his comrades in suffering, even as he had been forewarned that bitter experiences awaited him when he was called (ii. 6 ff., iii. 8 ff.). At xxxiii. 30 ff., he draws a striking picture of the way in which they received his word "as a very lovely song of one that hath a pleasant voice, and plays well on an instrument," and then did not act accordingly.

The outline of the *Book of Ezekiel* is exceedingly clear; the fact that the prophet speaks throughout in the first person is an additional evidence of its homogeneousness. The first main group (chaps. i.-xxiv.) contains visions, discourses and symbolic acts belonging to the time *before* the destruction of Jerusalem and (according to the dates given in chaps. i., viii., xx., xxiv.) arranged chronologically in the fifth, sixth, seventh and ninth years after the Captivity. In the second (chaps. xxv.-xxxii.) main group (most of) the oracles against external nations are brought together in geographical order, except that the larger cycle of predictions against Egypt is moved to the end. The following oracles are dated:— xxix. 1 in the tenth year; xxvi. 1, xxx. 20, xxxi. 1, in the eleventh year; xxxii. 1 and 17, in the twelfth year of the Captivity. The date at xxix. 17 introduces a sort of correction of the oracle against Tyre (chap. xxvii.). It is evident that this appendix was added to the already finished book, because the threatening against Tyre remains unaltered. The third group (chaps. xxxiii.-xxxix.) consists chiefly of discourses concerning the future, amongst which are the magnificent prediction of the quickening of the dead bones (*i.e.*, the people buried in the Exile) in chap. xxxvii., and the prediction of the final assault of the heathen powers, Gog and his allies, on the restored divine commonwealth (chap. xxxviii. f.). The only one of these oracles that is dated is chap. xxxiii. 21, in the twelfth* year. As a fourth main group, belonging to the twenty-fifth year after the Captivity, there follows finally chaps. xl.-xlviii., the great vision of the reconstitution of the divine commonwealth, especially of the temple and the cultus, in the Messianic Age.

With the exception of xxvi. 1, where, through a clerical error, the month (not the day of the month!) is missing, the dates are everywhere given according to year, month and day. This must have been noted down at the time by the prophet: in one case (xxiv. 2) he is expressly said to have done so. We know not to what extent Ezekiel added other kinds of remarks to these notes. We only know, from the thorough homogeneousness of language and thoughts, and not less from the occasional glances at later occurrences (such as the blinding of Zedekiah, xii. 13, the end of the kingdom, xix. 12 ff.) that the actual composition of the book took place during the later life of the prophet, and was not interrupted by any long intervals.

The verdict on Ezekiel's literary character was formerly influenced entirely by the assumption that he had before him the Pentateuch, with the priestly legislation at its head, in its complete form. On this assumption it was not possible to find many original thoughts in Ezekiel, and one could not but marvel greatly that he—a priest!—should come, in chaps.

---

* A mistake, no doubt, for the "eleventh year." Otherwise the messenger who brought to Tel Abib the news of the taking of Jerusalem was eighteen months in doing it.

xl.-xlviii., to recast, in many respects in fresh forms, the law which had long been held sacred. But we reach quite another conclusion when we yield to the force of facts and place the so-called Priests' Code of the Pentateuch in the exilic and post-exilic time. Ezek. xl.-xlviii. then becomes, not a re-modelling hard to understand, but the first sketch of the priestly legislation. The man who was supposed to be a bookworm becomes the creator of new ideas, the pioneer of a new order of things, a man of practical activity, and activity which produces an extraordinary result.

To estimate aright the position and the ulterior aims of Ezekiel we must look back upon the years since 623. The law-book found in 623 had put down the worship at the high-places (at all events after the building of the temple) as a transgression which must thenceforward be entirely forsaken. But the manner in which the priests of the high-places are recommended to the benevolence of the people, and in which the right is even conceded them at xviii. 6, to officiate as priests at Jerusalem, show that the Deuteronomic writer did not regard the worship at the high-places and everything connected with it as an inexpiable sin of the people. It seemed to him that it was not yet too late to reform and, by the zealous practice of a worship acceptable to God, to save the State. But the subsequent course of events pronounced a different verdict. Neither had the reforming zeal which was excited from above proved lasting—what idolatrous abominations in the temple Ezekiel could tell of in chap. viii.!—nor did the judgments which had come in the interval allow of the conclusion that the people's guilt had diminished. It is at this point that Ezekiel's ideas concerning the whole of the nation's past come in. To him, as chaps. xvi. and xxiii. set forth in more than forcible images, it was from the beginning an uninterrupted series of heathen abominations, an endless accumulation of inexpiable guilt. Hence there is no compassion for the guilty. Not till the city and the temple have been burnt, till famine and sword and exile have done their work, can there be any thought of showing grace to the scanty remnant which by that time will have been sifted again. And the replanting of this remnant, the re-establishment of the State and the cultus, must be done in forms which will exclude for ever a return to the so heavily punished abominations. "Holiness," *i.e.*, purity from every sort of stain, is to be the character of the new divine commonwealth, holiness, not merely of the temple, but of the whole circuit of the temple, indeed of the whole land and people. And the preservation of this holiness is guaranteed by a series of symbols and inviolable ordinances relating to the holy places, times, persons and actions. These ordinances, indeed, are not regarded as of equal importance with the legitimate worship of God, but they are the indispensable conditions of this. Ezekiel thus became the creator of the ceremonial law, the spiritual father of the Levitical tendency in Judaism. Its foundation-lines, as we have said, are to be seen in the nine last chapters of his book. It was a great mistake to see nothing but allegories and symbols in the demands which the prophet there makes. Where there are such, as at chap. xlvii. 1-12, they are easy to interpret. But most of the demands must be understood to be seriously intended by the prophet, and they were carried out in the priestly legislation, except where the power of traditional custom or other circumstances stood in their way. The most important of all the innovations is introduced in chap. xliv. 6 ff. Instead of the uncircumcised strangers who have hitherto done the menial work of the sanctuary the former priests of the high-places (and their descendants) are to do it in the future. They lose their priestly privileges: henceforth these are to be reserved for the sons of Zadok, *i.e.*, the offspring of the priestly families of Jerusalem. This demand of Ezekiel's is the root of the *distinction between Priests and Levites*, which Deuteronomy knows nothing of, whereas it plays an extremely important rôle in the Priestly Law. That alone is sufficient to show the proper position of the so-called Priests' Code—later than Ezekiel.

The assertion that, except in the last nine chapters, Ezekiel is quite destitute of originality, or that "the prophet was stifled by the writer" is only justifiable to this extent, that Ezekiel must really be styled the earliest of the "literary prophets" (in the narrower sense of the word). Not as though that operation of the Spirit of God, which Ezekiel in particular brings into such frequent prominence, were purely fanciful, or as though no nucleus of fact lay at the foundation of the visions. But those elements of the visions which cannot be put into a mental picture (cf. especially i. 11, 15 ff.), and those symbolical acts which cannot be performed (cf. iv. 4 ff.), can only be regarded as the literary expression of prophetic ideas. The prophetic discourses, however, are not lacking in new images and similes of all kinds, and over the whole there broods so profound a moral earnestness, so clear a consciousness of each man's responsibility for what he does and what he permits (chaps. xiv., xviii., xxxiii.), that it must be called a grievous wrong to the prophet when the preceding thirty-nine chapters are forgotten because of chaps. xl.-xlviii. He who laid the foundation of Leviticism is yet—quite in the spirit of the old prophets—acquainted with only *one* means of quickening the dry bones, and that is the breath of God which enters into them, brings the risen ones back to their native soil and there makes an everlasting covenant of peace with them (xxxvii. 14, 26).

2. LAMENTATIONS.

When we come to deal with the so-called "Law of Holiness" and the Priests' Code, we shall discover the form in which Ezekiel's programme of the future was carried out. We have first to do with a set of literary products in which not only the phraseology but also the spirit of Deuteronomy continued to work. To this class we assign the Lamentations, among the poetical productions; the Deuteronomistic revision of all the historical books, in the field of historiography; and, in that of prophecy, the consolatory speech of the "Great Unknown" (Isa. xl. ff.), and some other prophetic pieces which are now incorporated in the Book of Isaiah.

Lamentations, in the Hebrew Bible the third of the "Festival Rolls," or Megilloth (more precisely the Megillah of the 9th of Ab, the day of the burning of the temple), betrays in almost every part so lively a recollection of the closing period of the siege and taking of Jerusalem, that at least the greater portion of it can have been written by no one who was not an eye-witness or a younger contemporary of these events. The supposition that Jeremiah was the author is unknown to the Hebrew Bible. It first appears in the exordium of the Lamentations in the Greek (hence also in the Latin) Bible, and perhaps rests only on the erroneous interpretation of 2 Chron. xxxv. 25. Babylonia—not, as others preferred, Egypt—is in all probability the country where it was composed. Chaps. i.-iv. are alphabetical poems; and in chaps. i., ii., iv. each verse, in chap. iii. each set of three verses, begins with one of the twenty-two letters of the Hebrew alphabet (only that in chaps. ii.-iv. ʽ*Ayĭn* comes after *Pē*, as was originally the case in Ps. xxxiv. 18, 17). Besides this, there is in chaps. i.-iv. a special form of verse (the so-called Lamentation-verse or Qinah-verse, discovered by Ley and Budde), in which a short first clause is followed by a still shorter. In chaps. i. and ii. each of our verses consists of three Lamentation-verses; in chap. iii. of one; in chap. iv. of two. In chap. v. every verse has two clauses, but is differently constructed from those of chaps. i.-iv.

The older view, that all five poems are from the same hand, has of late been much shaken. After Stade (Geschichte des Volkes Israel, p. 701) had assigned chap. iii. to a much later time, Löhr (Die Klagelieder, Göttingen, 1891) distinguished between the poet of chaps. ii.-iv., who everywhere addresses the city and the author of i. and v., who, in adding these, aimed at making ii.-iv. available for divine service. In the Handkommentar (Gött., 1892), Löhr places the poet of ii.

and iv. about 570, the one of i. and v. about 530, whilst iii. is ascribed to a third, perhaps somewhat later, poet. Cornill also (Einleitung ins Alte Testament², p. 246 ff.; ³ ⁴, p. 231) maintains this undoubtedly correct distinction, in so far as to recognize only chaps. ii. and iv. as the "oldest and most valuable" part, and also traces chaps. i. and v. to one hand. In these, too, impressive utterance is given to the wretchedness occasioned by the invariably cheerless surroundings and the burdensome consciousness of a never-expiated guilt of the people.

To the same period, no doubt, belongs the splendid poem Deut. xxxii. 1-43, which at xxxi. 19 ff. is ascribed to God Himself, and at His behest is written out by Moses and Joshua, and at v. 30 is said to have been pronounced aloud by Moses to assembled Israel. But the poem itself contains nothing to necessitate the belief that it was composed by Moses, or in his day. The poet makes no secret of his far later standpoint when he describes the time of Israel's election and the bringing out of Egypt (v. 7) as "the days of old," treats the occupation of Canaan and the enjoyment of all the blessings of the fertile land (v. 13 ff.) as a historical fact, and (v. 15 ff.) represents the Divine rejection of Israel as the inevitable result of Israel's immeasurable apostasy and incurable ingratitude. Reproaches of this sort would doubtless apply to various centuries, and we can therefore understand how earlier critics deemed it possible to place the poem in the ninth or eighth century, and thus thought of it as accepted by the Jahwist (J) or the Elohist (E). A keener investigation of the contents (especially as regards the vocabulary) has shown the relationship in language and spirit with Jeremiah and Deuteronomy to be so striking as absolutely to forbid its being placed earlier than the end of the seventh century. When we also consider that, according to the only natural explanation of the conclusion (v. 36 ff.), the judgment on Israel has already been executed, and that now, on the other hand, vengeance is to be taken on the arrogant foes who have wickedly exceeded the Divine commission to chastise Israel, we are compelled by all this to place the poem in the Exile. With this it agrees that in v. 8, according to the original text which is preserved in the Greek Bible,* we meet with a view which cannot be certainly supported by any but exilic and post-exilic passages.

3. THE CLOSE OF THE DEUTERONOMISTIC HISTORICAL WORK.

As regards the products of the Deuteronomistic historiography, we must start from the fact adduced on p. 67 that Deuteronomy (apart from the still more recent additions, iv. 41-43, x. 6-9, xxxii. 48-52, xxxiv. 1a, 7-9) cannot have assumed its present form till the Exile. In all probability a yet more extensive work of redaction was very intimately connected with this, the blending of the compound *JE* (as to whose origin cf. p. 61 f.) with Deuteronomy, and the Deuteronomistic revision and expansion of the historical books from the Book of Judges to the Second Book of Kings.

In the four first books of the Pentateuch the traces of the Deuteronomist are comparatively infrequent. Most likely Gen. xxvi. 5, Exod. xiii. 3-16, xv. 25 f., belong to him, as well as Exod. xxxiv. 10b-13, Num. xxi. 33-35, and much else in the Pentateuch, which, for the sake of certainty, we have simply designated *R* (Redactor). The hand of the Deuteronomist is very noticeable in the Book of Joshua, and his additions are at times so closely interwoven with *JE*'s material that the analysis of the sources is attended with great difficulties, and not unfrequently must despair of a certain result. It is not so in the Book of Judges. The Deuteronomistic enlargements (designated *Rd* in the Survey) of the pre-Deuteronomic Book of Judges (on which cf. above, p. 21 ff.) can here be pretty certainly detected by various signs, not the

* Instead of "according to the number of the children of Israel," read "according to the number of the angels of God," and cf. Deut. iv. 19. As Israel is governed by Jahweh, so the heathen nations, according to His ordination and under His suzerainty, are ruled by inferior gods (cf. especially Ps. lxxxii.) or "princes" (Dan. x. 13 ff.).

least of which is their similarity to the corresponding portions of the Books of Kings. The idea that the Judges were actual lifelong rulers of the whole people, and the so-called "theocratic pragmatism," *i.e.*, the tracing all the people's fortunes to their religious behaviour, are to be attributed to this redactor, and next to these his chief feature is the fixed chronological scheme. This is founded on that calculation of the interval between the Exodus and the building of the Temple at 480 years, which we have mentioned above, p. 74. In our present Book of Judges 593 years are given to the same interval,* and this is due to the fact that the final redactor (see below), in opposition to the Deuteronomist's view, adds a number of years (110 in all) for Othniel and the so-called Minor Judges, and also the three years of Abimelech (according to ix. 22).

The redactor, designated *Ri*, in the Book of Judges seems to have brought his revision of the older histories down to the end of Samuel and Saul. In the Books of Samuel, apart from the chronological notices and other traces of his activity, there are some other characteristic pieces from a Deuteronomistic hand. Thus at 1 Sam. ii. 35 ff. there is an undeniable reference to the fate of the non-Zadokite priests after Josiah's reform of the ritual. The later origin of 1 Sam. vii. 3 ff. is shown by its ignoring (v. 13 f.) the oppression of Israel by the Philistines, which lasted down to David's time. In 1 Sam. xii. the reviser's hand appears to come out specially at the close. At 2 Sam. vii., apart from the general tone of the speech, it is most recognizable in v. 12 f. The original words (retained in v. 27) were: "*Thou* shalt not build me a house but *I* thee!" altered into, "Not *thou*, but thy son!" The latest Deuteronomistic insertion in the old David-Stories is 1 Kings ii. 1-9, the so-called Testament of David. The principal argument against its belonging to the David-Source (*Da*) is that in the latter the execution of Joab and Shimei is not ascribed to

* To the 390 years which we get by adding up the numbers in the Book of Judges we must add forty years each for Moses, Joshua, Eli, Samuel and David, and the three first years of Solomon.

David's orders but to other causes. It is difficult to say what end was contemplated by the interpolation. If Solomon, the builder of the temple, was to be thus freed from blood-guiltiness, David, on the other hand, was credited with such revengefulness, nay, treachery, that he lost as much as Solomon gained. On the (second) Deuteronomistic revision of the Books of Kings cf. above, p. 72 f. To it is probably to be ascribed the transplanting of 1 Kings i., ii. from its connection with the David-Stories (cf. above, p. 27) to the head of the Book of Kings.

3. Deutero-Isaiah (and Trito-Isaiah).

The connected historical work which originated in the pains taken by the Deuteronomistic redactors (for we can hardly think of only *one* hand as doing it all) embraced about two-thirds of all the matter in the historical books from Genesis to the end of the Second Book of Kings. All these supplements and revisions of the older literature bore, as we have several times remarked, the stamp of Deuteronomy, of legislation in the spirit of prophetism. That spirit was yet alive and capable of creative acts, as is evinced by a wonderful monument of its activity in the last quarter of the Exile, the so-called Deutero-Isaiah,[*] *i.e.*, chap. xl. ff. of our present Book of Isaiah.

It is mainly the great events of the time about 546 B.C., the overthrow of the kingdoms of Media and Lydia by Cyrus, which are more or less clearly reflected in chaps. xl.-xlviii. The time of consolation is come, the judgment on Judah is at an end. According to His primæval counsel, and the prophetic proclamation made long ago, the Almighty Incomparable God will

---

[*] This name (literally "Second Isaiah") is not meant to express the conjecture (which has actually been offered) that the author of these nine chapters was also called Isaiah, but simply to indicate that they form an independent second part of the Book of Isaiah.

bring His people home, and put to shame the idols of the heathen. He has chosen Cyrus as the instrument for chastising Babylon and delivering Israel. It is this deliverance which opens to Israel the possibility of fulfilling the mission for the salvation of the world entrusted to it by the eternal counsel of God, hindered by its own sins and blindness, but not on that account cancelled. With the renewal of the people its glory, as that of a priestly people, is to be manifested, and the worship of God in Spirit and Truth is to take the place of the dead service of works. The new Jerusalem is the prelude of a renewing of heaven and earth: the re-union of all the dispersed, everlasting salvation for the redeemed, and everlasting suffering for the ungodly, form the close.

But this gives only a slight idea of the overflowing wealth of prophetic ideas in these twenty-seven chapters. Two causes render it very difficult to give a precise statement of their contents. There is no strictly logical consecution of thoughts. Complaints and reproofs alternate with consolations and promises; words of hope and joy are followed by others, occasioned, probably, by fresh events, betraying a depressed mood. The external form also alternates between an exquisite prose and a purely poetic diction. The other difficulty is the ambiguousness of what is said concerning one of the weightiest ideas in the whole book, the "Servant of Jahweh." In one set of passages (xli. 8, xliv. 1, 21, &c.) this as certainly means the people of Israel, as in another (xlix. 5, l. 10) it is clearly distinguished therefrom. If, as is natural, we take these latter passages to mean the spiritual Israel, the truly theocratic-minded ones, to whom has been entrusted the mission, not only to the heathen but also to their own people, a fresh difficulty arises out of the famous section on the Undeservedly Suffering Servant of Jahweh, lii. 13 ff. The ascription of the individual traits to a plurality instead of to a single person is exceedingly difficult, for the prophet certainly belonged to the moral kernel of the people, and yet he sets himself (liii. 2 ff.) with the rest, in contrast to the Servant of Jahweh. But this is not all. After chap. liii. only *Servants* of Jahweh (in

7

the plural) are spoken of (liv. 17, &c.). Duhm ("Kommentar über das Buch Jesaja," Gött., 1892) attempted to solve the riddle by assuming that the so-called Ebed-Jahweh (treating of the Servant of Jahweh) Poems, xlii. 1-4, xlix. 1-6, l. 4-9, lii. 13—liii. 12, were written between 500 and 450, and therefore were subsequently incorporated with Deutero-Isaiah. Others have distinguished between the poet and Deutero-Isaiah, whilst holding that the poems were written contemporaneously with the latter. Others altogether dispute the separation of these poems from the work of Deutero-Isaiah.

The observation already made by Eichhorn that part of the utterances of Deutero-Isaiah can only be explained as belonging to the early days after the Return, has recently been repeated and thoroughly established. The only dispute about it is as to where the line is to be drawn between exilic and post-exilic matter. Stade (Gesch. Israels, ii. 70 f.) designates only chaps. lxiii.-lxvi. as at least revised, but the result reached by Kuenen (Einl., ii. 235 ff.), chiefly through observation of the style and language, is that the part brought from Babylon in 536 (probably xl.-xlix., lii. 1-12) was the nucleus of a collection which expanded still further, to which also its original author may have added, till at length, probably in the sixth century, the whole was united and in some measure arranged. This hypothesis may satisfactorily explain much that is surprising, but the idea that various hands have been at work from chap. l. onwards is a little suspicious, seeing that there is such far-reaching harmony both of thoughts and of form. Stade, therefore, and Cornill (Einl.,[2] p. 158 f.;[3] p. 160 f.) would only admit that chaps. lxiii.-lxvi. were supplemented or revised by another hand. And Cornill held it possible that chaps. xlix.-lxii. were not written out till after the Return (but by the same author as xl.-xlviii.). Duhm, on the contrary, ascribes lvi.-lxvi. to a Trito-Isaiah ("third Isaiah"), working about the middle of the fifth century.

The ascription of these twenty-seven chapters to Isaiah, son of Amoz, which is taken for granted, by Jesus Sirach (xlviii.

27), has not the slightest support in the text. Nowhere is there a trace of the author's wishing to pass for Isaiah. On the contrary, he describes the circumstances of the time in which he lived so clearly that only an exposition misled by false tradition could find prediction here. Jerusalem still lies in ruins: the people addressed still languish in exile (xl. 2, xliv. 26, xlv. 13, xlvii. 6, xlviii. 20, lii. 2 f., 11, lxiv. 9 f.). The Chaldæans, whose capital is Babylon, are the oppressors (xliii. 14, xlvii. 1, 5, xlviii. 14, &c.). Cyrus (Koresh; we meet the same form of the name at Ezra i. 1, 7 f., v. 13 ; 2 Chron. xxxvi. 22 f.) is the instrument of deliverance. Hence it is simply foolish to assert that by placing Deutero-Isaiah at the end of the Exile we make it out to be a forgery. In all probability the mistaken connection with the Book of Isaiah (which clearly ends with chaps. xxxvi.-xxxix!) is to be explained as follows. According to a Jewish tradition, which is still attested by the oldest German and French manuscripts, the original order of the prophets was this: Jeremiah, Ezekiel, Isaiah, and the Book of the Twelve. In this arrangement by the size of the books Deutero-Isaiah had its proper place betwixt Isaiah and Hosea. When Isaiah, on chronological grounds, was put at the head, the twenty-seven chapters which had no title were taken over with it, and thus a tradition was created which, in spite of its lack of foundation, has tenaciously asserted itself for many centuries.

5. ISA. XXXIV. f., XIII. f., XXI. 1-10.

Chaps. xxxiv. and xxxv. of the Book of Isaiah are of precisely the same tone and spirit as Deutero-Isaiah, and therefore are ascribed to him by many. They are a threat against the Edomites because of the wrong done by these to Jerusalem (when it was taken and destroyed: cf. Ps. cxxxvii. 7, Lam. iv. 21), and a promise to the exiles of a happy return to Zion. It is questionable whether the two chapters form *one* connected oracle: but there can be no doubt that it should be dated in the Exile or soon after.

The oracle of the fall of Babylon (Isa. xiii.-xiv. 23), also attributed to Isaiah, is of a somewhat different kind. As a specimen of poetry it is one of the most splendid creations in the realm of the Old Testament. This is specially true of the satirical song on the fallen King of Babylon (xiv. 4 ff.). As in Deutero-Isaiah, the historical background (especially at xiii. 19) is clearly to be distinguished from the prediction. The siege of Babylon by the Medes and Persians is close at hand, and with it the deliverance of the people who have been so long enslaved.

Finally, Isaiah xxi. 1-10 is placed by most in the same time (that of the overthrow of Babylon by the combined Medes and Persians; cf. verse 2). But the explanation of this difficult section by means of the relations prevalent about 710 B.C. is not altogether impossible, and consequently its derivation from Isaiah is not excluded.

6. The Law of Holiness.

All these prophetic voices, including Deutero-Isaiah, are of a different spirit from Ezek. xl.-xlviii. They were doubtless preceded by a work, the so-called Law of Holiness, in Lev. xvii.-xxvi., which is closely related to the chapters in Ezekiel. The name was given by Klostermann on account of the frequency with which the Divine commands are grounded on the proposition, "for I Jahweh am holy (xx. 26, xxi. 8, &c.), or "I am Jahweh, who hallows you (or 'them')." The characteristic which immediately strikes us is that of a priestly law, satisfying, above all things, the requirements of the ritual. The Deuteronomic demand that sacrifices should be brought to only *one* sanctuary, allowing, however, according to Deut. xii. 15, that animals might be slaughtered and eaten at any place, is now raised higher, so as to mean that every act of slaughter is to be regarded as a sacrifice, and consequently can only be performed at the one legitimate sanctuary. The unity of the cultus, which the Deuteronomic writer does not require till after the temple had been built, is therefore here carried back to the age of the Journey through the Desert. Then there follow in confused alternation regulations concerning the eating of blood and carcases, forbidden degrees of marriage and sins of unchastity, treatment of the sacrifices, the gleanings, the rights of neighbours in every conceivable relation, also the priests' duties, the celebration of the religious festivals, the Sabbatic year and the Year of Jubilee—all from the point of view that the trangression of these commandments defiles the land and violates the divinely willed holiness of the people, and thus of Jahweh Himself. And all these commandments are introduced as oral directions given by God to Moses that he might hand them on to Aaron and the people. According to the subscription, xxvi. 46, Mount Sinai is the scene of the revelation, and thus the sanctuary is the "tent of revelation" (Luther, "Die Hütte des Stifts"). The spiritual relationship with Ezek. xl.-xlviii. is of such a kind that this prophet has been held by famous critics to be the actual author of the Law of Holiness.

Although we have thus far spoken of this law-book as a literary unity, we must now point out that in it also very diverse constituents, and consequently a subsequent revision of an older original, have recently been demonstrated. Most scholars follow Klostermann in designating this original by H, *i.e.*, Law of Holiness; Dillmann uses S, *i.e.*, Law of Sinai; Kuenen, P^1, *i.e.*, first stratum of the Priests' Law. The only outstanding dispute concerning it is as to its extent. It has been shown probable that some other pieces (Lev. xi., some passages in xiii.-xv.; and according to Dillmann, Exod. xxxi. 13 ff.; Lev. v. 1-6, 21 ff.; Num. x. 9 ff., xv. 38 ff.) belonged to the original Law of Holiness. And within chaps. xvii.-xxvi. the boundaries between the original and the additions have been very differently drawn. According to Dillmann (Kommentar zu Num. bis Josua, p. 635 ff.) these chapters contain a redactor's amalgamation of two varying revisions of the Law of Sinai (which Dillmann believes to be very ancient). On the other hand, the most recent discussion of this complicated question (Bäntsch, Das Heiligkeitsgesetz, Erfurt, 1893) distinguishes between chaps. xviii.-xx. (II^1) as post-Deuteronomic but prior to Ezekiel, and the group later than Ezekiel, II^2 (chaps. xxi. and xxii.) and II^3 (chaps. xvii. and xxvi.). In any case the entire corpus received its present stamp from a hand which was most closely related to the author or authors of the Priests' Code proper. This comes out with especial clearness at xxiii. 36. In harmony with Deut. xvi. 15 and Ezek. xlv. 25, a seven-days' celebration of the Harvest Festival was here commanded originally (v. 34) : in accordance with the precept in the Priests' Code the reviser added the eighth day. But in spite of its points of contact with Deuteronomy, the original Law of Holiness was not so closely allied to it as to the Priests' Code, which was soon after taken in hand in the same spirit.

§ 6. THE POST-EXILIC PERIOD.

HAGGAI AND ZECHARIAH.—MALACHI.

THE edict of Cyrus (538) threw open the way home to the exiles. The hopes with which at least part of them trod it may be discovered in such prophetic utterances as Isaiah xxxv. and Zeph. iii. 14 ff. But grave hindrances were soon interposed which threatened the existence of the new colony and brought down the joyous spirit of those who had returned. According to Ezra iii. 10 ff. the foundation of the temple was laid soon after the Return: but it was not till after 520 that the building was more vigorously prosecuted. The contemporary prophets Haggai and Zechariah give us instructive glimpses into the circumstances and feelings of this latter period.

Both are mentioned at Ezra v. 1 and vi. 14 as zealous promoters of the building of the temple. Three of the four oracles of Haggai are devoted to this object; and all are dated precisely by the month and day of the second year of Darius (520). In i. 1-11 he exhorts Zerubbabel and the high priest Joshua to greater zeal in promoting the building, and contradicts the assertion that the time for this has not yet come. The appendix (v. 12 ff.) tells of the good result of this exhortation. In ii. 1-9 he consoles the leaders and the rest of the people, especially those who had seen Solomon's temple, for the poverty of the new building. The old promises are yet to be fulfilled: through them shall the glory of this second temple be greater than that of the first. In ii. 10-19 the prophet teaches that all sacrifices are useless if they neglect the duty of zealously prosecuting the building of the temple. The fourth oracle (ii. 20 ff.) promises Zerubbabel that when the heathen world is overthrown, *i.e.*, when the Messianic Kingdom dawns, he shall be a signet-ring in God's hand.

It is highly probable that Haggai himself was one of those who had seen the former temple: in that case he must have been more than seventy years old in 520. As a matter of fact, his whole manner of speaking is that of an aged man; even in more elevated passages it does not go beyond the bounds of prose.

Zechariah, the author of Zech. i.-viii. (the so-called Proto-Zechariah; we shall have to speak later of chaps. ix.-xiv., the "Deutero-Zechariah") is called son of Berechiah, son of Iddo, in i. 1, but at Ezra v. 1, vi. 14, son of Iddo. The latter statement can hardly have been meant to bring out prominently that the prophet belonged to the *priestly family* which was called after Iddo (Neh. xii. 4, 16). It is more likely that "son of Berechiah" Zech. i. 1, was subsequently interpolated: Kuenen conjectures that it was borrowed from an earlier title of chaps. ix.-xi., which assigned them to a Zechariah, son of Berechiah.

The Prologue (i. 1-6), dated in the eighth month of the year 520, exhorts the present generation not to neglect the call to repentance, like their fathers, who therefore had to experience the wrathful judgment of God. Connected with this are chaps. i. 7—vi. 8, the seven (or, if ii. 5 ff. is taken as an independent section, eight) Visions of the Night, dated from the 24th day of the 11th month of 520. Although seen in the night all these diverse images, which are explained to the prophet by an angel, issue in consoling promises relating to the complete restoration of Judah to favour and the humiliation of the heathen. The appendix, vi. 9-15, also gives a comforting promise concerning the Messianic time. The second main division (chaps. vii., viii.) contains a prophetic decision relating to the fasts which had hitherto been kept. Jahweh does not desire these fast days (which commemorate the taking of Jerusalem and the murder of Gedaliah): they should rather be turned into joyous festivals in expectation of the blessings of the Messianic time. Although Zechariah's language is somewhat more vivid than Haggai's he seldom rises above the forms of prose.

The last prophet who probably laboured before the great turning-point of the year 444 (see below) was Malachi. This name might be the shortened form of Malachiah (as in the Greek Bible), *i.e.*, " Jahweh's Messenger." But it has been truly observed that a new-born babe could scarcely be so called. Moreover Malachi is not called a prophet at i. 1, and the three superscriptions, Zech. ix. 1, xii. 1, Mal. i. 1, were obviously shaped by the same hand. Hence it can hardly be doubted that *mal'ākhī* (" my messenger ") i. 1, is only a catchword taken from iii. 1. It is an ancient, but assuredly idle, conjecture that no less a person than Ezra is here concealed.

The discourse of this unknown prophet rebukes the dishonouring of Jahweh by sacrifices unworthy of Him. And the curse is first to fall on the priests, who thus forget the high calling and privilege of Levi (ii. 1-9). Severe blame is then addressed to those who married heathen wives and put away " the wife of their youth," and those who blasphemed Jahweh by doubting His righteousness (ii. 10-17). But Jahweh will send His messenger (according to iii. 23, Elijah) to prepare His way; for He will soon appear to destroy manifold kinds of sinners amongst the people and to deliver the godly (chap. iii.).

The idea formerly prevalent that Ezra's activity is presupposed all through the prophecy has recently been contested,* with a view of showing that it must be placed earlier than Ezra. No doubt its insistence on the strict observance of the sacrificial precepts (i. 7 ff., 13 f., iii. 10) reminds us of the zeal for the law which originated with the oath to obey Ezra's priestly law-book. Yet there were legal precepts before Ezra: at iii. 22 attention is expressly called to the " statutes and ordinances " which God gave at Horeb, an obvious reference to Deuteronomy, even as the spirit and language of that law-book is elsewhere noticeable in Malachi. But the observances of such ritual laws as were extant had not hitherto been so strongly insisted on. It is difficult to believe that such offences as are rebuked at Mal. i. 7 ff. and 13 f. could have

* Especially by Stade, Geschichte Israels, ii. 133.

been committed after the engagement to observe the Priests' Law (444). Such circumstances also as are presupposed at ii. 11 ff. are incomprehensible after the Draconic measures of Ezra (Ezra ix., x.; about 457 B.C.). The very latest date possible would be that adopted by some recent writers, prior to Nehemiah's second residence (432), seeing that he also had to contend with mixed marriages (Neh. xiii. 4 ff.) and neglect of the tithes (Neh. xiii. 10; cf. Mal. iii. 10). Yet it remains more probable that Malachi is to be placed earlier than 458.

The peculiarity of this prophet's language, which, for the rest, is simple prose, like Haggai's and Zechariah's, is its predilection for a kind of dialogue between God and the people; so at i. 2, 6, 7; ii. 14, 17; iii. 7, 8, 13.

2. The Priests' Code and the Law-book of Ezra.—The Close of the Pentateuch and of the Historical Work extending from Gen. i. to 2 Kings xxv.

The programme for the theocracy of the future—we might briefly say, for the priestly commonwealth—was sketched by Ezekiel. The first attempt to carry out this programme was contained in the original Law of Holiness (see above, p. 100). But we have no knowledge as to the Law of Holiness obtaining official recognition in the worship at Jerusalem after the Return. Something quite different can be shown to have happened: even after the Exile the further development of the Priests' Law was most zealously pursued in the priestly circles which had remained behind in Babylon. We say "In the priestly circles." For it will appear that differences are not wanting which point to divergent theories and therefore to diverse hands and circles participating in the work. The priestly history and law-book in the Pentateuch was the product of various priestly schools in the period between 500 and 400 B.C., first at Babylon, then at Jerusalem. Apart from the "Law of Holiness," which was worked up into it, the following strata can be clearly distinguished: the Priests' Code proper (about 500); the "Law-book of Moses" (published 444), in all probability drawn up by Ezra himself; and the final redaction, occasioned probably by the blending of the Priests' Law with the older historical work (JED), about 400 B.C. But as regards the spirit which pervades them and the fundamental assumptions from which they start, *all* the parts bear so homogeneous a stamp that we have contented ourselves in the "Survey" with the common designation P, *i.e.*, Priests' Writing. This homogeneousness may justify us in attempting here to characterize the whole as it *now* lies before us.

The Priests' Writing begins, like J and E, with a preliminary history of the people. But it gives this in such extremely scanty outlines as to be only comprehensible when we think of the detailed representation in J and E as universally known. The Cosmogony (Gen. i.), in which the artistic arrangement of the six days' work and the highly developed idea of God are especially noticeable, is followed in chap. v. by a list of the patriarchs from Adam to Noah, then by an account of the Deluge in a quite different chronological framework from the Jahwist's, then by the so-called covenant with Noah (chap. ix.). This was succeeded by a Table of the Nations, of which only part is contained in chap. x., a list of the patriarchs from Shem to Abraham (chap. xi.), and quite short notices on the separation of Abraham from Lot and the birth of Ishmael. Only the Covenant of Circumcision with Abraham (chap. xvii.) and the purchase of the burying-place at Hebron (chap. xxiii.) are more fully treated; the death of Abraham, the sending of Jacob to Mesopotamia and his return, more briefly; and, with extreme brevity, Esau's separation from Jacob, Jacob's going down into Egypt, as well as his death, and his burial in the cave at Hebron. In this series of notices gaps can no doubt be perceived; before xxv. 26b the birth of Jacob and Esau, after xxviii. 7 something or other about Jacob's sojourn with Laban, must have been mentioned. In like manner Joseph must have been spoken of somewhere before xlvi. 6. But all these gaps were doubtless filled up with such scanty notices that the final redactor who in other places considered the Priestly Writing so carefully could dispense with them. There is, however, no more instructive example of the manner in which P takes for granted the contents of JE, and therefore simply recapitulates in the briefest form, than Gen. xix. 29. This one verse reproduces almost the entire contents of Gen. xviii. and xix.

In Exodus also the preliminary history down to the legislation at Sinai is somewhat scantily treated. But at chap. xxv. the great consecutive codes of law begin which extend almost uninterruptedly to Num. x. 28 (but see Exod. xxxii.-xxxiv.). After this, too, we meet with detailed laws and narratives from the same source, part of them closely interwoven with JE. An account of the death of Joshua in all probability formed its conclusion in the Book of Joshua (after long statements about the apportionment of the Holy Land amongst the several tribes and the boundaries of these); for Joshua xxiv. 29b, can scarcely be from any other source than P.

If we now ask for the signs which justify the ascription of whole chapters or even single verses and parts of verses to the Priestly Writing, a whole series of these can be mentioned (besides the avoiding of the divine name Jahweh down to Exod. vi. 2)—part of which are so characteristic and unmistakable that almost perfect unanimity has gradually been reached in this particular stratum of the Pentateuch and Joshua. One of the most notable signs is *the style*, with its unfailing breadth, its fondness for exhaustive details and "juristic formulating" (cf. Gen. i. 11 ff., 16 ff., xxvi. and xxviii.) and even for pure schematism (cf. Gen. v. 11, x. ff., Exod. xxxviii. 21 ff., Num. i. ii. xxvi. xxviii. xxix. xxxi. 26 ff., but, above all, chap. vii. 12 ff., where six verses are twelve times repeated). Corresponding to the preference for precise measures and numbers is the endeavour to provide the most precise chronological framework possible. Whilst the Jahwist contents himself with such general statements as Gen. xviii. 11, P calculates most particularly how old Abraham was at the Immigration (xii. 4b), at the birth of Ishmael (xvi. 16), at the institution of circumcision (xvii. 1, 24), at the birth of Isaac (xxi. 5), and at his death (xxv. 7). Elsewhere, too, the most precise chronological data all belong to *P*.

More important than these external features is the sharply marked religious standpoint of the Priests' Writing. We have already spoken of the elevated idea of God which meets us at the very outset in the cosmogony: "He said, Let there be light: and there was light." As the creative omnipotence of God here requires neither preparation nor medium so elsewhere His revelations are made simply by the word. The Jahwist does not shrink from remarkably human representations of God (Gen. iii. 8 ff., xviii. 1 ff., xxxii. 24 ff., &c.): but in the Priests' Writing the appearance of God on extraordinary occasions is only indicated as it were from afar (Gen. xvii. 22, xxxv. 9, 13). At Sinai the "Glory of Jahweh" (*i.e.*, His Revealing Appearance, which, however, only displays as it were a part or reflection of His complete personality) is veiled in a cloud (cf. Exod. xvi. 10, and especially Num. ix. 15 ff.). All closer description is carefully avoided, and only the comparison of Jahweh's glory with consuming fire is ventured on (Exod. xxiv. 17). Compare with this *JE*'s account, xxiv. 9 ff., of Moses, Aaron, Nadab, Abihu and the seventy elders beholding the God of Israel!

The extent to which the figures of the primæval history were already surrounded, in the view of the Priests' Writing, with a kind of saintly aureole is seen from the obviously intentional omission of *all* the traits which seemed to lower the dignity of the patriarchs. Jacob does not flee before the well-deserved vengeance of Esau, but is despatched to Mesopotamia by Isaac in perfect peace (Gen. xxviii. 1 ff.). Thus his fraud (chap. xxvii.) is not presupposed, and the brothers, therefore, dwell peaceably together after Jacob's return, and separate in friendly fashion, merely because their stock of cattle is so great (xxxvi. 6 ff.).

As to the far weightiest portion of the Priests' Writing, the laws, everything holds good which we have remarked above concerning the character of the Law of Holiness as the first comprehensive realization of Ezekiel's visions. Ezekiel's fundamental ideas are now carried out to their farthest consequences, and the legislation is expanded accordingly. It thus became possible for theories to be propounded—just for the sake of consistency—which simply could not be carried out (*e.g.*, the celebration of the so-called Year of Jubilee, Lev. xxv.), so that, as Jewish tradition admits, the attempt was never made.

The fundamental ideas themselves, which regulate every detail of the cultus and of civil life, are exceedingly simple. Strictly speaking, the entire ceremonial law aims at only *one* thing, that the citizen of the Divine commonwealth should testify by many actions his recognition of Jahweh as the Lord of all space, all time, all property, and all life. Hence all these should be hallowed to Him wholly and for ever, *i.e.*, appropriated to His sole use as His inviolable property. This being impossible, God contents Himself with the selection of a portion of space, time, &c., for absolute hallowing. Thus the theory is that *all* the land is Jahweh's property, but only *one* place, the tent of revelation with the holy ark, is absolutely holy, and, therefore, alone can serve as the spot where God is to be worshipped. This assumption is so seriously made that no kind of cultus seems conceivable in the whole period prior to the erection of the tent of revelation and the altar of burnt offering. The Priests' Writing knows of no altars or sacrifices in the patriarchal age, and, therefore, of no distinction between clean, *i.e.*, sacrificial, and unclean animals in Noah's ark (Gen. vii. 14 ff.; the Jahwist, vii. 2, is different). On the other hand, when the law is given at Sinai, the first thing for which provision is made (Exod. xxv. 8 ff.) is the construction of the holy place because it is the indispensable preliminary to the worship. We have already laid stress on the fact that God's abode in this sanctuary was not conceived of as the indwelling of His entire personality. But He has determined to reveal Himself henceforward, and to receive the sacrifices and offerings of Israel only at this place (which is naturally to be considered the prefiguration of the temple). The so-called

Kapporeth, the cover of the holy ark in the Holy of Holies, forms the most sacred centre (Exod. xxv. 22). Connected with it are the holy place and the court, gradually diminishing in their degrees of holiness. The Holy of Holies is to be entered by none but the high priest (at least so it seems according to Lev. xvi.; a somewhat freer theory is found at Num. xviii. 7), and that only on the great Day of Atonement; the holy place only by the priests (Num. iv. 5, xv. 20, xviii. 3), not the Levites.

The chief point in the theory of the *holy time* seems to be that rest days are to be set apart on which the people are not to encroach for their own advantage on the time hallowed to Jahweh. This applies to the weekly festival, the Sabbath, as well as the other feast days. And, indeed, the holier the day the more strictly is *all* work forbidden; on ordinary feast days nothing but their daily work (Lev. xxiii, 7 f., 21, 24, &c.), on the Sabbath and on the great Day of Atonement, work of every kind (verses 3, 30). In all this two things are noteworthy; the increased number of feasts and the tracing almost all of them to religious (theocratic) motives. The older laws are only aware of the duty of celebrating a feast to Jahweh three times a year (Exod. xxiii. 14, xxxiv. 23, Deut. xvi.), and these three are Nature Festivals, above all, Harvest Festivals. The seven days' Feast of Unleavened Bread in the month of Ears originally was regarded as the beginning of the harvest, according to Deut. xvi. 9, (cf. also Lev. xxiii. 10); the first day of the seven is the Passover, originally the Feast of the Presentation of the firstlings of cattle. The Feast of Weeks celebrates the prosperous conclusion of the corn-harvest; the Autumnal Feast (anciently "The Feast," absolutely), that of fruit and wine. In the Priests' Law (Lev. xxiii., Num. xxviii. 29) the Passover precedes the seven days of Unleavened Bread as an independent feast, and, together with them, is regarded as commemorating nothing but the Divine protection experienced by the people when they went out of Egypt. The autumn festival also lasts eight days, and is devoted to the memory of the dwelling in booths during the journey through the Desert. The only one which has no theocratic foundation in the Old Testament is the Feast of Weeks (Pentecost). There are the following new feasts: the Day of Memorial-Blowing on the first of the seventh month, and the great Day of Atonement on the tenth of the same month. The old feasts, like these new ones, are now precisely dated (Passover on the 14th of the first month; Tabernacles, from the 15th to the 22nd of the seventh month), whereas in earlier times each was proclaimed according to the state of the harvest. On seven of these feast-days (Lev. xxiii. 3 also prescribes it for all Sabbaths) there was to be a "holy assembly" of the whole people at the sanctuary—a requirement which could only be addressed to those who, like the post-exilic Jewish community, dwelt near the *one* sanctuary. Finally, the finishing touches given to the Sabbath celebration in Lev. xxv. are of special interest. Exod. xxi. 2 ff., is also acquainted with the freeing of Hebrew slaves at the end of six years' service, and xxiii. 11 with the abandonment every seven years (consequently not of all fields at the same time) of the products of the arable land to the poor and the beasts. Deut. xv. commanded that every seventh year should be celebrated as a year of release for Hebrew slaves and poor debtors. In the Priests' Writing an altogether new viewpoint emerges; the Sabbatic year is first and foremost a Sabbath, a rest time which the land itself celebrates to Jahweh. The fields must not be sown, the vine not pruned, the spontaneous growth not reaped. The ultimate consequence of the Sabbatic idea is the celebration of the year of Jobel or Jubilee (Lev. xxv. 8 ff.), every fiftieth year, *i.e.*, at the expiration of seven weeks of Sabbatic years. The Jubilee year is also a rest for the ground and a fixed point, when every kind of alienated property returns to the original possessor. The motive for this peculiar ordinance is clearly expressed at v. 23. No one is a real owner. All land is simply held in fief from Jahweh; the restoration to the man to whom it was first assigned is a recognition of Jahweh's suzerainty.

This brings us to the third of those fundamental principles of the Priests' Writing. Jahweh is the real Lord of all the property which Israel could boast of. A very large part of the precepts relating to sacrifices is concerned with the recognition of this fact. The older laws also know of gifts of firstlings, and presentations of sacrifices to Jahweh. But some of these gifts are very trivial (Deut. xviii. 3, xxvi. 2); and in part to be consumed by the offerer and his family at the sanctuary (as the so-called tenths, Deut. xiv. 22 ff., and the firstlings of cattle, xv. 19 ff.). The Priests' Code, on the other hand, prescribes that the breast and the right shoulder of all peace offerings, the whole of the flesh of all sin and trespass offerings, all the firstlings of cattle, and the first fruits of wheat, wine, oil, and dough, are to be given to the priests, besides which the Levites are to have the tenth of all fruits of the ground and of trees, and, according to Lev. xxvii. 32, even of the cattle. Finally, the principle that a portion of *all* property must be set aside for Jahweh is expanded into the theory that forty-eight cities, with the surrounding pastures, are to be assigned to the priests and Levites (Num. xxxv., Joshua xxi.)—in opposition to the older principle maintained by *P* himself at Num. xviii. 20, xxvi. 62.

At this point we may mention another far-reaching difference between the older custom and that of the Priests' Law as regards the sacrifices and offerings to Jahweh. According to the older idea sacrifice was the presentation to the Deity of enjoyable food. Nothing therefore could be offered except what serves for human nourishment (the only additional condition being that the gift must be the actual property of the offerer). Consequently the gladsome meal in praise and honour of the Deity, the "eating and drinking before the face of God," *i.e.*, at the sanctuary, was the principal thing. But in the Priests' Writing the renunciation of one's property comes into the foreground. The old sacrificial meals were regarded by it as offerings of secondary rank; the burnt offerings appear far weightier and more efficacious, and the sin and trespass offerings more so still. The flesh of the latter is "most holy" and can be eaten by none but the priests in a holy place. Perhaps the precise discrimination of these varieties of sacrifices is derived from an earlier period: but we have no reliable proof of their mention before the Exile. The great weight laid upon them is a striking evidence of the gloomy nature of the post-exilic cultus, of its pervasion with a deep penitence and desire for propitiation. The importance ascribed to an orderly service, carried out with painful observance of the ritual, comes out in another circumstance. The pre-exilic time was familiar with daily sacrifices offered by the king (2 Kings xvi. 15), but it is not till Ezekiel (xlv. 17, 22, &c.), that the daily and festival sacrifices are also offered on behalf of the community. In the Priests' Law (cf. the table of sacrifices, Num. xxviii. 29) the official sacrifices, *i.e.*, those offered by the priests in the name of the community, are so multiplied that 113 young bullocks, 1086 lambs, 36 rams, and 29 goats, are required yearly, each with its accompaniment of a fixed measure of meal and drink offering.

All *persons*, as well as space, time, and property are consecrated to Jahweh. This fourth fundamental thought finds expression partly in the consecration of the first-born, according to ancient tradition, partly in the imposition of the poll-tax (represented at Exod. xxx. 13 ff. as a payment by which those who had become forfeited to Jahweh might be redeemed), finally in the directions concerning the service of the priests and Levites. In pre-exilic times priestly functions were not confined to a distinct class. Every head of a household could and was accustomed to sacrifice; we are unhesitatingly told that David and Solomon (2 Sam. vi. 18, 1 Kings viii. 55) even blessed the people. The professional priest at the sanctuaries was chiefly needed to obtain oracles by means of the holy lot. But even at the greatest sanctuaries, such as Jerusalem, there was no "high priest" such as the Priests' Writing requires, but only a chief priest (two, under David and Solomon). He was one of the king's superior officials, and must strictly carry out his orders (2 Kings xvi. 10 ff.): like any other official he can be dismissed (1 Kings ii. 26). We learn too from such passages as Judges xvii. 5, 2 Sam. viii. 18, xx. 26, that the priesthood was in no way limited to those who were descended from Levi, although according to Judges xvii. 13, a Levite was preferred to any other priest. We have already spoken on p. 90 of the manner in which the legitimate priesthood was afterwards restricted by Deuteronomy to Jerusalem, and the foundation laid by Ezek. xliv. for the distinction between priests (sons of Zadok) and Levites (formerly priests of the high places). In the Priests' Writing this distinction is thoroughly carried out and incorporated into a well-devised system, in which post-exilic circumstances are as a matter of course everywhere implied. The following are the main features of this system.

Theoretically all Israel ought to perform priestly service. To say nothing, however, of other conditions, the requisite Levitical purity could not be maintained by all, and Jahweh therefore prescribed a substitute in the form of the "Sons of Aaron," *i.e.*, the priesthood hereditary in certain definite families. The tracing all these back to Aaron, or to his sons Eleazar and Ithamar, was evidently intended to enlarge the circle of the "Sons of Zadok." Reasons which we cannot ascertain must have made the recognition of some non-Zadokites inevitable. As the Zadokites were derived from Eleazar so were these others from Ithamar. If exacting demands were made on the ordinary priests with regard to their Levitical purity, much more were they on their head, the high priest (also a hereditary official). In his person the priestly, and at the same time kingly, people finds its most peculiar and completest embodiment. Especially is this so in the exuberant symbolism of his official dress (Exod. xxviii. 2 ff.). The blue and red purple of which his robe is made, and the golden diadem on his mitre, points to the royal dignity; the priestly character of the people is shown by the inscription on the diadem (Holiness to Jahweh) and the names of the twelve tribes engraved in precious stones and worn on the shoulder-pieces and the breastplate. Were it necessary

8 *

Num. xxxv. 25 would prove that all this declares the high priest to be the sovereign head of the priestly commonwealth in a manner which no one dreamed of for a royal official before the Exile, which never occurred even to Ezekiel. The rights of the avenger of blood expired at the death of the high priest. That is to say, a definite period of civil life terminates with him, as elsewhere with the death of the prince.

The official standing of the Levites, like that of the priests, flows from a divine arrangement made once for all. The only error in the still prevalent view is that it takes the Levites to be priests of a lower rank, because they (like Moses and Aaron) were of the tribe of Levi, and thus makes them to be the broad basis from which the priesthood proper rises with the high priest at the summit. But this is not the meaning of the Priests' Code. According to it they are a gift (Num. iii. 6, viii. 16 ff. &c.) presented by the people to the priests to wait upon them: hence, when they are consecrated they are to be presented, according to Num. viii. 9 ff., quite in the fashion of a so-called "wave-offering" to Jahweh (and to the priests in His stead). They, therefore, perform all the inferior duties at the sanctuary which should properly be done by the people itself, or rather by the first-born. This idea, that every individual Levite performs his service as representing one of the first-born, finds striking expression at Num. iii. 41 ff. There are only 22,000 Levites to represent 22,273 first-born. Two hundred and seventy-three therefore must be specially "redeemed." Consecration qualifies the Levites, not to officiate in the sanctuary, but to surround it, and thus, as a sort of protecting wall, to secure the profane multitude against the destroying holiness of Jahweh (Num. i. 53, &c.).

If we now collect from all this the sum of what is to be said concerning the fundamental ideas of the Priests' Writing and their execution it will, without contradiction, be briefly as follows. The idea that the Priests' Code was extant before the Exile could only be maintained on the assumption that no man knew of it, not even the spiritual leaders of the people, such as the priests Jeremiah and Ezekiel. This would be an enormous assumption; not less so is the other, that so deep and refined a symbolism, so exhaustive a carrying out of fundamental religious ideas had begun to be codified and then remained totally unregarded. Pray what could induce the sons of Zadok at Jerusalem not to introduce this law instead of the simple prophetic law in Deuteronomy? And what could move Ezekiel carefully to lay a new foundation when the whole building was there in most desirable form and extent? On the other hand everything appears in the best order and self-evident when we think of the codifications as arising in this order: Deuteronomy, Ezek. xl.-xlviii., Law of Holiness, Priests' Code. The latter, though, as we shall see below, not in its present form, obtained official validity through Ezra, and afterwards continued to be the standard of ritual and life and of the entire view of history amongst the Jews. In the gradually written expositions of Israel's laws of life it was *the last word.*

Only one possible question remains, and that refers to a leading point, the position of the Levites. According to Ezekiel xliv. 10 ff. the sentence which reduced the former priests of the high places to the inferior services of the sanctuary was a deserved punishment: according to the Priests' Code the service of the Levites, by virtue of a Divine appointment, is an honourable office of which they may be proud. How can these two views be reconciled? The history of the post-exilic period furnishes the answer. The non-Zadokites were so little inclined to take up the rôle assigned them by Ezekiel that, *e.g.*, not a single Levite was found at first amongst those who returned with Ezra in 458, and thirty-eight were only induced to accompany him by the special measures which he took (viii. 15 ff.). Again, in the narrative of the revolt of the Korahites, now blended in Num. xvi. with an older account of a political revolt of the Reubenites, we have a clear reflection of the vehement struggles (subsequently buried in deep silence) occasioned by the dislike the non-Zadokites felt to the manner in which they were employed in religious services. From this it is self-evident that the priestly circles were at least compelled to find another ground for the position of the Levites.

The extent of the original Priests' Code, drawn up in Babylon somewhere about 500, is uncertain. But it has at all events been shown to be very probable that it contained a law of worship in the shape of a history of the holy ordinances—the preliminary history also being included. The more detailed theories, such as the so-called Law of Sacrifice, Lev. i.-vii. (in which several strata are clearly distinguishable), to say nothing of Num. xxxv. and Joshua xxi., may therefore belong to a more and a most recent stratum.

The delay until 444 in introducing the Priests' Law is probably to be explained simply by the above-mentioned difficulty of the Levite question. It is extremely astonishing that Ezra, who, according to Ezra vii. 14, brought the law of God (*i.e.*, the form published in 444) with him from Babylon in 458, delayed publishing it for fourteen years. Obviously the fit time did not seem to have come till Nehemiah was installed as Governor. In the highly interesting authentic account of the introduction of the new law, Neh. viii.-x., two things are clearly presupposed. First (viii. 1), that the law-book had hitherto been kept by Ezra alone, and therefore had been brought by him from Babylon. In fact, in the commendatory letter which Artaxerxes I. gave to Ezra, the latter is plainly described as "the scribe," *i.e.*, the author of the Law of the God of Heaven. Secondly, that the contents were till then entirely unknown to the people. Official heralds must therefore summon the people to observe the Feast of Tabernacles in the new fashion (viii. 14 ff.). From this passage, with its appeal to Lev. xxiii. 40, we also learn that Ezra's law-book contained portions of the Law of Holiness. On the other hand, it clearly cannot have been identical with the whole of our present Priest's Writing, because Ezra could not in one breath have given the heterogeneous directions which we find in the various strata of the Priests' Code (cf., *e.g.*, Num. iv. 3 with viii. 24; Exod. xxix. 7, Lev. viii. 12, xxi. 10, in which passages Aaron alone is anointed, with Exod. xxviii. 41 and

Num. iii. 3: at Ezra ix. 4 it seems to be assumed that in the evening only a meal-offering is to be brought, whereas at Exod. xxix. 41, &c., a lamb is required). This shows that the earlier view of Ezra's law-book as identical with the whole of our Pentateuch is utterly untenable. On the other hand, it is easy to understand that, when a priestly law-book in Ezekiel's spirit had been observed for some decades, the work would be undertaken of uniting everything extant into *one* great corpus. But in doing this they were not content to blend Ezra's law-book with *JED* (see above, p. 94). All the codes were now adopted which had arisen in the priestly circles before and after Ezra,* partly as pendants to previously adopted sections (*e.g.,* Exod. xxxv.-xl. added to Exod. xxv.-xxxi.), partly as expansions of the fundamental thoughts. On the whole the redactor treated the older corpus (*JED*) with great consideration. He allowed its phraseology to stand even where it contradicted the historical account and the theories of the Priests' Writing. Thenceforward it was left to the Scribes to get rid of the difficulties which could not but arise from the blending of such manifold parts, all regarded as canonical. Elsewhere (*e.g.,* in the Deluge History, Gen. vi. ff.) the offence was removed by an apt interweaving of the various accounts. It is but seldom that the redactor seems to have resorted to the extreme measure, the omission of divergent accounts. This was certainly the case at Exod. xxxiii. 6, where *JE*'s account of the making of the Tent of Revelation could not possibly be retained in the midst of the two great sections of the Priests' Writing which were devoted to the same subject. But we have no means of knowing how the corpus, finally completed—probably before the close of the fifth century—was proclaimed canonical and binding in all parts. One thing only is beyond doubt: the canonization extended at first to the Pentateuch alone, excluding the Book of Joshua, although in this book also the blending of *P* with *JED* must

---

* The remarkable chapter, Gen. xiv., which seems to have been taken from a Midrash on the Patriarchal History, is also probably one of the additions due to the final redactor.

have been contemporaneous with the final redaction of the Five Books of Moses. For the Samaritans recognize the Pentateuch alone as a sacred book; hence, at the time when they received this from the Jews, the Book of Joshua must already have been reckoned in the second division of the sacred books. But this distinction between Law and Prophets stands in connection with the final redaction of the *whole* corpus, Gen.—2 Kings xxv.* It has left untouched the phraseology of the Deuteronomistic redaction (see above, p. 94 f.) almost everywhere in the historical books, from Joshua i. downwards, just as in the Pentateuch. The redactor (whom we designate *R* in Joshua, Judges, and the Books of Samuel) contented himself generally with inserting single verses. So at Judges iii. 1-3, vi. 7 ff.; seldom in the Books of Samuel (but cf. the thoroughly characteristic examples 1 Sam. vi. 15, 2 Sam. xv. 24). Some of these additions were religious verdicts, some chronological data or explanatory observations, sometimes they reconcile the contradictions between the various strata. Yet independent additions are not quite lacking, which must have been borrowed from popular tradition (thus probably at 1 Sam. xix. 18 ff.) or from later, edifying writings. 1 Sam. xvi. belongs to the examples of the latter class, and, especially, that recasting of an older model in the spirit of the Priests' Writing which is found in Judges xx. f. The additions made by the final redactor or redactors in the Books of Kings are designated *Z* in the "Survey." In such instances as 1 K. viii. 4b, they are unmistakable, and not less so in sections like 1 K. xii. 21 ff., and 33 ff. (cf. 2 K. xxiii. 16 ff.), or 2 K. i. 9 ff., which bear throughout the stamp of the Midrash (see below, on the Chronicles).

* As Meyer, *Die Entstehung des Judenth.* (Halle, 1896), p.216 ff., especially has shown, we are not to conceive of the process as one in which the Book of Joshua was separated from a previously existing Hexateuch, an independent literary work. The separation was effected by means of a deep cleft in the historical *united work* (from Gen.—2 Kings xxv.) after the account of the death of Moses.

3. The Work of the Chronicler (Ezra, Nehemiah, Chronicles).

The great work which arose from the efforts we have been describing set forth the course of history from the beginning of the world to the release of Jehoiachin (561 B.C.). Hence a work was still needed to tell of the re-establishment of the Jewish Commonwealth, and especially of the reforms made by Ezra and Nehemiah on the basis of the priestly lawbook. In the course of the fifth century this need was met by various monographs, which have been partially preserved for us in the Books of Ezra and Nehemiah. In their present form, however, these latter came from the hand of the Chronicler, and originally formed *one* whole with the two "Books of Chronicles" (literally, "of the events of the day," or "annals"). Indeed the Chronicler most probably edited first the Books of Ezra and Nehemiah, and afterwards subjected the older history to a revision. A work thus arose which described continuously the whole history from Adam to Nehemiah's second residence in Jerusalem, 432. This sequence, Chronicles, Ezra, Nehemiah, is supported by the fact that the close of the Chronicles, which breaks off in the middle of a sentence, is resumed and completed in the opening of the Book of Ezra. Probably the explanation of the present arrangement is that Ezra and Nehemiah (in whose case alone it was at first necessary) had already been received into the third part of the Canon when it was resolved to grant the Chronicler himself a place there.

We shall have to discuss more fully below the spirit in which the Chronicler edited the available sources, or in some cases himself wrote history. Let us first turn to the monographs on which he has drawn in the Books of Ezra and Nehemiah.* Leaving aside several isolated documents, these

---

* After the Chronicles had been separated from them Ezra and Nehemiah were still counted as one book by the Jews (as by *Josephus c. Apion* I. viii., and in the Talmud): Origen and the Latin Bible called them Ezra I. and II. On

consist of an Aramaic source from the middle of the fifth century (*Qa* in Ezra iv.-vi.), and of the personal Memoirs of Ezra and Nehemiah (*E* and *N*).

As to all these sources, it must be remarked that the Chronicler (respecting his own production, see below) evidently re-cast them, instead of always reproducing their phraseology, so that we have to distinguish in the "Survey" between, *Q*, *Qa*, *E*, *N*, and *q*, *qa*, *e*, *n*. Thus at the outset, Ezra i. 2 ff. the phraseology of the edict of Cyrus, compared with the form in vi. 3 ff., is open to grave suspicion. This is also true of certain terms in the letters of Tattenai, Darius and Artaxerxes I., chap. v. 7 ff., vi. 7 ff., vii. 12 ff.; but we gladly admit that most of the suspicions against these have been convincingly removed by E. Meyer ("Die Entstehung des Judenthums," p. 41 ff.). According to Neh. vii. 5, the authentic list of those who returned with Zerubbabel to Joshua comes from the Memoirs of Nehemiah. It is evident that the Chronicler borrowed it from that source (or, still more probably, from a historical work in which Neh. vii. ff. had been adopted), because Neh. vii. 73b, a half verse which really forms the beginning of chap. viii., is the continuation of Ezra iii. 1. The Aramaic source in Ezra iv. 8—vi. 18, and vii. 12-26, shows itself well informed; but the Chronicler has placed iv. 6-23 too early. For v. 6 refers to an event in the time of Xerxes (485-465 B.C.), and v. 7 ff. to the prevention by force (cf. v. 23!) of the fortification of Jerusalem with *walls* under Artaxerxes I. (about 445, since Nehemiah, according to Neh. i. 1, heard of it in the ninth month of that year). Not till v. 24 is the thread of v. 5 resumed.

The first part of the Book of Ezra is occupied with the events of 538-516. But chaps. vii.-xii. relate the home-coming of Ezra and a second band of exiles in the year 458, Ezra's own Memoirs being almost exclusively used. These Memoirs

---

the other hand, the Greek Bible reckons as Ezra I. an apocryphal Greek book (counted as Ezra III. in the Latin Bible) which originated in the last century before Christ. The so-called Fourth Book of Ezra is an apocryphon, probably from the time of Domitian, and is preserved almost exclusively in translations.

show themselves an excellent source, especially where their phraseology has been adhered to (Ezra vii. 27-34, chap. ix.); but some of the sources (especially Ezra x. and Neh. viii.-x.) which have passed through the hand of the Chronicler or his authority are also of great weight. The same is true of all parts of the Memoirs of Nehemiah, cupbearer to Artaxerxes I., who came to Jerusalem in 445 as the king's vicegerent, and by swiftly rebuilding its walls secured the sorely imperilled city against further assaults from its hostile neighbours. This "Narrative of Nehemiah, son of Hachaliah," dealing in Neh. i. 1—vii. 5, xi. 1, 2, xii. 31 f., 37-40 with his first residence (445-433), and in xiii. 4-31 with the second (432), lies before us in its original phraseology, and strongly fascinates us by its unpretentious, trustworthy description of events, and its manifestation of an energetic and, at the same time, truthful and pious personality. From the same source, no doubt, came xi. 4 ff., a list belonging to the time of Zerubbabel, recognized already by Ewald as the original continuation of vii. 73b. On the other hand, the authentic list in chap. xii. must have been mainly derived from the "Book of Annals," mentioned in v. 23, a chronicle which came down to Johanan, son (according to v. 22, grandson) of Eliashib, *i.e.*, to about the beginning of the fourth century.*
Whether the Chronicler (*i.e.*, the redactor of our Books of Ezra and Nehemiah) took the narrative of Ezra in Neh. viii.-x. from this source, or got his extracts as a whole from the Memoirs of Ezra and Nehemiah, must remain undecided.

If the Chronicler, up to this point, and especially in the Book of Nehemiah, limited himself to isolated additions or unessential alterations, he comes out in Chronicles † itself in

---

* It will, of course, be different if we think of v. 11 and 22 as taken from the same Chronicles. In that case the mention of Jaddua, the high priest, and "Darius the Persian" (*i.e.*, Darius III.) will compel us, with Meyer (Entstehung des Judenthums, p. 203 ff.), to come down to the time of Alexander the Great, and place the Biblical Chronicles considerably later.

† Luther adopted this name from Jerome (Chronicon totius historiæ divinæ). In the Greek Bible the work (for Chronicles originally formed only *one* book) is called Paraleipomena, *i.e.*, Things Passed Over: the Jews call it "Annals."

quite another sense as author. In the first part (1 i.-ix.) the history to David's time is given simply in the form of genealogies. The second part (1 x.-xxx.) treats of the history of David; the third (2 i.-ix.) of the history of Solomon; the fourth, finally (2 x.-xxxvi. 21), of the history of Judah, from the division of the Kingdom to the Babylonian Exile. On the conclusion (xxxvi. 22 ff., which is not completed till Ezra i. 3), cf. above, p. 121.

The Chronicles do not really aim at giving a history of Israel, but only of the Davidic dynasty, with special reference to the temple service. Their standpoint is that of the strictest Levitism, in a form which could not have been developed till the Priests' Law had long held sway. It is certain that the author was a Levite, and, indeed, a temple-singer or musician, because of the striking prominence which he gives to these. The way in which the Chronicler remodels the older history in the spirit of Levitism confronts us most characteristically in the passages where we can accurately check his description, by reference to the original in the Books of Samuel or Kings, of which he made use. We are chiefly struck there by the mechanical way in which the fundamental principle is carried out: every transgression brings on speedy punishment, and every calamity is a punishment for transgression. Cf. 1 x. 13 f., 2 xii. 1 f., xvi. 12 (in connection with v. 7 ff.); xix. 2 ff. (as a judgment on xviii. 2 ff.); xx. 35 ff. (in direct contradiction with 1 Kings xxii. 49 f.); xxiv. 2 (against 2 Kings xii. 3), and xxiv. 17 ff., as the cause of the calamity described in 23 ff.; moreover, xxv. 14 ff., 21; xxvi. 16 ff.; xxxiii. 11 ff. (where Manasseh's sins are duly punished, but at the same time, the continuance of his reign for fifty-five years is supposed to be explained by his conversion). According to xxxv. 21 ff., Josiah fell because he did not obey God's word, which had come to him through Pharaoh Necho.

Conversely, when there is indubitable prosperity, a blameless piety is implied. Hence the Chronicler says nothing about David's life as a freebooter or as Philistine vassal, nothing about his adultery and behaviour towards Uriah, nothing about the wretched proceedings in David's family, nothing about the manner of Solomon's accession, described in 1 Kings i. All this is doubtless a part of the attempt to surround David, the real originator of the temple building, with a sort of aureole. The only transgression ascribed to him is the numbering of the people, 1 xxi. 1, to which Satan had incited him. This narrative could not be dispensed with, because the consecration by David of what afterwards became the temple site was connected with it. For it was not to the idolater Solomon (although nothing is said of his idolatry itself), but to David, that everything was to be ascribed which was requisite for the preparation of the temple building and the arrangements of the worship. Not fewer than seven chapters (1 xxii.-xxvi. 28 f.) are devoted to the account of the collection of building materials (amongst which the gold and silver alone were worth nearly £450,000,000)* and the other preparations made by David. Indeed, the model of the temple and of all its vessels was given to Solomon by David, along with written instructions from the hand of Jahweh.

The statements as to the number of their warriors correspond to the mechanical view which makes the prosperity and power of the kings stand in precise relation to the degree of their piety. The most pious kings dispose of the largest armies. Thus David has more than one and a half million warriors, Jehoshaphat more than a million, Asa 580,000, Abiah 400,000 (against 800,000 Israelites, of whom half a million then fall in battle), Uzziah 307,500, Amaziah 300,000, Rehoboam only 180,000. As a matter of fact, these armies serve chiefly for pursuit, not for fight: cf. the striking examples, 2 xiii. 13 ff., xiv. 8 ff., and xx. 1 ff. Otherwise one of the leading principles of the theocratic theory would

---

* [Canon Rawlinson, in the Speaker's Bible, thinks the numbers given in the text of Chronicles corrupt, and says, "Estimated according to the value of the post-Babylonian Hebrew talent, the gold here spoken of would be worth more than one thousand millions of our pounds sterling, while the silver would be worth above four hundred millions." *Tr.*]

have been violated, namely, that all trust in weapons or other external means, instead of in the immediate interposition of Jahweh, is absolutely sinful. The instance last mentioned (2 Chron. xx.), a complete remodelling of 2 Kings iii. in the spirit of the so-called Midrash, is of altogether special interest. The precise meaning of this Hebrew word is "Investigation, Explanation." But in the history of Jewish literature it signifies a special class of writings which contain an instructive and edifying exposition of older (especially historical) books. The Chronicler himself 2 xxiv. 27, appeals to a "Midrash on the Book of Kings." In view of the above examples, it is self-evident that a Midrash of this kind cannot possibly pretend to be a historical narrative, although the popular view (and with it the Chronicler himself) may have confounded the two in early times.

Furthermore, it seemed quite self-evident to the Chronicler that the priestly law (as the law of Moses!) had been binding from the beginning, and therefore was to be regarded as the standard in judging of *all* proceedings. Where the facts would not fit in with the demands of the Priests' Code they were either set aside or corrected, the latter often in a very bold fashion. This was peculiarly necessary where the privileges of the priests and Levites were concerned, especially as the pre-exilic times, according to our explanation above, knew nothing of a distinction between the two: cf. 1 vi. 18 ff. (against 1 Sam. i. 1), xv. 2, 15, xviii. 17 (against 2 Sam. viii. 18); 2 vi. 13 (against the exemplar, 1 Kings viii. 22, cited in v. 12!); xi. 13 f.; xiii. 9 ff., and quite especially, 2 xxiii. and xxiv. 4 ff. (against 2 Kings xi. f.). With this assumption that the Priests' Law was in force it also corresponds that not only Hezekiah, but also other pious kings (thus Asa and Jehoshaphat) abolished the worship at the high places (which to the Chronicler was sheer idolatry like the Israelite bull-worship). Josiah did not wait till his eighteenth year, but took the reform of worship in hand in his twelfth year (*i.e.*, as soon as he was of age!). The account at 2 xxxiv. 8 ff. (taken from 2 Kings xxii.) will not indeed agree with this. But the Chronicler gets over the difficulty to a certain extent by making Shaphan, v. 18 (against 2 Kings xxii. 10) read "out" of the law-book. For the law-book is to the Chronicler identical with the whole Pentateuch, and Shaphan could not have read this through without a break.

No wonder then that very hard judgments have been pronounced respecting the trustworthiness of the Chronicles as a historical source, in fact that everything which goes beyond the older historical books has been declared an invention. But we shall come nearer the truth if we admit, first, that the Chronicler actually took part of his material from the sources he so freely cites, and, secondly, that amongst this material have been preserved all kinds of noteworthy and even incontrovertible traditions. As to the first point, it is no doubt true that tendency-narratives do not become more credible through being taken from any exemplar whatever. Yet it is quite a different thing for the Chronicler to have taken from his exemplars in good faith that which best corresponded with his own ideas and language and those of his surroundings, from what it would have been if he had *invented* narratives and then appealed to imaginary sources in order to create a false impression.

The character of the material enables us to form a fairly confident estimate of the precise character of the sources which the Chronicler adduces. The book most frequently cited is that of the Kings of Judah and Israel (or the Kings of Israel and Judah; also, abbreviated, "The Kings of Israel," or "History of the Kings of Israel"): the latest citation relates to Jehoiakim. This work cannot be identical with our Books of the Kings, but probably is the "Midrash on the Book of the Kings," adduced under this complete title at 2 xxiv. 27 (cf. also 2 xiii. 2). Hence it must have been a compilation in which (probably not before post-exilic times) the material of our Books of Samuel and Kings, and perhaps also matters from the so-called "great King's Book" (see above, p. 70 ff.) were re-modelled for the purpose of edification. Nor is it less probable that the freely cited monographs (1 xxvii. 24, xxix. 29; 2 ix. 29, xii. 15, xiii. 22, xxxiii. 19), perhaps also the biography of Uzziah by Isaiah (2 xxvi. 22), were only portions of that great Midrashic work, especially as the document adduced at 2 xx. 34 is expressly said to be "inserted in the book of the Kings of Israel." In similar fashion Isa. xxxvi.-xxxix. and 2 Kings xviii.-xx. are referred to at xxxii. 32.

In addition to the Midrashic matter there is some other documentary material (especially in the genealogies, chaps. i.-ix.), not preserved elsewhere, and possibly drawn by the Chronicler from good historical tradition. The decision as to the actual value of these notices must be reserved in each case for critical consideration. Unfortunately, though the text of Chronicles has in some instances been better preserved than that of its exemplars, it is on the whole in a very damaged condition.

Finally, with regard to the date when the Chronicles (with our present Books of Ezra and Nehemiah; see above, p. 121) were composed, 1 xxix. 7, where a computation referring to the Davidic period is made in Persian darics, would at once bring us to a very late period. Such an anachronism was not possible till that coinage had been current from time immemorial. The description of Darius Codomannus as "Darius the Persian" (Neh. xii. 22) also brings us down to the Greek period. With this it agrees that the high priest Jaddua, mentioned at Neh. xii. 22, is said by Josephus (Antiqq. XI., vii. 8) to have been in office under Alexander the Great. It depends chiefly on the textual criticism of 1 Chron. iii. 19 ff. whether we must descend still later (according to Kuenen, even into the last quarter of the third century). If the original text really knew of eleven generations after Zerubbabel the earliest date for the Chronicler must be about 250 B.C. But another interpretation of 1 Chron. iii. 19 ff. finds only 6-7 members mentioned after Zerubbabel, and thus leads to the dating of Ezra, Nehemiah, Chronicles about 300 B.C.

4. THE BOOK OF RUTH.—THE BOOK OF ESTHER.

The last products of Hebrew historiography which remain to be mentioned reflect once more the two main tendencies of Hebrew literature, the booklet of Ruth the prophetic, the Book of Esther the specifically Jewish-Levitical.

The Book of Ruth, designated by a Goethe as "the loveliest little epic and idyllic whole which has come down to us," cannot have been written till post-exilic times, as various traces show. Apart from certain linguistic signs of the Persian Age which do not indeed occur in the narrative but in the speeches of the actors, chap. iv. 7 especially proves that a considerable interval must have elapsed since Deut. xxv. 9; for the narrator has to explain, as practised in Israel "in former time," a custom which in Deuteronomy is assumed to be universally known. Moreover the origin of the booklet is well explained by the proceedings after Ezra's return (458). The merciless strictness with which Ezra (chap. ix. 1 ff.) enforced the banishment of *all* foreign wives evoked, in the families concerned, many a vigorous protest, which eventually proved most momentous to Jerusalem (see below, p. 195). And thus our idyll—perhaps on the ground of very intimate acquaintance with another Ruth!—probably aims at teaching the zealots that all foreign women do not lie under the same condemnation, but that there are those amongst them who are worthy of the highest praise for their true devotion to the God of Israel and to the members of His people. Ruth, the ancestress of the Davidic house, is proof enough of this.

If this is the precise tendency of the little book it must be admitted that the narrator could appeal to actual tradition in support of his main point, the descent of David from Ruth. The mention of Obed, iv. 17, is also in favour of this. But it cannot be decided whether this was a strictly historical tradition or rested only on a Midrash (on 1 Sam. xxii. 3). In any case it cannot be denied that free inventiveness was at work in the names of Elimelech's early-lost sons: Mahlon ("Sickness") and Chilion ("Vanishing"). But the booklet's historical value does not consist for us in its acquaintance with Elimelech's sons or with the progenitors and grandfather of David, but in its remarkable testimony to the meaning of "Religion in life," in Ezra's time, notwithstanding all Levitism. For if even the *whole* story were to be considered didactic poetry its colours are obviously taken from life, and the poem would thus be an honourable monument of the religion which could bring to perfection in the true Israelites such fruits, in the shape of a heartfelt piety and a self-sacrificing disposition.

Quite another spirit breathes upon us from the Book of Esther, the festival-roll of the Feast of Purim. We have no means of judging whether it is founded on any historical nucleus. What we read in it is a sort of historical romance, which nowhere bears the test if it is wished to regard it as a historical account. Chap. i. would suffice for a convincing proof of this. According to chap ii., Mordecai, who had been carried captive under Jehoiachin (597), lived with his niece under Achashverosh, *i.e.*, Xerxes, about 480. It is still less wonderful that Haman, chap. iii., instead of having Mordecai executed without delay, resolves to destroy *all* the Jews, and casts lots in the first month for all the eleven other months to ascertain the fittest day for the slaughter, than that immediately thereupon (eleven months beforehand!) the irrevocable death-warrant is published in all the provinces. And so the story moves marvellously on, the interest of it gradually heightened in most skilful fashion throughout chaps. iv.-viii., till the climax is reached in chap. ix., where the massacre of more than seventy-five thousand Persian subjects by the Jews is related, and Esther crowns the whole by obtaining the king's consent to a second day of slaughter.

The aim of the book is clearly stated at ix. 19 ff. It is to explain the origin of the Purim Festival in the month Adar. But the statement at iii. 7 that *pur* (presumably in Persian) is equivalent to "lot" cannot be linguistically established, besides which it was long ago* shown to be probable that the name is connected with the Persian Furdigan Festival, a Spring and New Year's Feast, which was also kept in memory of the dead, and on which the Persians still send to each other presents and sweets (cf. Esther ix. 19). As has already been said, it cannot be ascertained what other occasion the Jews had to celebrate this feast and to what extent a trace of this is still left in the Book of Esther. This only must be said: the book is a monument of the specifically Jewish spirit, as that spirit was gradually formed under the pressure of foreign rule in post-exilic times. This spirit is self-evidently not an irreligious one. The intentional avoidance of the Divine name (very conspicuously at iv. 14) is evidently due to the scrupulous dread of its being profaned amidst the licence of the feast. Yet the feast is one of thanksgiving for Divine protection granted to the people in a great distress in response to a three days' fast. The whole of it, however, expresses such national arrogance and such hatred of other nations as makes it easy to understand the strong objections to its canonicity which have been raised, not only amongst Christians, but even amongst the Jews (who, however, in later times have treasured this book more than all the prophets!). We shall judge rightly in the main if we criticise the book by the same standard as the Book of Judith. Both are, properly speaking, folk-tales, a self-glorification of the people, fitted thus to bring temporary forgetfulness of the misery of their bondage. But in opposition to the mistaken apologetic zeal which, for the sake of

---

* Cf. especially de Lagarde, Purim (Abhandlungen der Göttinger Gesellsch. der Wiss., 1885), who held that *furdigan* corresponds to the Persian *farwardigan*, the New Year Festival of the Magi (originally devoted to the Expulsion of Death. On the other hand Zimmern (ZAW, 1891, p. 157 ff.) traces Purim to the Babylonian *puchru*, *i.e.*, Assembly (of the gods on New Year's Day, to determine destinies). Mordecai may remind us of Marduk. Finally, according to Jensen (Zeitschr. für die Kunde des Morgenlands, 1892, p. 70; cf. also Dunkel, Schöpfung und Chaos, p. 309 ff.). Haman corresponds to the Elamite god Humman, Vashti to an Elamite goddess, Esther to Istar. [See also Wildeboer and his quotation from a later letter of Jensen's in the new Hand-Kommentar, now being edited by Marti. *Tr.*]

Jewish tradition, will concede to the Book of Esther equal worth and validity with the sayings of an Isaiah or Jeremiah, a Christian has the right to recall the Lord's word: "Know ye not what manner of spirit ye are of?"

We cannot venture beyond a conjecture as to when it was composed. 2 Macc. xv. 36 assumes that the day of Mordecai was observed in the period about 160 B.C. But this proves nothing, seeing that the Second Book of the Maccabees can scarcely have appeared before the Christian era. With this it agrees that Jesus Sirach seems not to have known the Book of Esther. The degree of aversion from other nations to which the book bears witness appears incomprehensible till after the Maccabean wars. Consequently it must be correct to put it in the second half of the second century B.C.

5. THE AFTER-GROWTHS OF THE PROPHETIC LITERATURE (OBADIAH, JOEL, JONAH, ISAIAH xxiv.-xxvii., ZECH. x.-xiv.).—THE CLOSE OF THE CANON OF THE PROPHETS.

Hitherto we have been following out the legislative and historical literatures to their farthest twigs. Now there remain three other classes of post-exilic writing to be discussed: the after-growths of the prophetic literature; the remains of the poetry proper (religious and secular) in the Psalms and the Song of Songs; finally, the products of the so-called "Wisdom Literature," in poetry and prose, *i.e.* (besides a considerable number of psalms), Proverbs, Job and Ecclesiastes.

The old opinion that Malachi was the last of all the prophets may have been correct to this extent that Malachi perhaps laboured by oral speech as well as in writing. All the prophecies which we find after him must be regarded as simply literary products. The chief proof of this is that (apart from the unique Book of Jonah) they are almost everywhere strictly dependent on the pre-exilic prophecies. This may justify the designation used above, "After-Growths of the Prophetic Literature." It is impossible to fix their chronological position more definitely: even the order in which we adduce them is founded merely on conjecture.

The threatening oracle of Obadiah against the Edomites doubtless presupposes the destruction of Jerusalem by the Chaldæans, v. 10-14. On the other hand the nine first verses must be derived from a far more remote time (possibly even from the ninth century), for Jeremiah makes use of them, chap. xlix. 14-16, 9, 10, 7, *i.e.*, in another order and altogether less exactly than in Obadiah. In our present Obadiah, therefore, a minatory prophecy against the Edomites, characterized by antique vigour of expression, is supplemented by a renewed threat which looks back on Edom's transgression in 586 and forwards to the recompense in the Messianic time. The manner in which Jahweh's Day of Judgment on *all* nations is expected at v. 15 brings us near to Joel and at all events into the fifth century. But it is questionable whether remnants of the ancient oracle have not also been preserved in v. 15-21, and equally so whether the name Obadiah, i. 1, is that of the supplementer or of the author of the original oracle. This oracle might have been occasioned by the revolt of the Edomites under Jehoram of Judah (about 845). But the hostility of the Edomites towards the Judæans was so frequently manifested on other occasions that we must despair of any nearer definition.

No less difficulty is found in placing the Writings of Joel, son of Pethuel, who sees in the irruption of a great plague of locusts the token of the [Judgment] Day of Jahweh and earnestly exhorts Israel to avert the outbreak of the Divine wrath by deep repentance. Jahweh does in fact hear their prayer (ii. 18 ff.). The promise of renewed harvest-blessing passes over in chap. iii. into a promise of other blessings in the Messianic time; the outpouring of the Spirit of God on all members of the nation of Israel and the final deliverance of Israel by means of the judgment on all nations in the Valley of Jehoshaphat.

From chaps. i. and ii. it results that the author lived in the vicinity of the temple and (on account of the great importance he ascribes to the meal and drink-offering, the fast and the assembly in the temple) in all probability was a priest. From his not mentioning the Aramæans and Assyrians amongst the enemies of the people it was long held that he belonged to the earlier, pre-exilic time. The remarkable silence of a Jerusalemite respecting the king was explained by the supposition that he lived during the minority of Joash of Judah (about 835). His position almost at the head of the minor prophets seemed also to recommend his being placed in the ninth century. But all these reasons have of late been almost universally recognized as invalid. Rather does iv. 2 ff., incontrovertibly presuppose the destruction of Jerusalem by the Chaldæans, and i. ii., the post-exilic community (ii. 16), in which there is no king and no princes, but simply elders (i. 14) and priests, "the servants of Jahweh" (i. 9, &c.), as leaders of the people: the fixed, official ritual of sacrifice also plays an important part. Corresponding to this there is no longer the least hint of idolatry or similar faults, and complete silence is maintained concerning the Kingdom of Israel. Israel, on the contrary, is now represented by Judah alone (ii. 27, iv. 2, 16). Finally let it be added that iii. 5 plainly refers to long-familiar prophetic utterances, in fact to Obadiah, 17 (perhaps also to Isaiah xxxiv.), that iv. 18 refers to Ezek. xlvii. and iv. 19 to Obad., 10, and no doubt will remain that Joel should be put about 400 B.C. There is nothing against this in the linguistic characteristics of the book (in the use, for example, of the Aramaic word for "End," ii. 20).

In the approximately contemporary *Book of Jonah* we have the only prophetic book which declares an important religious doctrine entirely in the form of a narrative. The hero of the story, Jonah, son of Amittai, is no doubt identical with the prophet of the same name who prophesied, according to 2 Kings xiv. 25, under Jeroboam II. (about 760). This does not mean that he was also the author of the booklet. Instead of this the narrator (iii. 3) does not conceal the fact that Nineveh in his time was a vanished power. The way in which the most astounding things (ii. 1, iv. 10) are related as though they needed no explanation shows clearly that the narrator was not concerned with the marvels but with the doctrines connected with them. Hence the only question is whether the whole should be regarded as a kind of parable or as a free adaptation of an old legend of the prophets. The latter is more probable because of the story's being attached to a definite historical person. But the teaching which the narrator purposes to give can only be found in the closing words, iv. 10 f. It simply runs : God willeth not the death of a sinner, but rather that he may turn and live. The threat of God's wrath once uttered is not a blind fate which must work itself out in any case : by repentance its recall can be procured—even by the heathen—and thus the Creator's purpose of love towards *all* His creatures retains its supremacy. The point of this teaching is evidently directed against the unspiritual, revengeful disposition of his fellow-countrymen, who thought they had a right to murmur at the continued delay of the sentence on Babylon and the heathen oppressors of Israel in general. Thus regarded, the little book is far from meriting the mockery of the injudicious, for it stands at the very topmost point of prophetic intuition, leaving a long way behind the idea of God which was cherished in the popular religion (the so-called "particularistic" view), and recalling such New Testament sayings as 1 Tim. ii. 4.

We are brought down to a later time, probably indeed to the beginning of the Greek period, by the very remarkable and extremely obscure chaps. xxiv.-xxvii. of the Book of Isaiah. Dim allusions to contemporary events (xxiv. 10, 14; xxv. 2 ; xxvi. 20 ; xxvii. 10) are woven into an inextricable whole with eschatological glimpses of the future (xxiv. 21 ff. ; xxv. 7 f.; xxvi. 19). The only certain point (from xxv. 10) is that the prophet writes in the immediate neighbourhood of the temple-hill and therefore in Jerusalem. A number of linguistic phenomena, in particular an almost boundless accumulation of plays on words, would be enough to demonstrate that, notwithstanding his impressive language and many profound thoughts, the prophet could not be identical with the Isaiah of the eighth century. Moreover, the attempt formerly made to place them prior to 588 or in the Exile is shipwrecked on the Biblico-theological character of these four chapters. Such theologumena as that of the annihilation of Death (xxv. 8) are unheard of in the earlier post-exilic time, and such utterances as xxiv. 21 and xxvi. 19, have their parallels only in very late psalms and the Book of Daniel.

The so-called Deutero-Zechariah, *i.e.*, Zech. ix.-xiv., must be regarded as one of the latest portions of all the prophetic books. These six chapters continued to be attributed to Zechariah, the contemporary of Haggai, in accordance with Jewish tradition, notwithstanding the special title in ix. 1 (which was afterwards imitated, as it appears, by a redactor at xii. 1 and Mal. i. 1), until the English theologian, J. Mede († 1638) ascribed Zech. ix.-xi. to Jeremiah, because of Matt. xxvii. 9 (where Zech. xi. 12 f. is evidently confused with Jer. xxxii. 6 ff.). On the other hand the Hamburg theologian, Flügge, 1784, wished to distinguish no fewer than nine distinct oracles in Zech. ix.-xiv. The constantly repeated attempts to solve the riddle led to quite discordant results. The right track already found by Eichhorn, was again forsaken, and—no doubt on attractive grounds—ix.-xi. were ascribed to a prophet of the time of Ahaz (that is about 735), xii.-xiv. to one of the time of Manasseh, or (by most) to the end of the seventh century. This solution of the problem was for several decades held to be indisputable till 1881, when Stade overthrew it by convincing arguments in the Zeitsch. für die Alttest. Wissenschaft (Years I. and II.). If Stade also has gone too far in asserting that Deutero-Zechariah is dependent throughout on pre-exilic and post-exilic prophets, he is right in maintaining that such passages as ix. 8, 11 ff.; x. 2, 6, 8 ff. refers to judgments executed in the distant past, especially to the banishment of the inhabitants of both kingdoms; that a form of Levitism is implied in xiv. 16 and 20 f. (cf. Exod. xxxix. 30) which is inconceivable till after Ezra's time, and, above all, that ix. 13 can only be explained of the Græco-Macedonian world-power. Assyria and Egypt, therefore, were veiled designations of the Seleucid and the Ptolemaic Kingdoms. We cannot hope for an exact interpretation of such passages as xi. 8 (formerly explained from 2 Kings xv. 8-14) and xii. 10 ff. (formerly referred to the prophet Uriah, Jer. xxvi. 20 ff., or to Josiah), especially as the allusions to current events are often closely interwoven with the eschatological glimpses, quite in the manner of Isa. xxiv.-xxvii.

Kuenen,[*] in particular (Einl.[2] ii. 411) has raised objections to Stade's final conclusion that the whole should be put about 280. According to him ancient fragments survive in chaps. ix.-xi. and xiii. 7-9, originating mainly in the eighth century (about 745 ff.), arranged by a post-exilic redactor partly in a peculiar fashion, and furnished with additions. And it really must be asked whether *every* mention of Ephraim (cf. especially ix. 10 and xi. 4-14) can be considered merely a filling up of the Messianic picture, although Ephraim itself had disappeared in the Exile long before the prophet's day. The mention of the teraphim and diviners (x. 2) is also very suprising for the Greek period. But the verdict on chaps. ix.-xi. as a whole is not altered by its being shown to be probable that there are fragments from an older time. Kuenen puts chaps. xii.-xiv. about 400. The bringing them down to the Greek time arose simply from the supposed unity of chaps. ix.-xiv. But this was not proved by Stade (who holds that chaps. ix. and x. contain a combination of the still unfulfilled older predictions and xi.-xiv. an elucidation of individual points and limitations). However this may be the

---

[*] H. Schultz, also, Alttestament. Theol.[5] (Gött., 1896), p. 49 [Eng. Trans., p. 70] supports the placing of chaps. ix.-xi. and xiii. 7 ff. in the anarchy after the death of Jeroboam II., and thinks that chaps. xii., xiii. 1-7, xiv. originated about 600 B.C.

uniting of Zech. ix.-xiv. with chaps. i.-viii., effected by Jewish tradition, must be explained in precisely the same way as that of Isa. xl.-lxvi. with chaps. i.-xxxix. The anonymous pieces, Zech. ix.-xiv. (or ix.-xi., xii.-xiv.) and Mal. i.-iii., perhaps after they had been reduced to their present shape by a redactor and provided with titles, were placed at the close of the minor prophets, till at last Zech. ix.-xiv. was erroneously regarded as a part of the immediately preceding book.

All that we have had to say about the prophetic writings of the post-exilic time ought to prove that prophecy cannot be affirmed to have expired with Malachi. But apart from Joel, Jonah, Isa. xxiv.-xxvii. and Zech. ix.-xiv., many other additions, besides isolated alterations in the older prophetic books, testify to the literary ardour which was devoted to prophecy and its products as late as the Greek period. Several of these after-shoots (*e.g.*, Isa. xxiii. 32 f., Micah vii. 7 ff., Jer. l. f., Hab. iii., Zeph. iii. 14 ff.) have already been mentioned in this Outline. The conclusion of Amos (ix. 8 ff.) is also counted by many moderns amongst the post-exilic supplements to the old prophetic utterances. The time of the translator of Jesus Sirach must be considered the lowest limit for the close of the *prophetic canon* as the second part of the Hebrew Bible (because he refers in his prologue to " the Law and the Prophets "). But there is nothing to prevent our dating the final redaction of the " Former and the Later Prophets " as early as the middle of the second century, B.C., although we know no more about any official act of canonization than in the case of the Pentateuch.

6. The Book of Daniel.

The Book of Daniel, which, on account of its position in the German [and English] Bible, is usually reckoned amongst the " Greater Prophets," belongs to another part of the Hebrew Bible and also to another class of literature.

Tradition looked upon it as the work of a Jewish exile who was brought up at the court of Nebuchadnezzar, and under him and his successors came to great honour. The book itself contains no statement that the whole was composed by Daniel. Yet in chaps. viii.-xi. he speaks in the first person, whereas in chaps. i.-vii. he is spoken of in the third. The contents of the book fall into two divisions: the Narratives (chaps. i.-vi.) and the Visions (chaps. vii.-xii.).

It has long been seen that if the narratives are considered to be accounts of actual events they lie open to the strongest possible objections, and the best-meant attempts fail to meet these. History knows nothing about a siege of Jerusalem in the third year of Jehoiakim (i. 1). The mention of the "Chaldæans" at Nebuchadnezzar's court (ii. 2, &c.) betrays a time when the old national name had at length assumed this quite special sense of Magi or astrologers. These "Chaldæans" speak* to Nebuchadnezzar in West-Aramaic instead of in that Babylonian language which is preserved in countless cuneiform inscriptions. Other unhistorical features are: The seven years' insanity of Nebuchadnezzar (iv. 30 ff.); Belshazzar as son and successor of Nebuchadnezzar and last king of Babylon; and Darius the Mede as successor of Belshazzar. All these are statements utterly impossible to a contemporary of the events of 608-536.

On the other hand all difficulties vanish at a stroke when the true character of the book is admitted: a work of comfort and exhortation belonging to the time when the Jews were sorely oppressed by Antiochus Ephiphanes IV. Indeed, the limit of its composition can be pretty accurately determined. At vii. 14 the re-dedication of the temple is still an object of expectation. It was accomplished in Dec., 165. The composition of the book must be placed before this limit, whether in the year 165 or just previously.

* The *Aramaic* part of Daniel, beginning at ii. 4, reaches to the close of the seventh chapter. From the misunderstanding of ii. 4 arose the quite erroneous designation of the West-Aramaic idiom (which Jesus and the Apostles also spoke) as the "Chaldæan Language."

Not only such facts as the silence of Jesus Sirach concerning Daniel, the very advanced development of the angelology and eschatology, the position of the book almost at the close of the Hebrew canon, but, above all, its peculiar contents, are accounted for by this theory. Everything contributes to a single end—the exhortation to endurance, endurance at any cost, in a dire distress which seemed to threaten the existence of the people and the ancestral religion. The author pursues this end in two ways. By the example of Daniel (who, according to Ezek. xiv. 14, 20, xxviii. 3, must have been a greatly lauded personality of ancient times) and his companions, he shows that God can guard from all harm the true confessors of His name and the zealous observers of His law, and can rescue them miraculously from the utmost conceivable mortal peril (chap. iii. !), so that heathen tyrants also are compelled to recognize His power and greatness. If this is the one aim of the narratives we can easily overlook the facts that Daniel, the scrupulous observer of the Dietary Laws (chap. i.) officiates as head of the *heathen* Magi, that he has not only to explain Nebuchadnezzar's dream but must first divine what it was (chap. ii.), that Nebuchadnezzar's conversion (ii. 46 ff.) is at once quite forgotten (chap. iii.), and many other points. The other method which the author uses is the form of the "Apocalypse," *i.e.*, the predicting by a prophet-voice of antiquity events which have already occurred. Thus in chaps. ii. and vii. the order and character of the four world-empires (Babylonian, Mede, Persian and Greek), and in chap. xi. the fortunes and conflicts of the Diadochi, down to Antiochus IV., are revealed with such fulness of detail that even in the first Christian centuries the real standpoint of the Apocalyptic writer was recognized by heathen critics.* The author evidently hoped (and certainly not without reason!) that by clothing his ideas in this form he

---

* This real standpoint also appears from chap. ix. Daniel is here troubled because the prediction of Jer. xxv. 11 has not been fulfilled. But at that time (about 538) not seventy years, but fifty at most had elapsed since the beginning of the Exile.

would make a deeper impression and the more surely attain his end. The form of an Apocalypse enabled him to bring out in the clearest fashion the thoughts on which he believed everything depended: all these disturbances and persecutions, all the bloody abominations and desecrations of things holy which God's people must experience, are but the immediate forerunners of the time of redemption when the blasphemers and destroyers will be judged and "the rule, power and might of the kingdoms under the whole heaven shall be given to the people of the saints of the Most High, and His kingdom shall be an everlasting kingdom" (chap. vii. 26 f.; cf. also xii. 1 ff.).

7. THE POETICAL BOOKS.

a. **The Psalter.**

Amongst the so-called "Poetical Books" *the Psalter*, the hymn book of the post-exilic Jewish community and the noblest Prayer Book of Christianity, takes by far the foremost place in regard to their significance for the history of religion.* In its present form it is a collection of 150† lyric (in part also lyric-didactic or elegiac) poems, the whole of which (including the "Marriage Song," Ps. xlv.) are religious in substance and were compiled for the promotion of the edification of the post-exilic community, especially in divine service. A hundred of them are ascribed to definite authors—one to Moses (Ps. xc.); seventy-three (eighty-three in the

---

* Jewish tradition regards the Psalms, Proverbs, and Job as poetical books in the stricter sense. These three are, therefore, accentuated on a different system from the remaining twenty-one books.

† The enumeration of the Psalms varies even in Hebrew manuscripts. In the Greek and Latin Bibles Ps. ix. and x. are correctly made *one*, also (incorrectly) Ps. cxiv. and cxv.: on the other hand Ps. cxvi. and cxlvii. (here again incorrectly) are divided into two. (Besides ix. and x., Ps. xlii. and xliii. are erroneously divided as well as Ps. cxvii. and cxviii. Ps. cviii. is a compilation from Ps. lvii. 8-12 and lx. 7-14.)

Greek Bible, which in other points also differs considerably from the Hebrew in the titles) to David; two (lxxii., cxxvii.) to Solomon; twelve (l., lxxiii.-lxxxiii.) to Asaph; one each to Heman and Ethan (lxxxviii., lxxxix.); ten (leaving out lxxxviii.) to the Korahites. Sixteen psalms have other titles: thirty-four ("the orphans") are entirely without. Seeing that by Asaph, Heman and Ethan, the Davidic choirmasters thus named (1 Chron. xv. 17) are doubtless meant, and that the Korahites are probably thought of as David's contemporaries, all the statements respecting psalmists, at least in Pss. i.-lxxxix (see below) must proceed from the assumption that no psalm is more recent than the age of David and Solomon. For the opinion that those titles were not originally intended to indicate the author but only to intimate that the psalm was to be apportioned to the division of the temple-choir named after David, Asaph, &c.,* is refuted by the title of Ps. xc. and, above all, by those of Ps. li. f., liv., lvi. f., lix. f., lxiii. This is also true of the theory that "of David, &c.," was meant to point to the Book of Poems named after David, &c., from which the psalm had been taken (Baethgen, Psalmen, p. vii.). "Of the Korahites" is the only title that can be satisfactorily explained (with Hupfeld) in this way.

The fact that psalms which can be shown to be late (cf., *e.g.*, in regard to Solomon, p. 14, above) are very often in the titles ascribed to definite authors on the ground of mere conjectures, and that in the above-mentioned psalms from li. onwards, events from the life of David (founded on the Books of Samuel) were alleged as the historical occasions for poems obviously belonging to the community, compels us to conclude that all these titles are later additions, and therefore have absolutely no validity in proving the authorship and date of the several psalms. As to David, we refer to the remarks above, p. 11. What is there said respecting the possibility of genuinely Davidic poems or fragments having passed from some pre-exilic Book of Songs into the post-exilic collections

---

* Thus de Lagarde, Orientalia, ii. 13.

of songs must now be yet further generalized: our present Psalter in all probability contains a fair number of pre-exilic songs or fragments of songs. To say nothing of the so-called Royal Psalms, xx., xxi., xlv., which can only be understood as songs from before the Exile, or of the manifold traces of antique phraseology, *one* circumstance in particular supports this. Such energetic denial of the necesssity of the sacrificial ritual as is found in xl. 7, l. 8 ff., and li. 18 f. (softened down with much trouble by the liturgical addition, v. 20 f.) could not have found its way into the temple hymn book till the psalms which contain it had long been clothed with a kind of canonical dignity. For the rest, however, the determination of the age of individual psalms depends mainly on subjective considerations, and is therefore easily liable to error. For the adaptation of the psalms to liturgical use must frequently (just as in our hymn books) have necessitated serious alterations of their original form. *How* idle the dispute concerning these annotations is must be clear above all others to the man who employs the psalms for the purpose for which they were collected. What in the world has the perennial edifying power of psalms like xxiii., xc., ciii., cxxi., cxxvii., and many others, to do with the question whether some post-exilic redactor was right or wrong in attributing them to David or Moses or Solomon?

It is now as good as universally admitted that the musical titles and annotations (almost all of them thoroughly obscure) are all connected with the temple music and the temple song of the post-exilic time, and therefore for the most part were later additions, if not actually added at the final revision of the Psalter. This explains how one and the same psalm (xiv. and liii.) received different titles when admitted into different collections. Express mention of the liturgical occasion is found in the titles of Ps. xxx., xxxviii., lxx., xcii., c.

The origin of our present Psalter in successive stages has gradually become clear through the observation of the following facts. The division of the Psalter into Five Books is attested from the second century A.D., although special (but always unvocalised) titles, such as "First Book," &c., may not have been added till much later in the Hebrew Bible manuscripts. The close of the several books is indicated at the end of Ps. xli., lxxii., lxxxix., cvi. by a so-called doxology (praise): the entire 150th Psalm serves as doxology to the Fifth Book. Since the doxology to Ps. cvi. seems to be cited at 1 Chron. xvi. 36, it was formerly concluded that the Chronicler must have been acquainted with the Psalter in its present form, along with the division into Five Books. But the opposite conviction has recently asserted itself with ever increasing force: the doxology in 1 Chron. xvi. 36 is original and therefore was added subsequently to Ps. cvi. in order to form a Fourth Book with the same number of psalms (seventeen) as the Third. After Ps. lxxii. comes the subscription (which the punctators regarded as part of the text), "The prayers of David, son of Jesse, are ended." Hence it is clear that the Third Book (Ps. lxxiii.-lxxxix.) is due to a redactor who wished to supplement a collection of Davidic poems by a gleaning of non-Davidic ones (already, however, ascribed to David's choirmasters). But closer observation of Ps. i.-lxxii. shows that this part also does not represent a homogeneous collection. In the first place, Ps. xlii.-xlix. (Korahite psalms)) and the Asaph-psalm, l., must originally have formed a whole with Ps. lxxiii.-lxxxix. The phraseology of the subscription after Ps. lxxii. (originally probably after Ps. lxxi.) shows that it can only have referred to Ps. iii.-xli. and li.-lxxi. For all these psalms are attributed to David except Ps. x., the second half of Ps. ix.,* Ps. xxxiii., lxvi., lxvii., lxxi.; and the Greek Bible also designates Ps. xxxiii., lxvii., and lxxi. as Davidic.

But the marking out of Ps. iii.-xli. by the concluding doxology

---

* That Ps. ix. and x. originally formed *one* psalm is seen from the alphabetic arrangement of the beginnings of the verses (to say nothing of the absence of a title to Ps. x.). In Ps. ix. the alphabetic arrangement is almost unbroken (down to the tenth letter); in Ps. x. it has been retained at least in v. 1 and v. 12 ff.

as a special collection is seen to be correct; first, from the two-fold admission of the same psalms (xiv. = liii.; xl. 14 ff. = lxx.), and then, from the following discovery of Ewald's. Whilst the First Book uses the divine name Jahweh 278 times and the name Elohim (God) only about seven times, when Jahweh might have been expected, Elohim preponderates to such an extent in Ps. xlii.-lxxxiii. as to stand two hundred times compared with Jahweh forty-three times. The only explanation, especially when xiv. and liii. have been compared together, is that some redactor, on account of religious scruples, attempted to replace the divine name Jahweh by Elohim in the separate collection xlii.-lxxxiii. (which, therefore, still lacked the gleanings of Korahite and other psalms, lxxxiv.-lxxxix.). He did not, indeed, quite attain his end, for Jahweh often asserted itself in the text alongside Elohim or Adonai (a specially striking instance at l. 1; cf. also lix. 6, lxviii. 19, lxxx. 5, 20).

The gradual growth of the Psalter is accordingly to be thus conceived: Ps. iii.-xli. formed the stem, as the first collection of Davidic poems, arranged about the time of Ezra. Towards the end of the Persian age a second collection of Davidic poems (li.-lxxi.) followed, together with poems by David's contemporaries (xlii.-xlix., l., lxxii., lxiii.-lxxxiii.), with a later gleaning (lxxxiv.-lxxxix.). The third collection (xc.-cl.) must have been made considerably later, and contained almost exclusively the later and latest psalms down to the time of Simon, the founder of the Asmonæan dynasty (142 ff., B.C.). The interval in time between the second and third collections is shown chiefly by the entire absence from Ps. xc.-cl. of the musical titles and annotations, which seem to have been quite familiar to so late a writer as the Chronicler. In the times after him there must have been so fundamental a transformation of the temple music that those ancient technical terms were altogether unknown to the Alexandrian (Greek) translation of the Psalms. Within the latest collection several connected groups may clearly be distinguished: thus Ps. xcii.-c., civ.-cvii., cxi.-cxvii., and especially the splendid group of the "Pilgrim Songs,"

Ps. cxx.-cxxxiv. It was, perhaps, the final redactor who prefixed to the whole collection the anonymous Psalms i. and ii. (which are still reckoned as *one* at Acts xiii. 33), the one as a kind of programme of the fundamental ethical ideas of the Psalter, the other of its theocratic and Messianic hopes. Yet one of them may have served as an introduction to an earlier collection. The above arrangement of the three collections does not imply that there were no subsequent dislocations, and especially that isolated Maccabæan psalms (thus, very probably, Ps. xliv. lxxiv., lxxxiii.), had not already made their way into the second collection.

The religious and religious-historical significance of the Psalter cannot easily be rated too high. The priestly law-book which Ezra had made the ruling power, by its extraordinary emphasis on all the *acts* which aim at external purity and propitiation in the cultus and in life, readily creates the impression that the entire age after Ezra gave itself up entirely to sacrifice and the ceremonial law, or, at any rate, saw in them by far the most important expression of religious need and feeling. Not as though the Priests' Law had wished the ceremonial law to be observed without a corresponding disposition, *opera operata*, without faith and personal devotion to God and one's neighbour. But there certainly is this far-reaching distinction that the genuine prophetic view, as we find it at Amos v. 25, Hosea vi. 6, Isa. i. 11 ff., Micah. vi. 6 ff., Jer. vii. 21 ff., in extraordinarily powerful testimonies, held sacrifice and external acts to be indifferent and unessential— a clear proof that as yet they knew nothing of a Divine appointment respecting these things. But the standpoint of the Priests' Code is that the sacrifices and external acts demanded by the law are the most excellent and absolutely indispensable expression of the disposition which pleases God.

From the Psalter we learn that alongside the legal tendency there ran another, not less powerful, which became of importance even in the temple-worship, and can only be described as a continuation and worthy exhibition of the prophetic world of thought. If we leave out Ps. cxix. the reference to the law in the Psalter is strikingly infrequent, and when it occurs it almost always (cf., *e.g.*, i. 2, xix. 8 ff., xxxvii. 31) has to do with the morally purifying and preserving operation, not the ritual significance, of the law. But what an abundance of evidences we have of every kind of most fervent and genuine religious feeling! There is heartfelt prayer and thanksgiving, world-conquering faith and trust, most blessed fellowship with God! Indeed, the above-mentioned genuinely prophetic view of sacrifice here finds (Ps. xl. 7, l. 8 ff., li. 18 f.) vigorous and, as we have already said, really astonishing expression in the worshipping community of post-exilic times. There are, too, in the Psalter many classical utterances of those loftiest expectations which, on account of their significance for all God's saving ways, surpass all other prophetic thoughts in importance—the idea of the Messianic Kingdom as a Kingdom of God which, thanks to the missionary vocation of Israel, embraces all the heathen, in short, the destiny of Israel's religion to be the world's religion.*

The correct estimate of the Psalter has been greatly promoted by the observation made long ago, but long and often forgotten again, that in a great number of psalms the speaker is not a single godly man but the godly community of the post-exilic time. This is connected with the fact that the individual is nowhere to be considered as the subject of religion but the people. The people was chosen by Jahweh, redeemed from Egyptian bondage by the mighty deeds of His arm, and thus made His people. Elsewhere it is called His first-born son (Exod. iv. 22; cf. Hosea xi. 1). It is to the people that the threats of judgment are addressed, as well as the promises of resurrection from the Exile and of the Messianic time. It would indeed be a mischievous exaggeration to recognize nowhere in the psalms the evidences of individual godliness, of individual religious experiences and needs, to

---

* Cf. Stade's excellent exposition of this point (in Zeitschr. für Theol. u. Kirche, ii. 1892, 369 ff.) which was formerly subjected to ill-founded criticisms in consequence of the critics holding much too mechanical a view of the idea "Messianic Prophecy."

think of everything as spoken *only* from the soul of the praying community. To say nothing of the possibility that many individual traits were suppressed or transformed when the poems were received into the Common Hymn Book, this thesis that the people is the subject of the Israelite religion greatly needs limitation, at least so far as post-exilic times are concerned. Jeremiah, in particular, prepared the way for the release of religion from its strait connection with State and nation: according to him (xxxi. 33) the "new covenant" was to become a reality in the inmost heart of every individual. It would thus be a perverted notion if we were absolutely to deny that there are "Individual Psalms," or to maintain that in the Congregational Psalms the poet has not a most vivid *personal* participation in the woe or joy of the whole. But this does not detract from the truth that a fairly large number of psalms, the interpretation of which formerly gave useless trouble, are lit up at once when taken as Congregational psalms: amongst others we assign iii., iv., vii., ix. f., xi., xiii., and very especially xxii., to this class.*

b. The Song of Songs.

We are carried into quite another world by those examples of lyric poetry which have been preserved in the "Song of Songs," or "Canticles." They did not make their way into the Canon without opposition, and no doubt they owe their admission to the two-fold fact that they were held to be Solomon's work, and could be allegorically interpreted throughout—in the Synagogue as referring to the relation between Jahweh and the Israelite community, in the

---

* The recognition that there are numerous Congregational psalms has been especially promoted in recent times by Olshausen, Reuss and Cheyne. We may also refer to the discussion of this question and of the underlying theoretic principles by Smend ("Ueber das Ich der Psalmen") in the Zeitschr. f. die alttest. Wissensch., 1888, p. 49 ff., the most thorough-going development of the theory of a Collective subject; and by Beer ("Individual- und Gemeindepsalmen," Marburg, 1894), who takes an intermediate position.

Christian Church to that between Christ and His Bride the Church. But a closer consideration of the phraseology compels us to reject unhesitatingly this allegorical interpretation as unworthy of God or Christ. That phraseology will not permit us to think of anything but the glorification of the bliss of earthly love, and that, predominantly, on its sensuous side. Alongside this, passages are not wanting which laud bridal or connubial love from a far higher point of view (cf. especially viii. 5 ff.). After the allegorical exposition was abandoned, these passages were used to justify the view that in the Canticles generally there is a glorification of monogamistic love as the fellowship designed by God, in contrast to all the distortions occasioned by the harem-system of the great. This view almost always went hand in hand with the theory that Canticles is a drama or opera which depicts in actions and reciprocal songs the bridal love of a country pair (a shepherd and the Shulamite), its forcible interruption by Solomon, who carries off the Shulamite to his harem, Solomon's fruitless wooing, the stedfastness of the Shulamite, and finally her happy reunion with her beloved. Countless attempts have been made* to divide the contents of the Canticles in this or some similar way into acts and scenes— mostly assuming that the MS. leaves have been transposed— and to apportion them to the actors (Solomon, the Shulamite, the shepherd), perhaps also to a second pair of lovers, finally to the men and daughters of Jerusalem (as choir). The smallest of the difficulties in the way of these attempts is perhaps this: none of the divisions are in any way indicated and consequently no two of the dramatizations coincide. The other difficulty is greater; the drama is unknown on genuine Semitic soil, especially in ancient times, and such converse between the bridal pair as is assumed in the Canticles is unheard of. It seems a far more natural theory that

* Recently, to mention only the most important, by Stickel (Berl., 1888), Bruston (Paris, 1891), Herzog (Berl., 1893), Martineau (in the American Journal of Philology, xiii. 3), and, in an exceedingly interesting way, by Rothstein (Halle, 1893).

Canticles consists of a number of distinct love-songs, whether by one or by several poets. But the riddle seems to us to have been completely solved by the explanations which Wetstein* has given, founded on his own observation of customs still in vogue amongst the Arabic population in Syria and Palestine. According to it Canticles contain marriage-songs (or fragments of such) as they are sung on the wedding-day and the next seven days, partly to the accompaniment of song and dances, by the bridesmen, the chorus of men and women, and the young pair themselves. These seven days are called "The King's Week," because the young bridegroom and the young wife during this time play the parts of king and queen, and receive the homage of the entire district and even of the neighbouring places, seated on a kind of throne which is erected for them as a seat of honour on the threshing-floor. It is remarkable how many enigmatic passages of the Canticles (*e.g.*, vii. 1 ff., as the accompaniment of the bride's sword-dance) are explained in an extremely simple fashion on this assumption. Amongst other things it thus becomes self-evident that neither has Solomon, iii. 7 ff., anything to do with the Solomon of history, nor is Shulamite (vii. 1) a proper name. Both designations are meant as comparisons, and in fact, Shulamite (in the Greek Bible "Shunamite") is an allusion to that Abishag of Shunem† who was appointed, as the most beautiful virgin then in Israel, to attend on the old man David. Budde's very true remark (at the close of the English Essay mentioned below) deserves special attention: all sorts of objectionable things in the Canticles must seem far more harmless and unexceptionable

---

* First in the Zeitschr. der deutschen morgenl. Gesellsch., 1868, p. 105 f., then in the essay on "Die Syrische Dreschtafel," in Bastian's Zeitschrift für Ethnographie (1873), and in Delitzsch' Kommentar über das Hohelied (Lpzg., 1875), p. 162 ff. Budde, in "The Song of Solomon" (New World, 1894, p. 56 ff.), as well as in the Preussischen Jahrbb., Oct., 1894, p. 92 ff., makes additional contributions to the explanation, founded on Wetstein's hypothesis.

† Stade, in the Gesch. Israels, i. 292, gave this unquestionably right explanation of the only once used name: see the more detailed proof in Budde, *loc. cit.*, p. 63 f.

if they belong to the class of ancient wedding customs and songs. For linguistic reasons, and especially on account of the use of various Greek words, the former part of the Greek period is the earliest to which these marriage-songs can be assigned.

8. The Monuments of the "Wisdom Literature."

a. Proverbs.

We must devote a final section to the monuments of the so-called Chokma (= Wisdom) Literature which have found admission to the Canon of the Old Testament. Here we leave the question untouched whether "the wise" formed a special guild in pre-exilic times (alongside the priests and prophets). Jer. xviii. 18 makes this highly probable, and certainly it was so in post-exilic times, as all kinds of clear traces show (cf. especially Prov. i. 6, xiii. 14, xxii. 17, xxiv. 3, Eccles. xii. 11). We are indeed left almost entirely in the dark as to the formation and constitution of these societies, the extent and the methods of their investigation. Thus much only is clear from numerous passages in the Book of Proverbs (i. 4, 8, ii. 1, iii. 1, iv. 1, &c.): the activity of the wise was devoted not only to consultations and discussions amongst themselves, but principally to the guidance of the young (the "Sons, *i.e.*, Pupils of the Wise"). But the Wisdom Books preserved in the Old Testament do at least give us some information respecting the subjects of their inquiry and teaching. The religion of Israel inherited from their fathers, is everywhere the foundation and pre-supposition, for "the fear of Jahweh is the beginning—it might also be rendered, the main thing in—knowledge"! (Prov. i. 7). But the ceremonial side of the religion, and with it the dependence on the priestly law, is almost entirely in the background: hence the prophetic tendency comes to the front. But this is the weightiest point: the religion on which Wisdom builds is no longer (cf. above,

p. 148) an affair of the people as a whole but of the individual. The teachings of Wisdom, the solution of the problems with which it deals, are to serve as guide-posts to direct the individual in wisely ordering, and really enjoying his life, and also for the quieting of painful doubts, the giving assurance as to comforting truths which concern individual human souls. More closely considered the three Old Testament Wisdom-books occupy themselves with the following topics: Proverbs, with all kinds of isolated rules for the conduct of life; the Book of Job, with a religious-philosophical discussion of the highest importance; finally Ecclesiastes, with the question whether a complete theory of the world in general is possible.

Chaps. x. 1—xxii. 16 are doubtless to be considered the kernel of the Book of Proverbs. At the head of this part stands the title, "The Proverbs of Solomon," which was afterwards (i. 1) transferred to the whole book. It proves that there was an ancient tradition, testified to at 1 Kings v. 9 ff. also, that Solomon was the prototype of the "wise," and, in particular, was the founder of Proverbial Wisdom. It is, indeed, altogether uncertain how many of the 375* verses, mainly in so-called antithetic (contrasted) parallelism, are to be attributed to Solomon himself (cf. the remark above, p. 13). "The Words of the Wise," chaps. xxii. 17—xxiv. 22, form the first appendix to this; the twelve verses, xxiv. 23-34, the second. These, too, so far as the title is concerned, make no claim to have been written by Solomon. There is a second principal collection in chaps. xxv. 1—xxix. 27, with the title, "These also are proverbs of Solomon which the men of Hezekiah, King of Judah, copied out." We cannot determine the source of this statement, which must be due to a later redactor, because of the "also." The frequent occurrence of the same proverbs in both divisions is against the theory that "the men of Hezekiah" in this way

---

* Behnke (Zeitschr. für die Alttest. Wissensch., 1896, p. 122) remarks that 375 is the numerical value of the consonants of *Sh^{e}lomoh* (Solomon, cf. x. 1): in like manner 136, the number of verses in the second collection, is the value of the consonants of the name *Chizqiyahu* (Hezekiah; cf. xxv. 1).

appended their own collection to the first principal collection of Solomonic proverbs (over 100 of the 541 proverbs in the entire book occur more than once). Moreover, it will be shown below that we must recognize a final revision of this part in the post-exilic age. There are the following appendices to the second main collection: — 1. The Words of Agur, the son of Jakeh (chap. xxx.). 2. The Words of King Lemuel (xxxi. 1-7.) 3. The Alphabetical Praise of the Virtuous Housewife (xxxi. 10-31). The assertion of Jewish tradition that Agur and Lemuel are mystical designations of Solomon is disproved at once by the linguistic character of those proverbs, which points rather to the later post-exilic time.

After the collection of which we have been speaking, or, at all events, the greater part of x.-xxix. had been finished, the prologue (i.-ix.) was added. It begins with a common title and short introduction to the whole book (i. 1-6): then it proceeds, partly with general exhortations to the appropriation of Wisdom, referring constantly to its blessed fruits, partly with warnings against various distinct sins and follies; it concludes with an impressive address by Wisdom herself, in which she solemnly invites to the meal which she has prepared (chap. viii. f.). This conclusion especially, with its peculiar personification of Wisdom, presupposes a long cultivation of speculation on the philosophy of religion, and the close of our present Book of Proverbs must therefore be placed not earlier than the middle of the fourth century. The numerous additions in the Greek translation of proverbs from other sources also show that after our Canonical Book of Proverbs had assumed its fixed form pains were still taken to extend and to alter it. We must also recognize that final revision of the older collections which has been indicated above, for in no other way can we explain the entire absence of any allusion to idolatry. Reuss has also correctly alleged as a mark of the post-exilic age the manner in which monogamy is everywhere taken for granted.

The assertion that the Proverbs, like a great part of the

Psalms, promoted "Religion in Life," requires a certain qualification. Alongside the many proverbs in which a profoundly religious disposition finds such splendid expression, as, *e.g.*, xxxi. 30, there is also a series which recommends rules for wise and even for merely prudent life, simply on the ground of a large experience. Common apophthegms, too, and actually a kind of riddle (xxx. 15 ff.), are not lacking: the poetry of culture (especially in the choice collection, chap. xxv. ff.) preponderates over popular poetry, the proverb in the narrower sense of the word. But the contents are nowhere such as to contradict the religious and moral key-note which is heard throughout.

b. The Book of Job.

Amidst all the controversy as to the date and aim of the Book of Job, there is one point on which absolute unanimity has ever prevailed: here we have one of the most magnificent creations of which the literary history of all times and all nations can tell, a creation so unique that an idle contest might ever be breaking out anew as to the precise class of poetry in which it is to be enrolled. And if in other didactic poems—for in any case the Book of Job is such—it is inevitable that the artistic form should suffer from the doctrinal aim, the Book of Job has not called forth such a criticism from anyone. The construction of the poem, as well as the solution of the problem, takes place before our eyes in such a fashion that (apart, of course, from some later additions), we never trace a falling off in the poet's creative power: on the contrary his speech displays its most impressive force at the end of the poem in the speeches of Jahweh.

The problem itself is none other than the question which includes *all* that can be objected against the moral character of the government of the world and the Divine ordering of human fortunes: "How is the suffering of the godly to be reconciled with the righteousness of God?" This, of course, does not deal with the troubles which the mere fact of being a man brings on every one without exception; all kinds of dangers, occasionally sickness and privation, manifold vexations and failures, death at the last. The question rather is: "How can God so often permit really godly men to be attacked with the sorest affliction of body and soul, leaving them to bear it in utter hopelessness to the end, whereas, on the other side, it is an indisputable fact that open despisers of God have often enjoyed to the end great and undisturbed happiness. Where, then, does Reason come in in the order of the world? Where does Divine Righteousness abide?"

This ceases to be a problem the moment that faith asserts itself in a future solution of all riddles, a righteous compensation hereafter, as is the case on the ground of the Christian hope of immortality. But the religion of Israel knew nothing of such a hope for the individual. It must suffice him if he attained to the natural limit of human life, and was not cut off "in the midst of the years." After that he became the property of the grave, and his unsubstantial shadow went down to the Underworld, and remained for ever unrelated to God and to the sorrow and joy of the world above.

So long as religion, in accordance with what we have said above, was indissolubly bound up with the needs, the fears and hopes of the nation as a whole, the problem treated in the Book of Job could not be felt in all its difficulty. Astounding experiences, therefore, whether of the whole nation or its individual members, did not cause men to take umbrage at the righteousness of God; the immediate future would, perhaps, provide a solution, whether the smitten ones themselves experienced it or not. But it was different when such problems began to be solved on what might be called independent ground, as problems of human life in general, outside the limits of the nation. Then first could he who believed in a Divine righteousness feel the inequality in men's fortunes to be a tormenting riddle. But he would be obliged, in the same measure, to look upon all earlier attempts to quiet doubt and solve the riddle as unprofitable evasions.

The question must have stood thus when the poet of Job

undertook its solution—certainly not for the sole reason that a special inclination towards philosophical speculation attracted him towards it, but because his inmost heart, his whole religious personality, was most mightily laid hold of by it. Nor does he seek the solution in the way of didactic exposition and demonstration, but clothes it with the outlines of a history; sets the problem, as it were, in personal form before our eyes, and illuminates it on all sides from widely different standpoints, till at length the mouth of God pronounces the decision.

The external organization—we might almost say the dramatic structure—of the poem is extremely simple and clear. The prose Prologue (chaps. i. and ii.) shows in Job a pattern of exemplary earthly happiness, and also of exemplary piety. The man who offers propitiatory sacrifices for sins which his children may possibly have committed is a really godly person: God Himself repeatedly bears testimony to this (i. 8, ii. 3). The question as to what tradition really said about Job, who is here represented as the owner of great herds in the land of Uz, is altogether trivial and without bearing on the understanding of the book. We merely know from Ezekiel (xiv. 14, 20), who mentions him along with Noah and Daniel, that his was one of those names of the past which were famous for their godliness. Our poet evidently means him and his friends to be thought of as non-Israelites: the problem is to be discussed outside the national soil of the religion of Israel. Naturally, this does not prevent specifically Israelite views and postulates of faith from appearing everywhere, more or less involuntarily. Yet the fiction is so far strictly adhered to, that not only the proper name of the God of Israel (Jahweh), but every direct reference to the history of the people, is avoided in the poetical part of the book.

The dramatic movement in the working out of the problem begins with the first assault which the Satan—a name suggested probably by the poetical use of it at Zech. iii. 1—*i.e.*, the Adversary, makes, attempting to cast suspicion on the unselfishness and so on the moral value of Job's piety.

God allows Satan to subject Job's external good fortune to a trial. He knows that it must end in the vindication of His servant. Swift strokes of ruin fall on Job from every quarter: in one day all his riches vanish. He holds his peace till the news of the loss of all his children comes suddenly upon him. Then he complies with the customary observances of sorrow, uttering at the same time words of prayer, the quiet grandeur of which cannot be enhanced by any addition or comment.

Satan's second assault moves God to abandon Job's body, but not his life, to a final trial. Job is attacked by a horrible, distressing, painful, and altogether hopeless disease. All the symptoms show that the form of leprosy known as elephantiasis is meant. Still he maintains his position with pious resignation against the bitter mockery of his own wife. But when his three friends have appeared and sat down in silence over against him seven days and nights, the grief which rages within gets the mastery at last. He breaks the silence with a monologue, in which he most vehemently curses the day of his birth, praises the earliest possible death as an enviable good fortune, and finally, sinking into melancholy, depicts the sweet rest and the equality of all who dwell in the Underworld.

The Prologue has, not improperly, been compared with the "Development" in a drama; and this "Development" is so masterly that it is difficult to understand how it could ever have been explained as a later addition to the original poem. By means of it the poet, with conscious art, has accomplished something which, quite apart from the increase of our artistic enjoyment of the poem, is also important for a right estimate of its religious value. The reader is placed at the outset on a firm and sure standpoint, from which he can observe the wavering conflict with most vivid sympathy, but without confusion. From the facts of which he has been told, he knows what Job and his friends do not know, that there are sufferings the reasons of which do not lie in the punitive wrath of God, but in His purpose of love. That is not a solution of the problem; we still miss the answer to the question how God's purpose of love can permit such an infliction of pain on His own. Yet it is a significant sign-post, indicating that in the issue of the dispute upright piety must at last vanquish prejudice and stupidity.

Job's first monologue (chap. iii.), which has brought us into the poetical part of the book (chaps. iii.-xlii. 6), is followed by the controversies, chaps. iv.-xxviii. Each of the friends speaks three times, in the same order, to be immediately refuted each time by Job. But in the third colloquy (xxii.-xxvi.), the material at the disposal of the friends is found to be so exhausted that Bildad, the second, contents himself with a brief embarrassed repetition of what has been said long before, and Zophar, the third, is quite silent. The standpoint of the friends is that of the current doctrine of retribution, in the form which had developed out of the distortion of the great truth proclaimed at Exod. xx. 5 f. There the ungodly are promised vengeance on their sins to the fourth generation; the pious, God's blessing to the thousandth generation. The popular view distorted this to mean that *all* sufferings are punishments, whilst continued good fortune is the reward of conduct pleasing to God. From immense suffering they logically deduced immense guilt; from special judgments, touching the body of the supposed pious man, secret faultiness. Hence the friends at first accuse the sufferer covertly, but, at last (xxii. 4 ff.), quite expressly, of having merited God's judgment by his sin. They endeavour to weaken Job's constant reference to those experiences of happiness and suffering, which do not correspond with their theory, by pretending that all the sinner's prosperity is only apparent and is destined to be suddenly shattered.

Job does not attempt to deny that he is a sinner in the sense in which all men are; but he is conscious that he has pursued an upright, pious course in thought, word and deed. The reference to universal human sinfulness cannot, therefore, in any way explain the enigma of his fate. The assertion of the friends that they have explained it is self-deception and malice. Convinced of this, Job talks himself into such bitterness in the first colloquy that his speeches several times (cf. especially ix. 22 f.) approach very near to blasphemy. But in his inmost soul his faith holds fast to that image of the wise and just God which he has borne in his heart so many years; in fact, he comes at last to invoke the Heavenly Witness of his innocence, the righteous God, to be his helper against the incomprehensible God who torments him without cause (xvi. 18 ff.). He struggles through to the rock-firm certainty (xix. 23 ff.) that God will at last take his part and bring his innocence to light. With such a certainty of victory, he gradually reduces to silence the attacks of his friends; but this does not bring him to a solution of the riddle itself. The concluding speech (chap. xxvii. f.) only reaches the result that God's doings are in any case Wisdom, but that He has kept this exclusively for Himself, and has merely given man such a share in it as finds expression in the fear of God and the avoidance of evil. As against the riddles of the course of the world, especially *such* experiences as Job had to undergo, there is nothing but a painful despair of winning knowledge. This being his view, Job's thoughts are again taken up sorrowfully with his former happiness and dignity (chap. xxix.); he contrasts with it his present unutterable misery, and then examines his past life (chap. xxx.) from a standpoint the moral elevation of which reminds us in many ways of the Sermon on the Mount. He had made no reply to the direct accusations of Eliphaz (in chap. xxii.): now the answer follows, and in a form which leaves but the one thought with the reader, that God must now indeed interpose for the sufferer and confirm the truth of his assertions. Job himself at the close solemnly summons Him, and his expectation is not disappointed.

But God's reply to him (xxxviii. 1 ff.) * out of the thunderstorm is something quite different from what he had repeatedly desired during the discussion, and, in part, had actually pictured to himself. A questioning and answering (xiii. 22) had hovered before his mind's eye, an occasion on which he

---

* On the subsequently interpolated Elihu-Speeches (chaps. xxxii.-xxxvii.), see more below.

could not only justify himself to God but God to him. Here, too, the poet displays all his greatness. Instead of a judicial process, which in any case must seem unworthy of God, he introduces God teaching the man, in a speech full of lofty irony, the foolishness, nay, the childishness of his demand. But the irony is not an annoying, absolutely repelling one. It aims simply at bringing the deeply wounded man into the right condition for the sure and speedy healing of his wound. And the solution of the riddle given in these Divine speeches is so clear and simple and thorough that no one who does not intentionally close his eyes can miss it. The God who from the beginning has ruled His creation with infinite glory and wisdom, ordering all things wisely, providing lovingly for every longing of the irrational creatures (xxxviii. 41 ff.), can cherish towards man also nothing but thoughts full of wisdom and love, although his ways may often be incomprehensible to human minds. If a proof were still needed that the poet wished to convey this teaching in the speeches of Jahweh it would be furnished by Job's answer (xl. 4 f. and xlii. 3 ff.). He recants and repents in dust and ashes, not because he has learnt that we must once for all despair of comprehending God's ways—*that* knowledge he had reached previously—but because God's appearance at the end had brought the assurance that the good man may ever take comfort in the wise and loving guidance of his God, notwithstanding every appearance to the contrary. This is the only view with which the Epilogue xlii. 7 ff. (again in prose) agrees.

The form which Job had wished justice to assume was unsuitable. But when he had humbled himself it is expressly admitted that he is perfectly right in not yielding against his own better knowledge and conscience to the unloving prejudice of his opponents. In fact, at their burnt-offering they need his intercession to avert the righteous anger of God. The complete re-establishment of Job's external prosperity (xlii. 10 ff.) is, of course, not a necessary element in the solution of the problem, but only a demand of "poetic justice." The reader's feelings require this demonstration that even in the concrete case to which the poet has attached the discussion and solution of the problem all controversy was at length hushed in perfect harmony.

Objections of some importance have been raised against the authenticity of some sections (especially xxvii. 7—xxviii. 28, and the descriptions of the hippopotamus and crocodile, xl. 15—xli. 26). But, with the exception perhaps of chap. xxviii., our idea of the whole is not affected by them. The same cannot be said of the Elihu-Speeches, chaps. xxxii.-xxxvii. These stand in absolutely irreconcilable opposition to the aim of all the rest of the poem. After Job's last great monologue, to which God's answer, xxxviii. 1, immediately attaches itself, Elihu enters suddenly upon the scene in order that, in four speeches addressed personally to Job, and differing very conspicuously from all the others even in form, he may read both the friends and Job a lesson. The former, because they could find no further answer; Job, because he dared to maintain that he was pure, instead of recognizing that his suffering was ordained by God for a wholesome discipline. We have already mentioned that in the heat of the dispute Job says what must needs wound a pious and reverent spirit. The author of the Elihu-Speeches was evidently offended because no one expressly and fitly corrected Job for this. But the idea that Job was so terribly punished beforehand for guilt which he contracted *in consequence of* his sufferings is utterly absurd, and therefore it certainly did not occur to the original poet, as we may see from i. 8, ii. 3, and, rightly understood, also from xlii. 7. That the speeches are interpolated is also clear from the fact that, in the further course of the poem, not the slightest notice is taken of this new champion.

As to the date when the book was composed, opinions have varied between the pre-Mosaic and the Maccabæan age. The many points of contact with Lamentations, Deutero-Isaiah, and, most especially, with the Prologue to the Proverbs, are not quite conclusive in favour of its belonging to the later, post-exilic age: for we usually assign the priority to the one side or the other, according to the judgment we have formed on other grounds, though a doubt may hardly be possible concerning such passages as xlii. 17 compared with Gen. xxv. 8, xxxv. 29. There is still a dispute, too, concerning the linguistic character of the book, although all kinds of indications of later speech are universally recognized. But, in the first place, it is an important fact that, according to what we have said on p. 155, the problem could not have been handled in *this* form till the individualistic treatment of religious questions had been freely cultivated. And, secondly, the angels appear in the Book of Job in a form which vividly reminds us of the Book of Daniel. They are called absolutely "the holy ones" (cf. Dan. iv. 14), although, according to iv. 18, xv. 15, they are subject to error and even to sin, and, according to xxi. 22, xxv. 2, they need the judicial interposition of God. On the other hand, they can intervene with intercessions for men (v. 1), as, in the Book of Daniel, the various nations are represented by special guardian-angels, hostile to each other. No doubt it is impossible to decide with certainty when these views became common property in Israel, and therefore we will not conceal the fact that distinguished students still date the book much earlier—about 500, or in the Babylonian Exile, or even in the period just prior to the Exile.

c. Ecclesiastes.

If the "Wisdom" of the Old Testament celebrated its loftiest triumph in the Book of Job, by solving a definite religious problem, "The Preacher," on the contrary, must be styled the final abandonment of the attempt to solve the riddle of existence with the means furnished by the Religion of the Old Testament, *i.e.*, above all else, without faith in a future compensation. The author's putting his doctrine into the mouth of Solomon, the prototype of all wise men, and all striving after Wisdom, is a very transparent literary disguise: the writer himself betrays its true character at i. 12. And the repeated bitter complaints that justice is badly administered, that injustice indeed prevails in the world, would not come very well from a reigning king. The theme of the whole is expressed at the very outset. Everything is vain, troublesome, and at the same time aimless. Vain is the striving after Wisdom, like that after property and pleasure. Man ever stands powerless in the presence of an inevitable and, to him, incomprehensible fate. And thus the only profitable counsel which one may perhaps venture to give (v. 17, &c.) is to get the better of the misery of existence by enjoying life rationally, doing this, however, in the fear of God, and with an abiding recollection of the reckoning which He demands.

The last-named condition shows that the Preacher is far from recommending the so-called Epicureanism as the highest worldly wisdom. The keynote of his reflections is rather an ethically earnest one, and his faith in God shows itself untouched by any kind of doubt. But it cannot be denied that in his case the decay of the Old Testament faith has made much progress, so that he vacillates helplessly from chagrin to doubt, from unsatisfactory grounds of comfort to worldly-wise considerations. We can nowhere speak of a fixed plan. The discourse is not unfrequently so full of contradictions that earnest attempts have been made to understand it as a dialogue between a doubting disciple and the master who corrects him, thus setting all the objections to the book aside at a stroke. The very debased Hebrew and the manifold tokens of the age of the Diadochi point to the middle of the third century as the date of Ecclesiastes. Doubtless it owes its admission to the Canon in face of great objections chiefly to the Epilogue (xii. 9 ff.). Though added in all probability by another hand, this seemed adapted to neutralize the objectionable features in the Preacher's deductions, and so to bring everything to a satisfactory issue. However that may be, we owe thanks to the compilers of the Old Testament Canon for not excluding even this book. It proclaims with clear voice the truth which was obviously beyond the ken both of its author and of the compilers of the Canon, that in it, and in *all* the books which had preceded, the last word of consolation and salvation for mankind had

11 *

not yet been spoken. They all are but forerunners and preparers of the way of that infinitely Greater One who has spoken it.

We are at the end. But we ardently desire, at the conclusion, to come to an understanding with those to whom the treatment of Old Testament Literature in this Outline, and, above all, the dissection of the books and documents into various constituents, has seemed new and startling, perhaps, indeed, highly objectionable. In large circles of the Evangelical Church every kind of inquiry which is strictly historical, and therefore critical, is still regarded as a "wrangling of science falsely so-called," the outcome of a conceited and unbelieving disposition, which consciously aims at the destruction of faith in the Scriptures and, with that, of the bronze foundations of the Church's faith as a whole. If there are those who in such inquiries seek their own glory and eagerly drag in the dust what is holy to others, they have their reward. But they who with earnest and upright soul strive to investigate the facts concerning the Holy Scriptures, so far as these are accessible to human knowledge, need no justification of their conduct. They know that they are not bound to give account to man, but to God. But in the interest of the many, who for the sake of an *unscriptural* view of Scripture have been troubled in conscience, three simple truths may now be mentioned. First, the experimental truth, that all attempts to distort or contradict historical facts for supposed reasons of faith have hitherto proved ineffectual in the end. There was a time when the allegorical exposition of Scripture was regarded as the rightful privilege, in fact the sacred duty, of a really orthodox theology. Our age no longer admits the faintest pretence to such a right. There was a time when the acknowledgment that the Hebrew vowel points originated at the same time as the consonants was reckoned amongst the signs of thorough orthodoxy. To-day such an acknowledgment would only be taken as the sign of boorish ignorance. May that other time not be far distant when the useless resistance to knowledge which can no longer be shaken by any exegetical devices will be universally and finally abandoned!

Secondly: it is a disingenuous mode of fighting, to point constantly at much which is still uncertain and disputed, and thus endeavour to keep up amongst the ignorant the impression that *no* scientific Scripture inquiry has ever brought anything to light except subjective opinions, to-day set up, to-morrow contradicted, the next day forgotten. No doubt there is much that is uncertain, much indeed which will never be determined. But that far more has been finally settled can only be denied by him who has formed his opinion without a glance at the actual condition of scientific inquiry. Such a glance renders impossible the odd notion that hundreds of earnest and truth-seeking men have agreed on a number of results purely out of the spirit of contradiction and unbelief.

And thirdly: the demand for the disavowal of actual (not merely imaginary!) historical facts and certainties, in the supposed interest of religious faith, is a gross contradiction of Evangelical and Reformed principles. And so much the more when faith is demanded for external traditions which—like the late Jewish ones in question—are demonstrably tarnished in so many ways by accidents and misunderstandings. It is therefore a simple duty of Christian truthfulness, in all those cases where our view of Holy Scripture, founded on those traditions, conflicts with indisputable facts, not to deny the facts, but to reform our view of Scripture. Every other way is an unbecoming criticism of God, to whom it seemed good that thus, and not otherwise, His revelations to Israel and the world should be made known. And not only unbecoming, but also shortsighted. In the end the conviction will and must make way that the theory of the development of Old Testament religion maintained by a great number of Evangelical inquirers of the present day, and also in this Outline, corresponds not only with the facts but also with the deepest interests of faith. Blamed by opponents as "Construction of History," it rather seeks to trace out truly the methods which God has followed with the chosen people. After tolerating for a while so many semi-heathen elements which were mingled with the religion of Israel as a national religion, they led to ever-growing clearness respecting the true and final ends of God. Prophetism and priestism, seemingly contradictory tendencies, had to join in helping to bring Israel to those ends for the salvation of the world. Prophetism is the medium of those fundamental ideas of the sublime dignity, holiness and righteousness, the grace and mercy, also, of God, the Lord and Judge of all the world. The Priestly Law provides the vesture without which these ideas could not fulfil their work of educating the as yet immature people. And the longer the Biblical inquirer's thought is absorbed in such contemplations of God's ways, the more willingly will he join in the confession with which the Apostle closes his examination of that Divine mystery which is involved in God's ways with Israel: "O the depth of the riches and the wisdom and the knowledge of God! Of Him and through Him and unto Him are all things. To Him be glory for ever! Amen."

II.

CHRONOLOGICAL TABLES FOR THE HISTORY OF THE ISRAELITES, FROM MOSES TO THE END OF THE SECOND CENTURY, B.C.

YEAR, B.C.	PALESTINE.—ISRAEL.	RISE OF THE MONUMENTS OF ISRAELITE LITERATURE.	CONTEMPORARY EVENTS IN THE ASSYRIO-BABYLONIAN EMPIRE.	CONTEMPORARY EVENTS IN EGYPT, ETC.
Before 4000				High culture in Egypt.
About 3500			In the fourth century kingdoms of the Proto-Chaldæans in Babylonia, with the capitals Uru (Ur of the Bible), Uruk (Erech, Gen. x. 10), Babila (Gate of God), Accad, Larsam, Kutha. Establishment of Semitic immigrants, down to about 3000.	Beginning of the series of Egyptian Kings with Mena (Menes, according to Ebers about 3892).
About 2000	A high stage of culture in Syria (including Palestine) resulting from the simultaneous influence of Egyptian and Babylonian culture.		About 2250, Babylon made capital of Chaldæa by Chammurabi. About 1900, the city of Asshur founded from Babylon (Gen. x. 8 f.).	*The Old Kingdom* of Memphis at its prime, under Sueferu, Khufu (Cheops), &c.
About 1600				Beginning of the five hundred years' dominion of the Hyksos (Shepherd Kings) at Tanis. Gradual expulsion of the Hyksos. *The New Kingdom.*

Year B.C.	Palestine.—Israel.	Rise of the Monuments of Israelite Literature.	Contemporary Events in the Assyrio-Babylonian Empire.	Contemporary Events in Egypt, etc.
About 1500			About 1500, dominion of the Kassites over North Babylonia.	Thothmes III.'s campaigns of conquest through Palestine to the Euphrates.
About 1400	According to the letters on clay-tablets from Tell el-Amarna (in cuneiform, found in 1887) to Amenophis III. and IV., Palestine was entirely subject to Egypt. Kingdom of the Cheta (Assyrian, *Chatti*, Heb., *Chitti*, Hittites), with Kadesh on the Orontes as capital.			
About 1350	Campaigns of conquest by the Cheta and prolonged conflicts with the Egyptians; at length a treaty with Rameses II. (Kingdom of the Cheta probably destroyed by Rameses III. about 1230).			Rameses I., Seti I., Rameses II. (the oppressor of Israel?).
About 1320	The people led out of Egypt by Moses. Establishment of the Israelites east of the Jordan.		Shalmaneser I. founds Calah (Gen. x. 11), the southern part of the city Ninua (Nineveh). which is mentioned in the eighteenth century.	
About 1280	Taking of Jericho by Joshua and gradual establishment of Israelite tribes amongst the Canaanites (Joshua i.-xii., Judges i.).			First mention of the people of Y-sir-'l (Israel), as dwelling in Palestine, on an inscription of the Pharaoh Merenptah, son of Rameses II.

1500-1110.

		Civil war and prolonged anarchy in Egypt under Seti II. and Setnekht.
		The Twentieth (Theban) Dynasty founded by Rameses III.
	About 1150, end of the dominion of the Kassites in North Babylonia.	
	About 1120, Tiglath Pileser I. of Assyria. Campaign against the Chatti (Hittites) and Babylonia.	
		About 1110, the King of Egypt pays tribute to the Assyrians.
About 1250	Assassination of Eglon, King of Moab, by the Benjamite, Ehud.	
	The Canaanite King (according to Judges iv. General) Sisera is vanquished in the Plain of Jezreel by part of the Israelite tribes under Barak and the "prophetess," Deborah, and killed by Jael.	Judges v. (the so-called Song of Deborah).
	Establishment of a part of Dan in Laish (Judges xviii.). Jerubbaal (Gideon) defeats the Midianites and founds the worship of the golden image of Jahweh at Ophrah (Judges vi.–viii.).	
	Abimelech, son of Jerubbaal, assassinates his brothers and rules three years as king over Shechem and the neighbouring towns. Rebellion and overthrow of the Shechemites. Abimelech at Thebez (Judges ix.).	Jotham's Fable (Judges ix. 7 ff.).
	Jephthah, of Gilead, defeats the Ammonites and in pursuance of a vow sacrifices his daughter (Judges xi.).	
	Samson, of Dan, champion against the Philistines.	

170 CHRONOLOGICAL TABLES FOR THE HISTORY OF THE ISRAELITES.

Year B.C.	Palestine.—Israel.	Rise of the Monuments of Israelite Literature.	Contemporary Events in the Assyrio-Babylonian Empire.	Contemporary Events in Egypt, etc.
About 1050	*Eli*, priest of Jahweh of Hosts (Jahweh Zebaoth) and of the holy ark at Shiloh. Samuel, of Ephraim, dedicated to Jahweh by his mother, ministers to Eli at Shiloh (1 Sam. i.-iii.). Loss of the holy ark in the fight against the Philistines. Eli's sons, Hophni and Phinehas fall. Eli†[Destruction of the sanctuary at Shiloh, Jer. vii. 14, xxvi. 6]; 1 Sam. iv. The holy ark is brought back by the Philistines to Bethshemesh and placed at last in Kirjath-Jearim (1 Sam. v. 1, vii. 1).		Decline of the Assyrian power. Babylonia independent. Tiglath Pileser's conquests on the Euphrates become in part the prey of the Aramæans.	
About 1020	*Saul*, the son of Kish, of Gibeah in Benjamin, anointed king by Samuel, defeats Nahash, king of Ammon, before Jabesh-Gilead (1 Sam. ix.-xi.). Philistine invasions. Saul's son, Jonathan, forces the Pass of Michmash: overthrow of the Philistines (1 Sam. xiii. f.).			Dispossession of the Ramessides by the elevation to the throne of the Theban High Priest, Herhor. After him, suzerainty of the Twenty-first (Tanite) Dynasty.

	From the period beginning about 1040 to towards the close of the tenth century, only isolated names are preserved, amongst which is a Nebuchadnezzar of Babylon.

Saul's campaign against Agag, king of the Amalekites. Discord with Samuel on account of Agag's having been spared (1 Sam. xiii.).

David, the son of Jesse, of Bethlehem, comes as a harper to Saul's court, to banish his melancholy, and becomes his armour-bearer (1 Sam. xvi.).

David's martial successes and friendship with Jonathan arouse Saul's jealousy. In spite of Saul's cunning David wins his daughter Michal, and, warned by Jonathan, escapes, with Michal's help, to Ahimelech of Nob and afterwards into the Wilderness of Judah. Saul has the priests of Nob killed by Doeg the Edomite: only Abiathar, son of Ahimelech, escapes to David (1 Sam. xvii.-xxii.).

David, as a freebooter in the Wilderness of Judah, although constantly pursued by Saul, shows magnanimity towards him (1 Sam. xxiii. f. and xxvi.).

David's transaction with Nabal and marriage of Abigail (1 Sam. xxv.).

172 CHRONOLOGICAL TABLES FOR THE HISTORY OF THE ISRAELITES.

YEAR, B.C.	PALESTINE.—ISRAEL.	RISE OF THE MONUMENTS OF ISRAELITE LITERATURE.	CONTEMPORARY EVENTS IN THE ASSYRIO-BABYLONIAN EMPIRE.	CONTEMPORARY EVENTS IN EGYPT, ETC.
	David flees to the Philistine king, Achish of Gath, obtains the town of Ziklag, and, as vassal of Achish, carries out forays in the South (1 Sam. xxvii.).			Increasing power of the caste of mercenaries (*Ma*) chiefly natives of Libya, under their own commander-in-chief.
	Incursion of the Philistines into the Valley of Jezreel. The princes of the Philistines compel Achish to send back David. He finds Ziklag plundered and burnt, but recovers the spoil from the Amalekites and gains over the leaders of Judah by sending them a share of the spoil (1 Sam. xxviii. 1, 2 : chap. xxix. f.).			
	Saul with the Israelites on Gilboa, seeks counsel from the Witch of Endor. Battle on Gilboa. Saul and his three sons fall. Care taken of their bodies by the inhabitants of Jabesh-Gilead. The whole west of the Jordan in the hands of the Philistines (1 Sam. xxviii. 4 ff., chap. xxxi.).			
About 1000	*David*, King of Judah, at Hebron (but in all probability vassal of the Philistines [2 Sam. ii. 1 ff.]).	David's Elegy on Saul and Jonathan (ii. Sam. i. 17 ff.).	About 1000, war between Assyria and Babylonia, followed by a long peace.	

1020–1000.

Abner, Saul's general, makes his son Eshbaal king over Israel at Mahanaim, and gradually reconquers (or receives as vassal?) from the Philistines the northern part of the country west of the Jordan. Fights between the Benjamites and Judahites at the Well of Gibeon. Asahel, brother to David's cousin and general Joab, is killed by Abner (2 Sam. ii. 8 ff.).

Abner, annoyed by Eshbaal, treats with David, but in the gate of Hebron is treacherously assassinated by Joab (Blood-revenge for Asahel!). 2 Sam. iii.

David's Elegy on Abner (2 Sam. iii. 33 f.).

Eshbaal † by assassination. David is anointed king of Israel by the leaders of the people at Hebron. He takes the Jebusite fortress on Zion and makes Jerusalem the royal residence. [The cuneiform name *Urusalim* is found as early as about 1400 B.C., in the clay-tablets found in 1887 at Tell-el-Amarna]. 2 Sam. iv., v. 1–16.

David defeats the Philistines (to whom till then he had probably been tributary) twice at Jerusalem (2 Sam. v. (17 ff.; cf. also xxiii. 8 ff.).

Abibaal of Tyre (2 Sam. v. 11, *Hiram*, usually therefore called Hiram I.) aids in the building of David's palace by sending cedars.

Year, B.C.	Palestine.—Israel.	Rise of the Monuments of Israelite Literature.	Contemporary Events in the Assyrio-Babylonian Empire.	Contemporary Events in Egypt, etc.
	Removal of the holy ark from Kirjath Jearim to Zion (2 Sam. vi.).			
	Three years' famine. David expiates the blood-guiltiness of the house of Saul by giving up seven of his descendants to the Gibeonites. Rizpah's deed. (2 Sam. xxi. The point in David's life as uncertain as that of the numbering of the people and the plague. 2 Sam. xxiv.).			
	Subjugation of the Philistines and Moabites; victory over the Aramæan king, Hadadezer of Zobah [and the Aramæans of Damascus?] Subjugation of the Edomites (2 Sam. viii.).			
	David's generosity towards Meribaal, son of Jonathan (2 Sam. ix.).			
	Hanun, King of the Ammonites, insults David's messengers, but is defeated at Rabbath Ammon, along with his allies (Aram, &c.) by Joab and Abishai. David himself defeats the Aramæans confederated under Shobach, Hadadezer's general, at Helam (2 Sam. x.).			

Joab besieges Rabbath Ammon. David's intercourse with Bathsheba, the wife of Uriah. The Uriah-letter. Nathan's Parable. The Birth of Solomon [Jedidiah] (2 Sam. xi.-xii. 25).	Nathan's Parable (2 Sam. xii. 1-4).	Namret, father of Shashanq, of the family of the Libyan Buiuwa, at the head of the caste of mercenaries.
David completes the conquest of Rabbah. Full subjection of the Ammonites (2 Sam. xii. 26 ff.).		
Absalom has his half-brother Amnon killed because of his violating Tamar, his sister, and flees to King Talmai of Geshur; Joab procures Absalom's pardon (2 Sam. xiii. and xiv.).		
Absalom's Insurrection at Hebron. David flees over the Jordan. His friend Hushai frustrates Ahithophel's counsel to Absalom (2 Sam. xv.-xvii.).		
David assisted by Barzillai. Battle at Mahanaim. Absalom †by Joab. David's lamentation for him (2 Sam. xviii.-xix. 9).		
David's return. Strife between the Judahites and Israelites as to the escorting of the King. The revolt of the Benjamite Sheba quelled by Joab (2 Sam. xix. 10—xx. 22).		

Year, B.C.	Israel.	Rise of the Monuments of Israelite Literature.	Contemporary Events in the Assyrio-Babylonian Empire.	Contemporary Events in Egypt, etc.
	Adonijah, oldest surviving son of David, seeks to become king, with Joab's help, instead of his decrepit father. Nathan (allied with the priest Zadok, &c.) obtains from David, through Bathsheba, the installation of Solomon (1 Kings i.).			
About 970	David †. Solomon's vengeance on Adonijah, Abiathar, Joab, Shimei (1 Kings ii. 16 ff.).			
	Solomon's marriage with a daughter of Pharaoh (1 Kings iii. 1). Organization of the administration by the institution of twelve overseers (1 Kings iv.). Importation of horses and chariots from Egypt and trade with that country (x. 26, 28). The Edomite Hadad's attempted revolt. Hostilities of Rezon, King of Damascus (1 Kings xi. 14-25).		Gradual recovery of strength by the Assyrian Empire under peaceful rulers.	Solomon's father-in-law, probably identical with Har Pasebchanu II., the last king of the Twenty-first (Tanite) Dynasty.

Year, B.C.	Israel.	Judah.	Rise of the Monuments of Israelite Literature.	Contemporary Events in the Assyrio-Babylonian Empire.	Contemporary Events in Egypt, etc.
	Solomon's arrangement with Hiram of Tyre. Building of the temple and palace on Zion by Israelite forced labourers assisted by Tyrian artists (1 Kings v.-viii.).		Solomon's speech in dedication of the temple (1 Kings viii. 12 ff.).		Hiram I. (in the Bible, II.), the friend of Solomon (and previously of David, according to 1 Kings v. 15), builder of splendid edifices at Tyre.
	Buildings for the fortification of Jerusalem (ix. 24). The Ephraimite Jeroboam's attempted insurrection (1 Kings xi. 26 ff.).				
	Voyages to the gold-land Ophir with Hiram's men (ix. 26; x. 22). Solomon's wealth and works of art (x. 16 ff.). The fame of his wisdom (v. 9 ff.); Visit of the Queen of Sheba (x. 1-13).		The Blessing of Jacob (Gen. xlix. 1-27). The Book of the Wars of Jahweh (Num. xxi. 14). The Book of the Upright Ones (Joshua ix. 12 f.; 2 Sam. i. 18). The original form of the Balaam-Discourses (Num. xxiii. f.).		
	Solomon.† His son Rehoboam, by his hard answer to the people's complaints at Shechem, drives the rest of the tribes (except the southern part of Benjamin) to revolt				About 943, Expulsion of the Tanite Dynasty by Shashanq (cf. p. 176, and 178): he marries his son Uasarken [I.] to Ramaka, daughter of Pasebchanu II.

178 CHRONOLOGICAL TABLES FOR THE HISTORY OF THE ISRAELITES.

Year, B.C.	Israel.	Judah.	Rise of the Monuments of Israelite Literature.	Contemporary Events in the Assyrio-Babylonian Empire.	Contemporary Events in Egypt, etc.
	against the house of David (1 Kings xii. 1-19).				
933 to 912	*Jeroboam* I., son of Nebat, returns from Egypt (cf.1Kings xi. 40), and becomes monarch of the Northern Kingdom (Israel in the stricter sense; also called the Kingdom of the Ten Tribes, or, after the principal tribe, Ephraim), with Shechem as its capital (but already at xiv. 17; xv. 21, &c., Tirzah appears as the royal residence). Worship of the golden bulls (images of Jahweh!) at Bethel and Dan (1 Kings xii. 20, 25 ff.).	933-917 *Rehoboam*, King of Judah. 928 Jerusalem pillaged by Shishak (Shashanq), King of Egypt (1 Kings xiv. 21 ff.). Continual wars with Israel (xiv. 30). 916-914 *Abijam*. Wars with Jeroboam (1 Kings xv. 1 ff.).	The (Ephraimite) Hero-Stories (*II¹* & *II*) in the Book of Judges.		Campaign of conquest by the Pharaoh Shashanq, founder of the Twenty-second (Bubastid) Dynasty, against Palestine (and also against Israel, according to the evidence of the numerous names of towns on a wall of the temple at Karnak).
912 to 911	*Nadab*, son of Jeroboam, murdered by Baasha of Issachar during the siege of Gibbethon. Extermination of the house of Jeroboam (1 Kings xv. 25 ff.).	913-873 *Asa*. Measures taken against idolatry (xv. 9 ff.).	The Jerusalem Stories of David (*Je*: 2 Sam. v.-vii. and ix.-xx.). The David Stories (*Da*) in 1 Sam. xvi. 14 ff.-1 Kings ii.	913-890 Rimmon-Nirari of Assyria (893 Beginning of the Assyrian Eponym Canon which is still extant).	The successors of Shashanq I.: Uasarken I., Takeleth I., Uasarken II., Shashanq II.

933-877.   179

Date	Israel/Judah	Biblical	Assyria	Damascus/Tyre
911 to 888	*Baasha*, son of Ahijah, King at Tirzah (xv. 33 ff.). Baasha blockades Jerusalem from Ramah. Asa purchases the help of Benhadad I. of Damascus. Baasha obliged to retreat by the invasion of the Aramæans. Asa destroys Ramah and fortifies Geba and Mizpah (1 Kings xv. 16 ff.).	The Saul - Stories (S) in 1 Sam. ix. ff.).	899-884 Tiglath-Ninep II. of Assyria.	Benhadad I, son of Tabrimmon, King of Damascus.
888 to 887	*Elah*, son of Baasha, murdered by Zimri at Tirzah. Extermination of the house of Baasha.			
887	*Zimri*, for seven days King at Tirzah, besieged by Elah's general, Omri, burns himself and the palace (xvi. 8 ff.).		883-859 Assurnatsirpal, the builder of the north-west palace at Calah, in the south of Nineveh.	
[887] 883 to 877	*Omri*, proclaimed king by the army in the camp at Gibbethon: sole king, after the death of Zimri and the rival king Tibni (xvi. 16 ff., 21 ff.). Building of Samaria as a new capital on a strongly fortified hill (xvi. 24).			855-854. Ethbaal (Ithobal), King of Tyre, father-in-law of Ahab of Israel.

12 *

Year, B.C.	Israel.	Judah.	Rise of the Monuments of Israelite Literature.	Contemporary Events in the Assyrio-Babylonian Empire.	Contemporary Events in Egypt, etc.
	Ahab, son of Omri, marries Jezebel, daughter of Ethbaal, King of Tyre. Jezebel patronizes Baal-worship in Israel. The prophet Elijah is zealous for the worship of Jahweh, flees from Jezebel's vengeance, opposes Ahab because of the judicial murder of Naboth the Jezreelite (1 Kings xvi. 29 ff.; xviii. 1-19; xxi. 1 ff.; but cf. also 2 Kings ix. 25 ff.).		The original form of the "Book of the Covenant" (Exod. xxi.-xxiii.; cf. xxiv.7). If there is a trace of it in 2 Chron. xvii. 9 it did not originate till Jehoshaphat's time.	876 Tribute paid by the Phœnician towns, Tyre, Sidon, &c., to the Assyrians.	Chemosh-melech, father of Mesha, King of Moab, vassal of Israel.
857	Benhadad of Damascus with thirty-two "kings" besieges Samaria, is defeated by a sally of the Israelites and again in the following year at Aphek, surrenders to Ahab and on making certain promises is released (1 Kings xx.).			858 to 829 Shalmaneser II. Numerous campaigns against the Aramæans, Babylon, &c.	Hadadezer of Damascus (in the Bible, Benhadad [II.]).
854	In spite of the dissuasion of the prophet Micah, son of Imlah, Ahab, along with Jehoshaphat of Judah (who was probably vassal of Israel), marches to Ramoth Gilead which was besieged by the Aramæans, and falls in the battle (1 Kings xxii.).			854 Shalmaneser defeats at Karkar the Aramæans of Hamath and Damas-	

857-842.

Date	Events	Literature	External
			...cus and (as vassal of the Damascenes?) Ahab of Israel.
851	Revolt of the Moabites. Ahaziah, son of Ahab, dies from a fall (2 Kings i. 2 ff.). The attempt to renew the Ophir voyages fails.		Monumental tablet of Mesha of Moab (in Paris), found in 1869, the oldest monument in so-called Phoenician characters.
853 to 812	Joram, son of Ahab. Activity of Elisha, the prophet called by Elijah (1 Kings xix. 19 ff.). The communities of prophets at Bethel and Gilgal (2 Kings ii.-viii. 15). Campaign of Joram and [his vassal?] Jehoshaphat and the King of Edom against Mesha of Moab. Mesha offers his firstborn son on the wall [probably of Kir Heres]. Withdrawal of the Israelites (2 Kings iii.). Renewed invasions of the Arameans of Damascus under Benhadad. Sudden relief of Samaria when hard pressed (probably by an invasion of the Assyrians) (2 Kings vi. 21 ff.).	The Jahwistic Historical Source (J) in the Pentateuch and Joshua.	Campaigns of Shalmaneser against Babylonia and (850 to 816) against Hadadezer of Damascus.
849-42	Jehoram, married to Ahab's daughter Athaliah. Revolt of the Edomites and of the town of Libnah.	The Ephraimite Narratives (E) in 1 Sam. iv.-vi.	About 815 Hazael, Benhadad's successor (through murder? cf. 2 Kings viii. 15).
812	Ahaziah.		

Year, B.C.	Israel.	Judah.	Rise of the Monuments of Israelite Literature.	Contemporary Events in the Assyrio-Babylonian Empire.	Contemporary Events in Egypt, etc.
842	Campaign of Joram with Ahaziah against Hazael of Damascus. Joram, wounded at Ramoth Gilead, returns to Jezreel. Joram's general, Jehu, anointed king in the camp at Ramoth Gilead by Elisha's orders, kills Joram and Jezebel at Jezreel (2 Kings ix.).	Ahaziah, wounded by Jehu's command, during his flight from Jezreel, † at Megiddo (2 Kings ix. 27 ff.).		842 Campaign of Shalmanezer II. against Hazael of Damascus.	
842 to 815	Jehu, King of Israel (as vassal of the Assyrians!) exterminates the entire family and all the adherents of Ahab in Jezreel and Samaria, kills Ahaziah's forty-two brothers at Beth Eked, wins over Jonadab, son of Rechab, destroys in Samaria the Baal worshippers and Baal worship (2 Kings x.). Severe oppression of Israel by Hazael of Damascus (2 Kings x. 32; cf. viii. 11 ff.).	842 Ahaziah's mother, *Athaliah*, becomes queen after exterminating the house of David. Joash, son of Ahaziah, saved by his aunt Jehosheba (according to 1 Chron. xxii. 11, wife of the chief priest Jehoiada) and concealed six years in the temple (2 Kings xi. 1 ff.). Jehoiada, supported by the body-guard, proclaims the seven-year old Joash king. Athaliah killed. Extermination of the Baal-worship in Jerusalem (2 Kings xi. 4 ff.).	The N source in Judges xvii.-xix.?	842 "Tribute of Jehu, son of Omri (!)". Israel long continued to be the "Land of Omri" to the Assyrians. 839 Hazael of Damascus vanquished by the Assyrians. 833-29 Campaigns of Shalmanezer II. in the East.	Hazael of Damascus, for many years the tormentor of Israel (see under Jehu).

			823-11 Samas-Rimmon of Assyria (817 Beginning of the so-called Administration Lists, *i.e.*, the Eponym Lists with Notes, down to 728). Campaigns against Babylonia. Hazael of Damascus takes Gath.
	836-797 *Joash* (Jehoash). Rearrangement of the expenditure of the temple-revenues (2 Kings xii. 1-16). Hazael of Damascus diverted from attacking Jerusalem by an immense tribute from Joash (2 Kings xii. 18 ff.).		
814 to 798		*Jehoahaz*, son of Jehu. Israel weakened to the very uttermost by Hazael of Damascus (2 Kings xiii.).	
			810-782 Rimmon-Nirari of Assyria. Campaigns against Media and (806-803) against Aramæans and Phœnicians.
	Joash † by conspirators.		The [Ephraimite] Blessing of Moses, Deut. xxxiii.
	797-779 *Amaziah*. Victory over the Edomites and taking of Sela (2 Kings xiv. 1 ff.).		797 Victorious campaign in the West (against Damascus, Israel, Tyre and Sidon).
798 to 783		*Joash*, son of Jehoahaz. Elisha.† Victory over Hazael, son of Benhadad II. (2 Kings xiii. 10 ff.).	

Year, B.C.	Israel.	Judah.	Rise of the Monuments of Israelite Literature.	Contemporary Events in the Assyrio-Babylonian Empire.	Contemporary Events in Egypt, etc.
	Battle at Beth-shemesh. Amaziah defeated by Jehoash and taken. Breaches in the walls of Jerusalem; increased tribute of Amaziah (2 Kings xiv. 8 ff.).		Ephraimite Stories of Prophets concerning Elijah (*Pr*) in 1 Kings xvii. ff., xxi. Ephraimite Narratives (*E*) in 1 Kings xx., xxii.; 2 Kings iii.[?], and vi.-x. Ephraimite Stories of Prophets concerning Elisha (*Pr*) in 2 Kings ii., iv.-vi., viii., xiii.— Isa. xv.-xvi. 12.		
783-743	*Jeroboam II.*, son of Jehoash. Reconquest of the territory occupied by the Aramaeans. The last flourishing period of Israel's history (2 Kings xiv. 23 ff.).	779 Amaziah † at Lachish, by conspirators. 779-740 *Azariah* (Uzziah). Re-conquest of the harbour of Elath on the Red Sea. Azariah at last leprous. Jotham co-regent (2 Kings xiv. 17 ff., xv. 1 ff.).	Amos. The Elohistic Historical Source (*E*) in the Pentateuch and Joshua. The Ephraimite Stories of Samuel and Saul (*SS*) in 1 Sam. viii. ff.	775 Campaign of the Assyrians against Syria. 771-754 Assurdanilu of Assyria. 763, June 15th, Eclipse of the sun. 753-746 Assurnirari.	Flourishing period of the (Ethiopic) Kingdom of Napata on the Upper Nile. Piankhi of Napata conquers Upper Egypt. Tefnakht of Sais brings the petty princes of Lower Egypt under his dominion, but at last succumbs to Piankhi (about 770).

743	Zechariah, son of Jeroboam II.; assassinated at the end of six months by Shallum at Ibleam (2 Kings xv. 8 ff.). Shallum, son of Jabesh; assassinated at the end of one month by Menahem at Samaria (2 Kings xv. 13 ff.).		
		747 Beginning of the era of Nabonassar in Babylon (and of the Ptolemaic Canon). 745-728 Tiglath Pileser III. (in the Bible also Pul), King of Assyria. Tribute of Damascus, Tyre, Hamath.	Expulsion of the Ethiopians from Egypt.
		(*Hosea*, son of Beeri (chaps. i. to iii., according to i. 4, under Jeroboam II.; chaps. iv.-xiv. under Menahem).	
743 to 737	Menahem, son of Gadi. Tribute to the Assyrians raised by taxing the 60,000 men of war (2 Kings xv. 17 ff.).		
		Beginning of Isaiah's activity. [Isa. ii.-v., vi., xvii. 1-11.]	
		742-40 Siege and taking of Arpad by the Assyrians.	Bocchoris (Bokemanf; Twenty-fourth Dynasty). Renewed invasion of the Ethiopians.
	740-736 *Jotham*. Building of the upper gate of the temple.		
		? Blending of the Hero-Stories and the Stories of the so-called Minor Judges (*vi*) to form the pre-Deuteronomic Book of Judges.	
		738 Tribute of Menahem of Samaria (also Rezin of Damascus and Hiram).	

YEAR, B.C.	ISRAEL.	JUDAH.	RISE OF THE MONUMENTS OF ISRAELITE LITERATURE.	CONTEMPORARY EVENTS IN THE ASSYRIO-BABYLONIAN EMPIRE.	CONTEMPORARY EVENTS IN EGYPT, ETC.
737 to 736	*Pekaliah*, son of Menahem † by Pekah (2 Kings xv. 23 ff.).				
736-730 735	*Pekah*, son of Remaliah. Pekah allies himself with Rezin of Damascus against Judah (Syrian-Ephraimite War). Rezin takes the harbour of Elath. Threatened with an assault on Jerusalem (Isa. vii. 1 ff.), Ahaz purchases the assistance of Tiglath Pileser (2 Kings xvi. 5 ff., 17 ff.).	736-728 Ahaz.	Isa. i. (?), vii.-ix. 6, xi. 1-9.	734 March of Tiglath Pileser to Palestine (see Israel). 733 and 732 Damascus besieged and taken by Tiglath Pileser. Rezin killed (2 Kings xvi. 9).	
734	A considerable portion of the inhabitants of northern Israel and the land east of the Jordan deported by the Assyrians (2 Kings xv. 29 ff.).			Homage and Tribute of Jauchazi (Ahaz). Hanno of Gaza, &c. (see Judah).	
		732 Ahaz does homage to Tiglath Pileser at Damascus; sends to Uriah the priest the model of an altar to be copied (2 Kings xvi. 10 ff). Activity of the prophet Isaiah.	Isa. ix. 7 ff.	731. Campaign against Babylonia. 728 Tiglath Pil. under the name Pul (Poros in Ptolemy), King of Babylon. 727-723 Shalmanezer IV.	About 728: Founding of the Twenty-fifth (Ethiopic) Dynasty by Sabaco (till 717).

737-722.

730 to 722 (?)	*Hosea*, son of Elah, assassinates Pekah (by order of the Assyrians?), vassal of Shalmanezer IV.		Campaign of the Assyrians against Luli (Eluleus) of Tyre, and Hosea ("Ausi") of Samaria (see Israel).
	727-699 *Hezekiah*, vassal of the Assyrians. Removal from the temple of the brazen serpent of Moses. Victory over the Philistines (2 Kings xviii. 1-8).	Micah i.-iii.	722-706 Sargon (in the Bible mentioned only at Isa. xx. 1), King of Assyria.
725 (?) 722	Hosea negotiates secretly with Sewe of Egypt, and on this account is imprisoned by Shalmanezer IV. Samaria taken by Sargon after three years' siege; 27,280 carried captive. Colonization of the depopulated land by settlers from the East. Origin of the mixed race of Samaritans (2 Kings xvii. 1-6, 21-34). [Later transplantations of colonists to Samaria by Esarhaddon about 675 (Ezra iv. 2) and Asnappar (?), according to Ezra iv. 10.]	? Construction of the Siloah-tunnel (Sirach xlviii. 19; but perhaps there is a reference to the tunnel as early as Isa. viii. 6).	Isa. xiv. 24 ff.; xvii. 12 ff.; xxviii. 1-6.
			721 Merodach Baladan conquers Babylon, but is vanquished by Sargon.
			720 Battle at Raphia. Sargon vanquishes Sabi (Sewe) of Egypt and takes Hanno of Gaza.
		Isa. xix. (?)	717 Destruction of the Hittite Kingdom of Carchemish.
			716-705 Shabataka, King of Egypt.

YEAR, B.C.	JUDAH.	RISE OF THE MONUMENTS OF ISRAELITE LITERATURE.	CONTEMPORARY EVENTS IN THE ASSYRIO-BABYLONIAN EMPIRE.	CONTEMPORARY EVENTS IN EGYPT, ETC.
714? (701?)	Sickness and recovery of Hezekiah. Embassy of Merodach Baladan of Babylon (2 Kings xx.; the date 2 Kings xviii. 13ᵃ [Isa. xxxvi. 1] must have originally referred to the events in 2 Kings xx. [Isa. xxxviii. f.]).	Isa. x. 28 ff., xx.	715 Tribute of the "Pharaoh" to Sargon. 711 Taking of Ashdod by the Tartan, i.e., the Commander-in-chief of the Assyrians (Isa. xx. 1). 710 War of Sargon with Merodach Baladan. 709 Sargon, King of Babylon. 705-681 Sennacherib, King of Assyria.	
705	Revolt of Hezekiah from Sennacherib. Alliance with Egypt-Ethiopia in spite of Isaiah's dissuasion (Isaiah xxx., xxxi.). Hezekiah keeps in prison at Jerusalem King Padi, who had been expelled from Ekron because he was a loyal vassal of the Assyrians.	Isa. xiv., 29 ff., xviii. (?), xxviii.-xxx.	704 War with Merodach Baladan; Babylon taken (703?).	704-685 Taharka, Isa. xxxvii. 9. (Tirhakah), King of Ethiopia and Egypt.

Date				
701	Sennacherib during his campaign against Egypt devastates Judah, takes forty-six cities, threatens Jerusalem from Lachish by despatching a strong army. Hezekiah sends an enormous tribute to Lachish, but, encouraged by Isaiah, refuses to surrender Jerusalem. Dissolution of the Assyrian army by the pestilence (2 Kings xviii. 13 ff., 17 ff. [parallel to this xix. 10 ff.], 35).	Isa. xxxi., xxxvii. 22 ff. (?) i. (?) xxii. (?). The Source N in Judges xvii.-xviii.	Subjugation of the Phœnician cities, except Tyre, under Sennacherib.	The Egyptians defeated by Sennacherib at Altaku. Ekron taken.
643 to 641	*Manasseh* (vassal of the Assyrians), favours the worship of the images of Jahweh (and other gods?) which Isaiah (and Hezekiah?) opposed, as well as other heathen doings. Children sacrificed (to Jahweh or heathen gods?). Manasseh's murders (of the prophetic party?) (2 Kings xxi. 1 ff.).	Micah. vi. 1-vii. 6. Nahum. Written sources of Deuteronomy (?) (see below, under 628.) Blending of the Jahwist and Elohist (in the Pentateuch and Joshua) into JE.	692 Destruction of rebellious Babylon by Sennacherib. 681 Sennacherib murdered by his sons. 681-668 Esarhaddon. Rebuilding of Babylon. 668-626 Assurbanipal (Sardanapalus of the Greeks).	670 Egypt conquered by the Assyrians. Taharka vanquished by the Assyrians; end of the Ethiopian dominion (about 662). 663-610 Psammetichus. 655 End of the so-called Dodecarchy.
643 to 641	*Amon,†* by conspirators (2 Kings xxi. 19 ff.).			
640 to 609	*Josiah*, raised to the throne by the people.	About 630 Zephaniah, chap. i. 628 Calling of the Prophet Jeremiah (Jer. i.). Speeches belonging to the time of Josiah (ii.-vi.).		Scythian invasion of Hither Asia.

Year, B.C.	Judah.	Rise of the Monuments of Israelite Literature.	Contemporary Events in the Assyrio-Babylonian Empire.	Contemporary Events in Egypt, etc.
		Deuteronomy (whether in the form of the so-called original Deuteronomy, or already as a combination of several older writings).	Strengthening of the kingdom of Media by Phraortes and Cyaxares. 625 Nabopolassar, independent King of Babylon.	Egypt at length opened to the Greeks also.
622	Josiah pledges all the people to the law-book found in the temple by the chief priest Hilkiah (in the main preserved in our Deuteronomy). On the basis of this law (cf. especially Deut. xii.) he undertakes a thorough purification of the ritual in and around Jerusalem (abolition of the high-places, and all the remains of heathen ceremonies). Celebration of the Passover in accordance with the new law (2 Kings xxii. 23).	Habakkuk. Zeph. ii.–iii. 13.		
609	Josiah † in the battle at Megiddo against Pharaoh Necho. Jehoahaz, son of Josiah, deposed at the end of three months by Pharaoh at Riblah and taken to Egypt. Increased tribute of Judah to Necho (2 Kings xxiii. 31 ff.).			609 Pharaoh Necho II. (609-594) defeats Josiah, is beaten by Nebuchadnezzar at Carchemish on the Euphrates.

608 to 597	*Jehoiakim* (till then Eliakim), son of Josiah, made king by Necho; vassal of Egypt (2 Kings xxiii. 34, 36 f.). Jeremiah threatens the destruction of Jerusalem, is arrested in the temple (Jer. xxvi.).	Jeremiah's speeches in chaps. vii.-xx. (mainly), xxi. 11 ff. xxiii. 9 ff. (?). Chap. xxv. [xxvi.], xlv.-xlix. (?).	608 Nabopolassar of Babylon allies himself with Cyaxares of Media. Destruction of the Assyrian kingdom, and (606?) its capitals Nineveh and Asshur.
605	Jehoiakim, after the battle at Carchemish, vassal of the Chaldæans (2 Kings xxiv. 1).	Jer. xi.-xiii. 27. First writing out of Jeremiah's predictions by Baruch, burned by Jehoiakim, renewed and increased by Jeremiah (Jer. xxxvi.).	605 Nebuchadnezzar (whilst crownprince) totally defeats Pharaoh Necho at Carchemish on the Euphrates. The Egyptians lose all foreign conquests.
602	Jehoiakim revolts from Nebuchadnezzar. Devastation of Judah by hostile invasions (2 Kings xxiv. 2 ff.).	First redaction of the Books of Kings (by *Dt.*). Jer. xiv. 1-17, xviii. 35.	604-562 Nebuchadnezzar King (of the Chaldæans) in Babylon.
597	*Jehoiachin*, son of Jehoiakim, reigns three months. Siege of Jerusalem. Jehoiachin surrenders, with the whole court, to the Chaldæans, and is brought to Babylon. Pillage of the temple and the palace. *First Deportation* of numerous princes, priests (Ezekiel amongst them), and seven thousand men of war (2 Kings xxiv. 8-16). Amongst the names is that of Josiah's son, Mattaniah.	Jer. xxii. 20 ff.	Conquest of Elam by the Persians.

192 CHRONOLOGICAL TABLES FOR THE HISTORY OF THE ISRAELITES.

Year, B.C.	Judah.	Rise of the Monuments of Israelite Literature.	Contemporary Events in the Assyrio-Babylonian Empire.	Contemporary Events in Egypt, etc.
597 to 586	Zedekiah raised to the throne by Nebuchadnezzar.	Jer. xxiii. 1-8, xxiv. [xxviii., xxix.], xxvii., xxx. and xxxi. (?).	Magnificent buildings of Nebuchadnezzar at Babylon.	594-89 Psammetichus II. Pharaoh.
		593 Ezekiel's consecration to the prophetic office.		
588	In spite of Jeremiah's dissuasions Zedekiah, relying on Egypt, rises against Nebuchadnezzar. One and a half year's siege of Jerusalem (briefly interrupted by the advance of Pharaoh Hophra). Jeremiah, suspected of being a deserter, is imprisoned, consulted by Zedekiah, remains a prisoner in the court of the guard (Jer. xxxvii.).	[Jer. xxi. 1-10, xxxiv. 8 ff.]. [Jer. xxxii. 1-xxxiv. 7].		588-570 Pharaoh Uaphrahet (Hophra of the Bible, Apries of the Greeks).
	Jeremiah delivered out of the cistern by Ebed Melech.			
586	Great famine in Jerusalem. Storming of the city. Zedekiah, flying to Jericho, is seized and brought to Nebuchadnezzar at Riblah. His sons killed before his eyes, himself blinded and led in chains to Babylon.	[Jer. xxxvii.-xliii. 7].	586-73 Unsuccessful siege of Tyre (under Ithobal II.) by Nebuchadnezzar (cf. Ezek. xxix. 17 ff.).	Solon (Archon since 591) organizes the Athenian constitution.

597-568.

					570 Amasis with Hophra.
City and temple reduced to ashes by Nebuzar-adan. *Second Deportation* of prisoners to Babylon, with the works of art and vessels of the temple. Executions at Riblah (2 Kings xxv.; cf. Jer. lii.).	Jeremiah, spared by the Chaldeans, resorts to Gedaliah, who has been made Governor of the remnant at Mizpah by Nebuchadnezzar (Jer. xl. 1 ff.).	Gedaliah, and those with him, murdered by Ishmael, at the instigation of Baali, king of the Ammonites (2 Kings xxv. 22 ff.; Jer. xl. 7-xli. 18).	Flight of the remnant to Bethlehem, and, notwithstanding Jeremiah's dissuasion, to Egypt (Jer. xliii. 1-xliii. 7). Jeremiah apparently soon afterwards dies in Egypt (the legend says, stoned at Tahpanhes by the Jews).	[Jer. xliii. 8-xliv. 30]. 573 Close of the Book of Ezekiel (only xxix. 17 ff. an Appendix of 571). Lamentations. Combination of Jeremiah's predictions with the narratives concerning him (enclosed in [ ] above) forming the Book of Jeremiah (by Baruch?).	568 Campaign of Nebuchadnezzar against Amasis of Egypt.

Year, B.C.	Judah.	Rise of the Monuments of Israelite Literature.	Contemporary Events in the Assyrio-Babylonian Empire.	Contemporary Events in Egypt, etc.
561	Evil Merodach shows favour to Jehoiachin after nearly thirty-seven years' imprisonment (2 Kings xxv. 27 ff.).	The "Song of Moses," Deut. xxxii. 1-43.	561-60 Evil Merodach (Babyl. E. Marduk).	
		Conclusion of our present Deuteronomy with the Deuteronomistic redaction (Dt), probably contemporaneous with the blending of JE (in the Pentateuch and Joshua) with D; also the Deuteronomistic redaction of the Book of Judges (Ri) and the Books of Samuel (Dt) and Kings (Dt^2) to form one great historical work.	559-56 Nergal Sharezer (Neriglissar).	
			558 Cyrus, son of Cambyses I., king of Persia.	
	A portion of the Exiles in Babylonia lapse into idolatry (cf. passages as early as Ezek. xiv. 3 ff., xx. 32), Jer. x. 1, Isa. lxv. 1.	Nucleus of the "Law of Holiness" (in Lev. xvii.-xxvi.).	555-539 Nabonidus (Babyl. Nabunaid), last king of the Chaldæans.	

Date			
	552 Alliance of Nabonidus with Crœsus of Lydia.		
	550 Cyrus conquers Ecbatana, Astyages taken. End of the Median Kingdom.	Isa. xl.-xlv. (or to lxii.?). Isa. xxi. 1-10?, xiii. 1-xiv. 23. Chap. xxxiv. f.	Amasis allied with Sparta. Crœsus (and Nabonidus?) against Cyrus.
	546 Battle at Sardis; Crœsus and his Egyptian auxiliaries vanquished by Cyrus. End of the Lydian Kingdom.		
	539 Cyrus' attack on Babylon and victory at Rutum; Nabonidus taken prisoner; Babylon (where in all probability Belshazzar, son of Nabonidus, was commandant) taken.	Zeph. iii. 14 ff.	538-529 Cyrus, king of Persia, also king of Babylon.
538	The Edict of Cyrus permits the Jews to return.		
	First bringing back of 42,360 Jews and 7,537 bondmen by David's descendant, Zerubbabel, and the priest, Joshua (Ezra ii., Neh. vi. 7 ff.).		
	Erection of the altar of burnt offering. The Samaritans, repulsed from taking part in the building of the temple, prevent the building during the lives of Cyrus and Cambyses (Ezra iv. 1-v. 21).		

13 *

196 CHRONOLOGICAL TABLES FOR THE HISTORY OF THE ISRAELITES.

Year, B.C.	Judah.	Rise of the Monuments of Israelite Literature.	Contemporary Events in the Assyrio-Babylonian Empire.	Contemporary Events in Egypt, etc.
	Establishment of the High-priesthood (Haggai and Zechariah the first witnesses to there being a high-priest, namely, Joshua).		529-522 *Cambyses*, king of Persia, &c.	525 Egypt, conquered by Cambyses in the battle at Pelusium, continues to be a Persian satrapy till 332.
520	Vigorous prosecution of the building of the temple under the influence of the prophets Zechariah and Haggai. Renewed interruptions stopped by Darius because of the Edict of Cyrus (Ezra v. 1-vi. 14).	Haggai (Sept., till Dec., 520). Zechariah I., 1 ff. (520); i. 7-vi. 15 (519); chap. vii. ff. (518).	521-486 Darius I., after Hystaspis, Gaumata the Magian had been killed, king of Persia. Darius conquers rebellious Babylon.	
516	Dedication of the second temple (Ezra vi. 15 ff.).	About 500. Composition of the Priests' Code proper (P) in Babylonia. Isa. lvi.- (or at all events lxiii.-) lxvi. Malachi.		Beginning of the rising of the Greeks in Asia Minor against Darius. 490 Battle of Marathon.
	The Judæans accused to Xerxes by the Samaritans (Ezra iv. 6).		485-465 Xerxes (Achashverosh of the Bible).	

		Partial blending of the Priests' Code with the Law of Holiness.	480 Battle of Thermopylae and Naval Fight at Salamis.
			465-424 Artaxerxes I., Longimanus (in the Bible Artasastha).
458	The priest and scribe, Ezra, authorised by Artaxerxes I., brings back about 1500 Judæans and Benjamites (Ezra vii. and viii.).	The Aramaic Documentary-Source (Q^a) in Ezra iv.-vi.	The rising of the Egyptians against the Persians (since 462), aided by the Lybians and an Athenian fleet repressed by the satrap Megabyzus.
	The merciless dissolution of all mixed marriages (Ezra ix. and x.) involves the Jewish colony in serious internal discords, and in animosities with their neighbours, and finally (as may be concluded from Ezra iv. 7 ff. and Neh. i.) occasions the destruction of the walls of Jerusalem.	The Book of Ruth.	The culminating point of poetry, plastic art, and painting at Athens.
445	Nehemiah, cupbearer of Artaxerxes I. at Susa, is sent to Jerusalem with royal authority as governor, and in spite of the hostility of Sanballat, Tobiah, Geshem, &c., completes the re-fortification of Jerusalem in fifty-two days (Neh. ii. 1-vii. 3).		

198 CHRONOLOGICAL TABLES FOR THE HISTORY OF THE ISRAELITES.

Year, B.C.	Judah.	Rise of the Monuments of Israelite Literature.	Contemporary Events in the Assyrio-Babylonian Empire.	Contemporary Events in Egypt, etc.
	Publication of the "Law-book of Moses" (i.e., the Priests' Code, enlarged with other pieces) brought by Ezra from the Exile. Celebration of the Feast of Tabernacles in accordance with the new law, and engagement to observe the latter confirmed by signing names (Neh. vii. 73ᵇ–x. 40).	Oldest collection of Congregational hymns (Ps. iii.–xli.).	Increasing influence of foreign (especially Greek) mercenaries in the Persian army.	
	Solemn dedication of the new walls (Neh. xii. 31 ff.).	Memoirs of Ezra (E) in Ezra and Nehemiah.		
432	Nehemiah's second residence in Jerusalem. Reform of all kinds of abuses (Neh. xiii. 4 ff.). Banishment of Sanballat's son-in-law; according to Neh. xiii. 28 the banished man was a son of Jehoiada, grandson of the high-priest, Eliashib; according to Josephus (Antiqq. XI., vii. 2, and viii. 2 ff.), a great-grandson of Eliashib, called Manasseh.	Obadiah? (Founded on an older oracle [v. 1-9]).		
		Memoirs of Nehemiah (N) in the Book of Nehemiah.	423-404 Darius II., Nothus, king of Persia.	
	About 400, the high-priest, Johanan, murders his brother Joshua in the temple; as a punishment the Persian Governor imposes a heavy tax on the lamb for the daily offering (Antiqq. XI. vii. 1).	About 400. Conclusion of the Pentateuch by the blending of JE, D, and P, probably connected with the final redac-	404-359 Artax. II., Mnemon.	431-404 Peloponnesian War. Activity of Socrates at Athens. Activity of Plato at Athens.

432-311.   199

Year	Jewish History	Literature	Political History	Other
	About 350 many Jews were transported to Hyrcania, probably for taking part in an insurrection against the Persians.	tion of the historical work which extends from Gen. i. to 2 Kings xxv. Final redaction of the Book of Proverbs. Joel? Jonah? End of the Persian Period: Collection of the 2nd and 3rd Books of the Psalms. Job?	359-338 Artax. III. Ochus. 336-331 Darius III. Codomannus defeated by Alexander the Great.	Building of the Samaritan temple on Gerizim after the acceptance of the Pentateuch from the Jews.
332	The Jews submit to Alexander the Great; Palestine under Macedonian Governors. Onias I., high-priest.	Canticles? Isa. xxiv.-xxvii.? Additions of all sorts to the older prophets.	323 Alex. the Great † at Babylon. Perdiccas regent († 321). Continual wars between the Diadochi.	323-285 Ptolemy I., Lagos, founder of the dynasty of the Lagidæ at Alexandria.
321	Ptolemy Lagos surprises Jerusalem. Many Jews transported to Egypt.			
320	Antigonus conquers Palestine.			
312	Through the battle of Gaza Ptolemy Lagos becomes master of the country.		Commencement of the Seleucid dominion in Syria and Babylonia, with Seleucus I., Nicator (312-280).	(In Italy, Wars of the Romans with the Samnites, 343-290).
311	Palestine again under Antigonus.	Psalms of the Greek Period.		

CHRONOLOGICAL TABLES FOR THE HISTORY OF THE ISRAELITES.

Year, B.C.	Judah.	Rise of the Monuments of Israelite Literature.	Contemporary Events in the Assyrio-Babylonian Empire.	Contemporary Events in Egypt, etc.
301	In consequence of the battle of Ipsus Palestine again under Ptolemy. Prosperous period under the mild rule of the Ptolemies.	The historical work of the Chronicler (Ezra—Nehemiah—Chronicles). Zech. ix.–xiv. ?		
			280-279 The Gauls invade Macedonia and Greece. The remnant of them become mercenaries of the King of Bithynia, and then populate the district afterwards called Galatia.	285-246 Ptolemy Philadelphus. In his reign the Priest Manetho of Sebennytos writes three books of Egyptian history (arranged in thirty-one Dynasties).
264 to 248	Renewed struggles for Palestine between the Syrian and the Egyptian kingdoms.	Ecclesiastes?		
248	Marriage of Antiochus III. with Berenice, the daughter of Ptolemy Philadelphus (Dan. xi. 6).	Translation of the Pentateuch into Greek (according to the later fable, by 70 [72, precisely] interpreters): this lays the foundation for the so-called Alexandrian Translation or Septuagint.		246-221 Ptolemy III., Euergetes.
	Fresh conflicts between Ptolemy III., Euergetes and Seleucus Callinicus (Dan. xi. 7 ff.).		224-187 Antiochus III., the Great. In Greece most flourishing time of the Ætolian League; its conflict with the Achæan League, which had been revived in 280.	
218	Antiochus III., the Great, overruns Palestine, but at the	About the middle of the third century, Conclusion of the Second Part of the Hebrew Canon, the Nebiim or Prophets.		221-204 Ptolemy IV., Philopator.

202	Battle of Raphia is forced to withdraw, by Ptolemy IV., Philopator (Dan. xi. 10 ff.).		201-181 Ptolemy V., Epiphanes.
200	Palestine conquered by Antiochus III., by Scopas, general of Ptolemy V., Epiphanes,		(Since about 280) Most flourishing time of Alexandrian learning (the "Grammarians" and Glossators).
198	again by Antiochus III. (Dan. xi. 13 ff.)		
197	Cleopatra, daughter of Antiochus III., espoused to Ptolemy V. (Dan. xi. 17.) Palestine continues under Syrian (Seleucid) rule.	196 Flamininus proclaims the freedom of Greece at the Isthmian games.	
		About 180, Composition of the Wisdom of Jesus Sirach (precisely; Jesus, son of Sira) in the Hebrew language.	181-146 Ptolemy VI., Philometor, according to Josephus, c. Apion, II. 5, entrusted his whole kingdom to the Jews. The Jews, Onias and Dositheus, commanded the Egyptian army.
		187-175 Seleucus IV., Philopator, murdered by Heliodorus.	
176	Seleucus IV., Philop., stirred up by the temple-superintendent Simon (through his hatred of the high-priest Onias III.), attempts unsuccessfully to get possession of the temple treasure by means of Heliodorus (Dan. xi. 20).		
175	Antiochus IV. (Dan. xi. 21-45) begins to Hellenize Judea by force. The high-priest Onias III., the head of the strictly legalistic party (the *Chasidim*, i.e., Pious), is compelled by order of		175-164 Antiochus IV., Epiphanes, the tormentor of the Jews.

Year, B.C.	Judah.	Rise of the Monuments of Israelite Literature.	Contemporary Events in the Assyrio-Babylonian Empire.	Contemporary Events in Egypt, etc.
171	Antiochus to make way for his brother Jason (literally, Jesus), the head of the Greek party. Jason expelled by Menelaus, the assassin of Onias III.		The third Macedonian war of the Romans against Philip III.	170-164 Ptolemy VI. reigns along with his brother Ptolemy (VII.) Physcon, who was afterwards expelled from Egypt.
170	Jason surprises Jerusalem; Antiochus, returning from Egypt, takes vengeance (169) on the inhabitants and plunders the temple.			
168	Antiochus, with savage cruelty, prosecutes the extirpation of the Jewish religion and customs. Sabbath observance, circumcision and the possession of the Book of the Law, forbidden on pain of death. Razing of the walls of Jerusalem; Syrian garrison in the strongly fortified castle. Compulsory heathen sacrifices in all the cities of Judea. In Dec., 168, erection of an altar of Olympian Zeus, to whom the temple was now dedicated, on the altar of burnt offering at Jerusalem ("The abomination of desolation," Dan. xi. 31, xii. 11).			

167	The priest Mattathiah at Modin (now *el-Mediye*, E. of *Lydda*), kills an official of Antiochus and with his five sons organizes the insurrection. Destruction of the heathen altars. Putting to death of the renegade Jews.	
166	Mattathiah †. His son Judas, the "Maccabæan," repeatedly defeats Syrian generals (Gorgias at Emmaus, 165 Lysias at Beth Zur), and occupies Jerusalem with the exception of the castle.	165 or shortly before, the Book of Daniel.
165	December. Solemn dedication of the re-purified temple.	
	Victorious campaigns of the Jews in the neighbouring lands.	
164	Lysias defeats the Maccabæans at Beth-Zachariah, S. of Jerusalem; Siege of Zion.	164 Antiochus V., Eupator, Lysias guardian and regent.
163	Lysias grants to the Jews the free exercise of their religion.	
162	Demetrius I. nominates as high-priest Alcimus, the head of the Hellenistic party. Conflicts between Alcimus and Judas. The latter defeats Nicanor, the general of Demetrius, at Kaphar Salama, and then completely at	162-150 Demetrius I. (Soter) procures the murder of Antiochus V. and Lysias.

Year, B.C.	Judah.	Rise of the Monuments of Israelite Literature.	Contemporary Events in the Assyrio-Babylonian Empire.	Contemporary Events in Egypt, etc.
161	Beth-Horon (Nicanor†). Alliance of Judas with the Romans. Judas † in the unfortunate battle with Bacchides, the general of Demetrius. Rule of the Greek party under the high-priest Alcimus.			Onias the high-priest flies from Jerusalem and, appealing to Isa. xix. 17 ff., founds a Jewish temple at Leontopolis, where worship continued till 73 A.D.
161 to 143	*Jonathan*, brother of Judas, wins preponderance for the Maccabæan party	The Book of Esther.		
153	and, at the solicitation of Demetrius, garrisons Jerusalem: he is nominated high-priest by Alex. Balas and invested with purple and diadem. The Greek party set aside.	About 150, the Five Books of Jason of Cyrene on the Maccabean Wars (from which the Second Book of Maccabees was extracted in the first cent. A.D.).	Demetrius falls before Alex. Balas.	
145	Jonathan, hitherto a partizan of Alex. Balas, extorts from Demetrius II. an increase of territory and freedom from taxation, but then passes over to the side of Trypho (see column iv.), but is taken prisoner by the latter in Ptolemais and afterwards murdered.		147 Demetrius II., rival king: 145 king. In opposition to him Antiochus (VI.), son of Alex. Balas, was soon set up as rival king by his guardian Trypho.	146-117 Ptolemy VII., Physcon (cf. above, p. 202), according to *Josephus, c. Apion*, ii. 5, persecutor of the Jews (in the so-called Third Book of the Maccabees the same act is ascribed to Ptolemy IV.).
142				
142 to 135	*Simon*, Jonathan's brother, high-priest and prince, obtains from Demetrius the recognition of the independence of Judea (in 142 the computation of time by the years of Simon begins).			

141	May, 142. Simon's entry into the citadel of Jerusalem, surrendered by the Syrians.	
	Simon, by the people's decision, *hereditary* high-priest, general and prince (Dynasty of the Asmonæans),	Collection of the Fourth and Fifth Books of Psalms and Close of the Psalter.	Trypho, after the assassination of Alexander VI., rival king to Demetrius.
139	recognized by the Romans,	? The Book of Judith (originally in Hebrew).	138-128 Antiochus VII., Sidetes.
135	murdered by his son-in-law, Ptolemy.		
135 to 105	*John Hyrcanus I.*, son of Simon, submits to Antiochus VII., Sidetes, but under the weak Demetrius II. conquers, subsequently to	About 130, the Proverbs of Jesus Sirach translated into Greek by the author's grandson.	Demetrius II. king again.
128	a portion of the surrounding countries, and compels the Idumæans to be circumcised. Judæa entirely independent of Syria.		124-113 and 111-96, Antiochus VIII., Grypos, and along with him, 113-95, Antiochus IX., Cyzicenus.
	About 120 John Hyrcanus subdues the Samaritans and destroys their temple on Gerizim.		
108?	Conquest and Destruction of Samaria.	About 90, the First Book of Maccabees. Towards the end of the century, "The Wisdom of Solomon."	
105 to 104	*Aristobulus I.*, son of John Hyrcanus, high-priest and *king*.		
78	Alex. Jannæus, brother of Aristobulus, king.		

III.

MEASURES AND WEIGHTS, MONEY, THE COMPUTATION OF TIME IN THE OLD TESTAMENT.*

1. Measures and Weights.

1. **Measures of Length.** By far the most frequently mentioned measure of length is the *cubit* (Heb. *'ammā*, which also means "elbow" or "fore-arm"). It was divided into two spans (*zereth*, 1 Sam. xvii. 4, &c.), each of these containing three palms (*tōphach*, Exod. xxv. 25, &c.), of four fingers each (*'eṣba'*, 1 Kings vii. 15).

Ezekiel (xl. 5, xliii. 13) founds the measure of his future temple on a cubit which is a cubit and a handbreadth of the ordinary standard long. Hence it is usually, and probably with justice, assumed that in place of the smaller cubit which had gradually become prevalent he restored "the old measure," by which, according to 2 Chron. iii. 3, the temple of Solomon was built. But it is uncertain whether the Hebrew measures are to be identified with the Egyptian or the Babylonian. Amongst the Egyptians the great or "royal" cubit, (7 handbreadths or 28 digits) amounted to 525-528 millimetres, and therefore the small one (6 handbreadths) to about

---

* On this section cf. especially J. Benzinger, Hebräische Archäologie (Freib. i. B. u. Leipzig, 1894), p. 178 ff.

450 mm. But the great or "royal" cubit of the Babylonians comes to about 555, the small or common cubit to about 495 mm. Hence the difference is not great. In determining the common Hebrew cubit there is an uncertainty of between 45 and 49 centimetres, and in that of Ezekiel between 52 and 55 centimetres.

The following larger measures of length are mentioned:—

a. The Rod (*qanè*, precise meaning, *reed, cane*), which measured, according to Ezek. xl. 5 (cf. also xl. 3, 7 f., xlii. 16 ff.), six great cubits, *i.e.*, according to the above, about 3 metres and 20 or 30 centimetres.

b. The Length (*kibrā*, only in the connection *kibrath 'éreṣ*), *i.e.*, a length of land, Gen. xlviii. 7, and 2 Kings v. 19, or *kibrath hā'āreṣ*, the length of the land. In all three cases the context shows that it is a short distance, and can scarcely be a definite measure.

The superficial measure *ṣèmed* also (*yoke*, literally, *team*), which is applied to arable land at 1 Sam. xiv. 14, and to vine-growing land at Isa. v. 10, is probably a mere approximate reckoning of as much land as can be ploughed in a day with a team of oxen.

2. Measures of capacity. With the exception of the '*ómer* and its equivalent, the '*iśśārōn*, *i.e.*, "tenth" (see below), all the Dry and Liquid measures are formed on the sexagesimal system, and there can therefore be no doubt that they came from Babylonia, from which country this system spread over Syria and Palestine several centuries before the immigration of the Hebrews. The measures mentioned in the Old Testament are:

Chōmer (Isa. v. 10, translated "Malter" by Luther, in all other passages "Homer"), only mentioned as a Dry Measure, = 364·4 litres [In the Oxford "Helps to the Study of the Bible" the earlier Homer is stated to = 293·760 litres, or 8·081 bushels, and the latter 214·200 litres, or 5·893 bushels].

Kor (1 Kings v. 2, &c., Dry Measure; Ezek. xlv. 14, for Liquid), of the same contents as the Chomer.

Lèthekh, only at Hosea iii. 2 (as a Grain Measure), according to the (perhaps merely conjectural) tradition, half a chomer, i.e., 182·2 litres.

'*Ēphā* (Isa v. 10, &c., translated "Scheffel" by Luther; Prov. xx. 10, "Mass"; often also "Epha"), the most frequently mentioned Dry Measure; the tenth part of a chomer (Ezek. xlv. 11) = 36·4 l. At Ezek. xlv. 13 the sixth part of an 'epha is mentioned.

Bath (at Isa. v. 10 Luther renders "Eimer," elsewhere "Bath"), only for liquids; the tenth part of a kor (Ezek. xlv. 14), and therefore of the same contents as the 'epha, = 36·4 l.

Sĕā, in the Old Testament only for Dry Measure; a third of the 'epha = 12·14 l.

Hīn, Liquid only; a sixth of the bath = 6·07 l.

'*Ōmer* (*Gomer*), a measure which is only found in the so-called Priests' Code (Exod. xvi.); a tenth of the 'epha, therefore = 3·64 l. The definite explanation at Exod. xvi. 36 proves that the name was not employed till late. Elsewhere in the Priests' Code the same measure is called

'*Iśśarōn*, *i.e.*, tenth (of an 'epha). Consequently in the 'Omer or 'Issaron the Decimal System (though not till the Priests' Code) triumphed over the old system, according to which the 'epha fell into fractions or multiples of six.

Qab, only at 2 Kings vi. 25 ("the fourth part of a cab"); the third of a hin, the sixth of a sea, the eighteenth of a bath or 'epha = 2·2 l.

Log (only at Lev. xiv. 10 ff, as Oil Measure), the fourth of a qab = 0·50 l.

3. Weights. Like the Measures of Capacity, the System of Weights, which the Hebrews doubtless adopted from the Canaanites, was of Babylonian origin, and it, too, is founded on the sexagesimal system: 1 talent = 60 minae = 3600 shekels. The Babylonians distinguished between the heavy and the light talent, as well as between the heavy and the light mina; in each case the light weight contained only half of the heavy. But another distinction was also made between the *royal weight* (according to the standard

weights found in the ruins of Nineveh, 1 heavy talent = 60·6 kilos., and therefore a heavy mina was about 1 kilo.) and the *common weight*. The latter (probably older) system made its way amongst the Hebrews and others, and we must calculate the statements concerning weights in the Old Testament according to it: the talent (Heb. *kikkār*, literally, *circle*) = 58·944 kilos.; the mina (Heb. *manê*), the sixtieth part of a talent = 982·4 grammes; the shekel (Heb. *shéqel*), the sixtieth part of a mina = 16·37 grammes. The following fractions of the shekel are mentioned:—The half-shekel (Heb. *béqa‘*, Gen. xxiv. 22, &c.), the quarter-shekel (1 Sam. ix. 8), and the *gērā* (*i.e.*, "grain," = $\frac{1}{20}$ shekel). A distinction also is drawn between the heavy and the light shekel, &c., in this common weight; the light shekel comes into consideration especially with reference to money (see below).

But as it happened with the measures of capacity so here also a change to the decimal system is found, in that the mina is reckoned as 50 instead of 60 shekels. This does not mean that the shekel was made heavier but that the mina and the talent received a lighter denomination. Traces of this reckoning are first found in the Old Testament at Ezek. xlv. 12 (where the direction, "And ye shall reckon the mina at 50 shekels" [see critical note on Ezek. xlv. 12, in Kautzsch's Die Heilige Schrift] obviously introduces something fresh); again, in the Priests' Code, Exod. xxxviii. 25 ff. (1 talent = 3000 shekels; hence the mina = 50 shekels). At 2 Chron. ix. 16 the mina seems to be reckoned as 100 shekels, for the weight of Solomon's golden targets is stated at 300 shekels, instead of 3 minae (1 Kings x. 17). Probably, however, we have here, as is so frequently the case with the Chronicler, an intentional enhancing of the traditional statement.

The division of the shekel into 20 gerahs, like the new computation of the mina, seems to have first become customary in Ezekiel's time, for he lays special stress on it at xlv. 12 (see above). With this it corresponds that the proportion is invariably repeated in the Priests' Code

14

(Exod. xxx. 13, Lev. xxvii. 25, Num. iii. 47, xviii. 16) when the "holy weight" is prescribed. The "holy weight" (lit. "shekel of the sanctuary"), according to the view of the rabbis, is contrasted with the common weight, supposed to be half as heavy; in reality, with the somewhat lighter silver shekel which was current as a coin (see below).

2. MONEY.

Apart from the introduction of Persian coins after the Exile (see below), the precious metals were employed as the medium of exchange by weighing out the amount (Gen. xxiii. 15 f.: cf. also Isa. lv. 2) in the balance (Jer. xxxii. 9). It is no doubt probable that even in early times pieces of determinate weight, provided perhaps with some stamp, were in circulation. The silver quarter-shekel, 1 Sam. ix. 8, points in this direction, perhaps also "the pieces of silver," Gen. xlii. 25, 35, as well as the *qĕsîṭā*, Gen. xxxiii. 19, Josh. xxiv. 32, Job xlii. 11, which can only be explained, especially in the passage in Job, as pieces of metal of definite weight. But seeing that the weighing of pieces of metal to a definite weight, according to all the indications, was a private affair, and therefore furnished no guarantee of correctness, the re-weighing of these pieces, at least in the case of large sums, was inevitable. The predominance of silver as the medium of exchange is evidenced by the fact that *kèseph*, "silver," in the wider sense of the word, may mean "money" or "payment" (Exod. xxi. 11) in general.

Naturally the money was weighed out in ancient times in accordance with the prevalent scale of weights (see above): here, too, the shekel, as sixtieth (or 50th) part of the mina and three thousand six hundredth (or 3000th) part of the talent, was the unit. But as the circulation of metal pieces of definite weight became more common it must have been felt more and more keenly that it was very awkward to reckon the gold shekel in terms of the silver shekel, or *vice versâ*, whilst the relative values of gold and silver remained fixed in the proportion of 1 to $13\frac{1}{3}$. According to the *great common weight* (see above, p. 209) a shekel weighed 16·37 grammes, according to the *small* weight about 8·18 grammes. A silver piece, therefore, of about 109 gr. corresponded with a gold shekel of the latter weight; a silver piece of 218 gr. to a gold shekel of the heavy weight. The difficulty of reckoning was relieved by the production of a unit of silver, a piece which either weighed $\frac{1}{10}$th (in Babylonia, &c.) or $\frac{1}{15}$th (almost everywhere in Phœnicia, as well as among the Israelites) of the silver piece corresponding to the gold shekel: hence if we take the small common weight as the basis it would amount to 10·91 or 7·27 gr., and with the larger common weight as the basis 21·82 or 14·54 gr. These silver pieces also commonly bore the name shekel, although in reality they were 1·83 or 0·91 gr. less than the shekel of weight or gold shekel.

The first evidence that the Israelites actually made the silver shekel equal to $\frac{1}{15}$th (not $\frac{1}{10}$th) of the weight of the gold shekel multiplied by $13\frac{1}{3}$ is furnished by the division into half and quarter shekels which is also found in other places* where the shekel was fixed at $\frac{1}{15}$th of the above weight. It is shown further by the actual weight of the (stamped) shekels of the Maccabæan period which have been preserved in fairly considerable numbers. This varies between 14·50 and 14·65 gr.: 14·55 gr. has therefore been taken as the average.

Both in gold and silver the mina was reckoned as containing 50 shekels, not 60 as in the older weight, and the talent 60 such minae (and therefore 3000 shekels). If we put the

---

* If Exod. xxx. 13 fixes the so-called poll-tax at half a shekel and Neh. x. 33 at a third of a shekel, Nehemiah perhaps adheres to the Persian system, which was constructed on the tenth of a shekel standard and accordingly (cf. Benzinger, *loc. cit.*, p. 193) divided the shekel into thirds, not into halves and quarters. On the other hand, the Maccabæan system, which, according to the above, was constructed on the fifteenth of a shekel standard, again demanded the half shekel as poll-tax (cf. Matt. xvii. 24 ff., where the didrachma or double drachma corresponds to the value of half a shekel).

value of the gold shekel at about £2, and that of the silver shekel at about 2s 8d,* then—

1 Gold shekel = 16·37 gr. = £2
1 Gold mina = 818·6 gr. = £100
1 Gold talent = 49·11 kilos. = £6000
1 Silver shekel = 14·55 gr. = 2s 8d
1 Silver mina = 727·5 gr. = £6. 13s 4d
1 Silver talent = 43·65 kilos. = £400

The following stamped coins are mentioned in the Old Testament:—

1. The *Daric* (Heb. ădarkōn), introduced by Darius I. (521·485), a gold coin of 8·40 gr. (*i.e.*, about $\frac{1}{60}$th of the light Babylonian mina), and therefore worth about £1. 2s* : cf. Ezra viii. 27 (about 458). At 1 Chron. xxix. 7, the computation by darics is pre-supposed even for David's time, a proof that the coin must have been in circulation for a very long time.

2. The *Drachme* (Heb. darkĕmōn), Ezra ii. 69 (Neh. vii. 70 ff.). From a Phœnician inscription found in the Piræus in 1888, in which *darkemon* and *adarkon* stand beside each other, it is clear that they are not names of the same coin, as used to be thought. Cf. Ed. Meyer, Die Entstehung des Judenthums (Halle, 1896) p. 196 ff. He estimates the gold drachme, in case the Persian system is followed, at 4·3 gr., = about 12s.

According to 1 Macc. xv. 6, the Jews first obtained the right to coin money in 139-138 B.C., under the high-priest and prince, Simon.

3. Computation of Time.

1. The Year. The ancient Hebrew year was a *solar*† year

---

* [Cf. Helps to the Study of the Bible, p. 150. *Tr.*]

† At Gen. vii. 11, viii. 14 (in the Priests' Document) the length of the Deluge Year is reckoned from the 17th day of the 2nd month of the 600th year of Noah to the 27th day of the 2nd month of the 601st year. This presupposes that in the primæval period they reckoned by lunar years of 354 days, and therefore had to add eleven days to complete the solar year (the traditional length of the Deluge.)

of twelve months. This follows partly from the names of certain months, in so far as they are suitable to definite seasons, and partly from the assignment to definite months of the feasts which depend upon the harvest. In pre-exilic times the year began in autumn (Exod. xxiii. 16, xxxiv. 22); in all probability there is a reminiscence of this in the appointment of the new moon (*i.e.*, the first day) of the seventh month as the "Day of Trumpet Blowing" (Lev. xxiii. 24, Num. xxix. 1). During the Exile, in accordance with the Babylonian system, the beginning of the year was transferred to the spring; the manner in which Exod. xii. 2 emphasizes the Passover month as the first month of the year shows plainly how much this was felt to be an innovation.

2. The Months. In spite of and contemporaneously with the computation by solar years (see above) the computation by lunar months (from new moon to new moon) of twenty-nine to thirty days each, adopted from the Canaanites, asserted itself amongst the Israelites.* It is an evidence of this that the expression for "new moon" (*chōdesh*) was partly used for the first day of the month and partly for the "month" in general, and eventually quite displaced the antique Semitic designation of the month (*yèrach*)). Of the old Hebrew (or Canaanite) names of the months, too, it happens that only four have been preserved, namely,

'*Ābīb* (Exod. xiii. 4, xxiii. 15, xxxiv. 18, Deut. xvi. 1), in full, *Chōdesh hā-.Ībīb*, *i.e.*, the month of ears, the seventh (according to later reckoning, the first) month.

Ziv (1 Kings vi. 1-37), the month of the brilliance [of flowers], the eighth (later, second) month.

'*Ēthānīm* (1 Kings viii. 2), *i.e.*, probably, the month of the constantly flowing [brooks], the first (later, seventh) month.

Būl (1 Kings vi. 38), the second (later, eighth) month.

---

* Although we have no evidence for it in the Old Testament the twelve lunar months (= 354 days can only have been made up into a solar year of 365 days by the deliberate insertion of an intercalary month (in the later Jewish calendar, the second or latter Adar as a thirteenth month.)

In the time immediately preceding the Exile the number of the month took the place of its name; this is universal in Ezekiel, in the later portions of the Book of Jeremiah, in the Books of Kings (where the names of the months, 1 vi. 1, 38, viii. 2, already seemed to require explaining), as well as in Haggai and Zechariah. But, together with the numbers, Zechariah already uses twice the new, Babylonian-Syrian names (i. 7, vii. 1); five others are incidentally mentioned in the Books of Esther, Ezra and Nehemiah. The complete list of names is:—

		Approximately, middle of
1.	Nīsān (Neh. ii. 1, Esth. iii. 7).	March to April.
2.	'Iyyār	April to May.
3.	Sīvān (Esth. viii. 9)	May to June.
4.	Tammūz	June to July.
5.	'Ab	July to August.
6.	'Ĕlūl (Neh. vi. 15)	August to September.
7.	Tishrī	September to October.
8.	Marchesvān	October to November.
9.	Kislēv (Zech. vii. 1, Neh. i. 1)	November to December.
10.	Tēbēth (Esth. ii. 16)	December to January.
11.	Shĕbāt (Zech. i. 7)	January to February.
12.	'Ădār (Ezra vi. 15, Esth. iii. 7, and often)	February to March.

3. Weeks and Days. With the exception of Gen. xxiv. 55 (supposing that the ten days there is to be regarded as a reference to the division of the month into so-called decades), the week of seven days (*shābūa'*, i.e., a seven [of days] is always taken for granted. The days were reckoned from sunset to sunset (but cf. Gen. i. 5-8, &c., where the days are reckoned from morning to morning). In all probability the time from morning to evening was divided into twelve hours, which were longer or shorter according to the season. It is in favour of this opinion that, although there is no expression for "hour" in the Heb. Old Testament, we are told that Ahaz

set up a sun-dial in Jerusalem, probably after an Assyrian pattern.

The night was divided into a first (Lam. ii. 19: "Beginning of the night-watches"), middle (Judges vii. 19), and last (Exod. xiv. 24) watch of the night; according to 1 Sam. xi. 11, the last was also called the morning watch.

IV.

LIST OF OLD TESTAMENT PROPER NAMES, ACCOMPANIED WITH AN EXACT TRANSLITERATION OF THEIR HEBREW FORMS.

The Hebrew *consonants* are transliterated as follows:—'Aleph by ', Bēth, &c., *b, g, d, h, v, z* (a quite soft *s*, not at all resembling the German ʒ), *ch* (something like *ch* in the German "Rachen" [or Scotch loch], *ṭ* (the hardest *t*), *y, k* (when aspirated, *kh*, something like the German *ch* in Rechen, Blech, &c.), *l, m, n, s,* ' (a peculiar guttural), *p* (aspirated, *ph*), *ṣ* (an emphatically pronounced *s*), *q* (a strong *k*, formed at the back of the palate), *r, ś* (to be spoken as the common *s*) *sh, t*. No notice is taken in the transliteration of the *h* which is added at the end (especially of feminine words in *ā*), as a mere vowel letter, *i.e.*, as pointing to a preceding vowel.

The long vowels are represented by ā, ē, ī, ō, ū; the short by *a, e* (unaccented Seghol; accented Seghol by è), *i, o, u*. The so-called *Sheva quiescens* is not noticed; *Sheva mobile* is represented by ĕ, the so-called Chateph-sounds by ă, ĕ̈, ŏ; *Pathach furtivum* (always after a long vowel) also by ă.

Hebrew words as a rule have the accent on the final

LIST OF OLD TESTAMENT PROPER NAMES. 217

syllable; an accented penultimate syllable is indicated in the following list by an accent; and in such cases the accented *e*, *i*, *o*, *u* (*é*, *í*, *ó*, *ú*) is always a long vowel, but accented *a* (*á*) is such only in *yáhu*, ... *yáresh*, ... *máveth*, ... *pá'u*.

Aaron, *Ahărōn*
Abarim, *Ăbārīm*
Abdon, *Abdōn*
Abel (place name), *Ābēl*
Abel (man's name), *Hĕbel* (breath)
Abiah, *Abiyyā* (also *Ăbiyyáhū*, *Ăbiyyām*
Abiathar, *Ĕbyāthār*
Abigail, *Ăbīgáyil*
Abihu, *Ăbīhū'*
Abimael, *Ăbīmā'ēl*
Abimelech, *Ăbīmĕlekh*
Abishai, *Ăbīshay*
Abner, *Ăbnēr*, also *Ăbīnēr*
Abraham, *Abrāhām* (*Ăbrām*)
Absalom, *Abshālōm*
Accad, *Akkad*
Accho, *Akkō*
Achish, *Ăkkīsh*
Achmetha, *Achmĕthā* (Ecbatana)
Achor, *Ākhōr*
Achshaph, *Akhshāph*
Achzib, *Akhzīb*
Adam, *Ādām* (man)
Adama, *Ădāmā*
Admah, *Admā*
Adonijah, *Ădōniyyáhū*
Adoraim, *Ădōráyim*
Adrammelech, *Adrammĕlekh*
Adullam, *Ădullām*
Adummim, *Ădummīm*

Agag, *Ăgāg*
Agur, *Āgūr*
Ahab, *Ach'āb*
Ahasuerus, *Ăchashvērōsh* (Xerxes)
Ahaz, *Āchāz*
Ahaziah, *Ăchazyā*, *Ăchazyáhū*
Ahiah, *Achiyya*, *Ăchiyyáhū*
Ahikam, *Ăchīqām*
Ahimaaz, *Ăchīmá'aṣ*
Ahimelech, *Ăchīmĕlekh*
Ahithophel, *Ăchīthóphel*
Ai, *Ay*, also *Ayyā*
Ain, *Ayin*
Ajalon, *Ayyālōn*
Akrabbim, *Aqrabbīm*
Almodad, *Almōdād*
Almon, *Almōn*
Amalek, *Ămāléq*
Amasa, *Ămāsā*
Amaziah, *Ămasyā*
Ammon, *Ammōn*
Amnon, *Amnōn*
Amorite, *Ămōrī*
Amos (the Prophet), *Āmōs*
Amoz (father of Isaiah), *Āmōṣ*
Amraphel, *Amráphel*
Ana, *Ănā*
Anab, *Ănāb*
Anak, *Ănāq*
Anakim, *Ănāqīm*
Anamim, *Ănāmīm*
Anathoth, *Ănāthōth*

Anim, *Ănīm*
Aphek, *Ăphéq*
Ar, *Ār*
Arab, *Ărāb*
Arabian, *Ărab*
Arad, *Ărād*
Aram, *Ărām*
Ararat, *Ărārāt*
Arba, *Arba'*
Argob, *Argōb*
Ariel, *Ărī'ēl*
Arkite, *Arkī*
Arnon, *Arnōn*
Aroer, *Ărō'ēr*, also *Ar'ōr*
Arpad, *Arpād*
Arphaxad, *Arpakhshad*
Artaxerxes, *Artachshashtā*
Arubboth, *Ărubbōth*
Arvadite, *Arvādī*
Asa, *Āsā*
Asahel, *Ăsāh'ēl*
Asaph, *Ăsāph*
Aschenaz, *Ashkĕnaz*
Ashdod, *Ashdōd*
Asher, *Āshēr*
Ashera, *Ăshērā*
Ashima, *Ăshīmā*
Ashtaroth, *Ashtārōth*
Askelon, *Ashqĕlōn*
Asshur, Assyrian, *Ashshūr*
Astarte, *Ashtōreth*
Ataroth, *Ăṭārōth*
Athaliah, *Ăthalyā*
Ava, *Avvā*
Azazel, *Ăzā'zēl*
Azekah, *Ăzēqā*

218 LIST OF OLD TESTAMENT PROPER NAMES ACCOMPANIED

Baal, *Bá'al* (Lord)
Baalath, *Bá'ălath*
Baal Gad, *Bá'al Gād*
Baal Hamon, *Bá'al Hāmōn*
Baal Hermon, *Bá'al Chermōn*
Baal Meon, *Bá'al Mĕ'ōn*
Baal Perazim, *Bá'al Pĕrāşīm*
Baal Shalisha, *Bá'al Shālīshā*
Baal Zephon, *Bá'al Sephōn*
Baasha, *Ba'shā*
Babel, Babylon, *Bābĕl*
Bahurim, *Bachūrīm*
Bala, *Bălā*
Balaam, *Bil'ām*
Balak, *Bālāq*
Bamoth, *Bāmōth*
Barzillai, *Barzillay*
Baruch, *Bārūk* (blessed)
Bashan. *Bāshān*
Bathsheba, *Bath-shĕba'*
Bedan, *Bĕdān*
Beer, *Bĕ'ēr*
Beeroth, *Bĕ'ērōth*
Beersheba, *Bĕ'ēr Shĕba'*
Beesh-terah, *Bĕ'esh-tĕrā*
Bel, *Bēl*
Bela, *Bĕla'*
Belshazzar, *Bēlsha'ṣ-ṣar*, also *Bēlṭsha'ṣ-ṣar*
Benaiah, *Bĕnāyā, Bĕnāyàhū*
Benhadad, *Ben-hădad*
Benjamin, *Binyāmīn*
Bered, *Bĕred*
Berothai, *Bĕrōthay*
Besor, *Bĕśōr*

Betach, *Bĕṭach*
Beten, *Bĕṭen*
Beth-Anoth, *Bēth-'Anōth*
Beth Arabah, *Bēth [hā-]'Ărābā*
Beth Arbeel, *Bēth 'Arbē'l*
Beth-Azmaveth, *Bēth-'Azmāveth*
Beth Aven, *Bēth 'Āven*
Beth Barah, *Bēth Bārā*
Beth-Birei, *Bēth-Bir'ī*
Beth-Cherem, *Bēth-Kĕrem*
Beth Dagon, *Bēth Dāgōn*
Bethel, *Bēth-'Ēl*
Beth Emeq, *Bēth-'Ēmeq*
Beth Ezel, *Bēth-'Eṣel*
Beth Gader, *Bēth-Gādēr*
Beth Gamul, *Bēth-Gāmūl*
Beth Hanan, *Bēth-Chānān*
Beth Haram, *Bēth-Hārām*
Beth Hoglah, *Bēth-Choglā*
Beth Horon, *Bēth-Chōrōn*
Beth Jeshimoth, *Bēth-[hā-]-Jĕshīmōth*
Beth-le-Aphrah[R.V.], *Bēth-lĕ-'Aphrā*
Beth-lebaoth, *Bēth-lĕ-Bā'ōth*
Bethlehem, *Bēthlĕchem*
Beth-nimrah, *Bēth-Nimrā*
Beth-pazzez, *Bēth-Paṣṣēṣ*

Beth-palet, *Bēth-Pĕleṭ*
Beth Peor, *Bēth-Pĕ'ōr*
Beth Rehob, *Bēth-Rĕchōb*
Beth Shean, *Bēth-Shĕ'ān*
Beth-Shemesh, *Bēth-Shĕmesh*
Beth-Shitta, *Bēth-ha-Shiṭṭā*
Beth-Tappuah, *Bēth-Tappūăch*
Bethuel, *Bĕthū'ēl*
Beth-Zur, *Bēth-ṣūr*
Betonim. *Bĕṭōnīm*
Bezek, *Bĕzeq*
Bezer, *Bĕṣer*
Bilhah, *Bilhā*
Boaz. *Bō'az* (in him [is] strength)
Bochim, *Bōkhīm*
Bor Hasira, *Bōr Hassīrā*
Bozkath, *Bosqath*
Bozrah, *Boṣrā*
Buz, *Būz*

Cabul, *Kābūl*
Cain, *Qáyin*
Cainan, *Qēnān*
Calah, *Kĕlach*
Caleb, *Kālēb*
Calneh, *Kalnē, Kalnè*, also *Kalnō*
Canaan, *Kĕnáʻan*
Caphtor, *Kaphtōr*
Carchemish, *Karkĕmīsh*
Casiphia, *Kāsiphyā*
Casluhim, *Kaslūchīm*
Chaldæan, *Kasdīm*
Chebar, *Kĕbār*
Chedorlaomer, *Kĕdōr-la'òmer*
Chemosh, *Kĕmōsh*
Chephira, *Kephīrā*

WITH AN EXACT TRANSLITERATION OF THEIR HEBREW FORMS. 219

Cherethites and Pelethites [ha], Kĕrēthī [veha] Pĕlēthī
Cherith, Kerīth
Cherub, Kĕrūb, pl. Kĕrūbīm
Chinnereth (Chinneroth), Kinnĕreth, Kinnĕrōth
Chittim, Kittīm (pl. of Kittī)
Chisloth Tabor, Kislōth Tābōr
Chushan Rishathaim, Kūshan Rish'ătáyīm
Cush, Kūsh
Cuth, Cutha, Kūth, Kūtha
Cyrus, Kōresh

Daberath, Dăbĕrath
Dagon, Dāgōn
Damascus, Dammĕ́seq
Dan, Dān
Daniel. Dānīyyēl, Dānī'ēl
Daric, Ădarkōn (but Darkĕmōn = Drachme)
Darius, Dārĕyāvesh
David, Dāvīd
Deborah, Dĕbōrā (bee)
Dedan, Dĕdān
Delilah, Dĕlīlā
Diblathaim, Diblāthayim
Dibon, Dībōn
Diklah, Diqlā
Dinah, Dīnā
Dinhabah, Dinhābā
Dizahab, Dī Zāhāb
Doeg, Dō'ēg
Dophkah, Dophqā
Dor, Dōr

Dothan, Dōtháyin, Dōthān
Dumah, Dūmā
Dura, Dūrā

Ebal, 'Ēbāl
Eben-ezer, 'Eben hā 'Ēzer
Eber, 'Ēber
Eden, 'Ēden, 'Ēden
Edom, 'Ĕdōm
Edomite, 'Ĕdōmī
Edrei, 'Edrĕ'ī
Eglath, 'Eglath
Eglon, 'Eglōn
Ehud, 'Ēhūd
Ekron, 'Eqrōn
Elah, 'Ēlā
Elam, 'Ēlām
Elath, Eloth, 'Ēlat, 'Ēlōth
Elealeh, 'El'ālē
Eleazar, 'El'āzār
Elhanan, 'Elchānān
Eli, 'Ēlī
Elias, 'Ēlīyyā, 'Ēlīyáhū
Eliezer, 'Ĕlī'ezer
Elim, 'Ēlīm
Elishah (people), 'Ălīshā
Elisha (prophet), 'Ĕlīshā
Elkosh, 'Elqōsh
Ellasar, 'Ellāsār
Elon, 'Ēlōn
Eltekeh, 'Eltĕqē
Emim, 'Ēmīm
Enam, 'Ēnām
Endor, 'Ēn Dōr
Engannim, 'Ēn Gannīm
Engedi, 'Ēn Gĕdī
Enoch, Chănōkh
Ephraim, 'Ephráyim
Ephrath, 'Ephrāth

Ephron, 'Ephrōn
Erech, 'Erekh
Esarhaddon, 'Esarchaddōn
Esau, 'Ēsāv
Eshcol, 'Eshkōl
Eshean, 'Esh'ān
Eshtaol, 'Eshtā'ōl
Esthemo[a], 'Esthĕmō, Esthĕmō'ā
Esther, 'Estēr
Etham, 'Ēthām
Ethan, 'Ēthān
Ethbaal, 'Ethbā'al
Ether, 'Ēther
Euphrates, Pĕrāt
Eve, Chavvā
Evil Merodach, 'Ĕvīl Mĕrōdakh
Ezekiel, Yĕchezqē'l
Ezion Geber, 'Esyōn Gĕber
Ezra, 'Ezrā

Gaash, Gā'ash
Gad, Gād
Galilee, Gālīl, Gālīlā
Gallim, Gallīm
Gamaliel, Gamlī'ēl
Gareb, Gārēb
Gath, Gath
Gaza, 'Azzā
Geba, Gĕba'
Gebal, Gĕbāl
Gebim, Gēbīm
Gedaliah, Gĕdalyā
Geder, Gĕder
Gederah, Gĕdērā
Gedor, Gĕdōr
Gehazi, Gēchăzī
Gerar, Gĕrār
Gerizim, Gĕrizzīm
Gershom, Gershon. Gērshōm, Gērshōn
Geshur, Gĕshūr
Gezer, Gĕzer

220   LIST OF OLD TESTAMENT PROPER NAMES ACCOMPANIED

Gether, *Gĕther*
Gibbethon, *Gibbĕthōn*
Gibeah, *Gibʻă*
Gibeon, *Gibʻōn*
Gideon, *Gidʻōn*
Gihon, *Gīchōn*
Gilboa, *Gilboʻă*
Gilead, *Gilʻād*
Gilgal, [*ha*]*Gilgāl*
Giloh, *Gīlō*
Girgashite, *Girgāshī*
Gittaim, *Gittáyim*
Gob, *Gōb*
Golan, *Gōlān*
Goliath, *Golyath*
Gomer, *Gomer*
Gomorrah, *ʻAmōrā*
Gozan, *Gōzān*
Goshen, *Góshen*

Habakkuk, *Chăbaqqūk*
Habor, *Chābōr*
Hachmoni, *Chakhmōnī*
Hadad, *Hădad*
Hadadezer, *Hădadʻezer*
Hadashah (town), *Chădāshā*
Hadassah, *Hădassā*
Hadid. *Chādīd*
Hadoram, *Hădōrām*
Hadrach, *Chadrākh*
Hagar, *Hāgār*
Hagarenes (pl.), *Hagrīm*
Haggai, *Chaggay*
Halah, *Chălach*
Halhul, *Chalchul*
Ham, *Chām*
Haman, *Hāmān*
Hamath, *Chămāth*
Hammon, *Chammōn*
Hanani, *Chănānī*
Hanes, *Chānēs*
Hannah, *Channā*

Hapara, *Hăppārā*
Hapharaim, *Chapharáyim*
Hara, *Hārā*
Haran, *Chārān*
Harod, *Chărōd*
Havilah, *Chăvīlā*
Havran, *Chavrān*
Hazael, *Chăzāʻēl*
Hazar Addar, *Chăṣar ʻAddār*
Hazarmaveth, *Chăṣar Māveth*
Hazazon Tamar, *Chăṣaṣon Tāmār*
Hazeroth, *Chăṣērōth*
Hazor, *Chāṣōr*
Hebrew, *ʻIbrī*, pl., *ʻIbrīm*
Hebron, *Chebrōn*
Helbon, *Chelbōn*
Helkath, *Chelqath*, *Chelqāth*
Heman, *Hēmān*
Hena, *Hēnaʻ*
Hepher, *Chépher*
Hermon, *Chermōn*
Heshbon, *Cheshbōn*
Hezekiah, *Chizqiyyā*
Hilkiah, *Chilqiyyā, Chilqiyyāhū*
Hinnom, *Hinnōm* (usually *Ge Hinnōm*, or *Ge Ben H.*, Valley of the Son of Hinnom)
Hiram, *Chīrām*
Hittite, *Chittī*, pl. *Chittīm*
Hivite, *Chivvī*, pl. *Chivvīm*
Hobab, *Chōbāb*
Holon, *Chōlōn*
Hophra, *Chophraʻ*
Hor, *Hōr*
Horeb, *Chōrēb*
Hormah, *Chormā*

Horonaim, *Chōrōnáyim*
Hosea, *Hōshēʻă*
Hul, *Chūl*

Ibleam, *Yiblĕʻām*
Iddo, *ʻIddō, Yeʻdō*
Ijon, *ʻIyyōn*
Indian, *Hōddū*
Isaac, *Yiṣchāq*
Isaiah, *Yeshaʻyāhū*
Ishbosheth, *ʼIsh Bósheth*
Ishmael, *Yishmāʻēʼl*
Israel, *Yiśrāʼel*
Issachar, *Yiśśākhār*
Ithamar, *ʼIthāmār*

Jabal, *Yābāl*
Jabbok, *Yabbōq*
Jabesh, *Yābēsh*
Jabin, *Yābīn*
Jabneh, *Yabnĕ*
Jachin, *Yākhīn* (He [God] establishes)
Jacob, *Yaʻaqōb*
Jael, *Yāʻēl*
Jahaz, *Yăhaṣ, Yáhṣā*
Jair, *Yāʼīr*
Jakan, *Yăʻăqān*
Janoah, *Yănōăch*
Japhet, *Yépheth*
Japhia, *Yāphīăʻ*
Jarmuth, *Yarmuth*
Jashobeam, *Yāshobʻām*
Jattir, *Yattīr*
Javan, *Yāvān*
Jazer, *Yaʻzēr*
Jebus, *Yĕbūs*
Jebusite, *Yĕbūsī*
Jechoniah, *Yĕkonyā, Yĕkhonyāhū*
Jeduthun, *Yĕdūthūn*
Jehoahaz, *Yĕhōʼāchāz*

Jehoash, *Yĕhō'āsh*
Jehoiachin, *Yōyākīn*, *Yĕhōyākhīn*
Jehoiada, *Yōyādā'*, *Yĕhōyādā'*
Jehoiakim, *Yōyāqīm*, *Yĕhōyāqīm*
Jehoram, *Yĕhōrām*
Jehoshaphat, *Yōshāphāt*, *Yĕhōshāphāt*
Jehu, *Yēhū'*
Jekabzeel, *Yĕqabsĕ'ēl*
Jephthah, *Yiphtāch*
Jeremiah, *Yirmĕyāhū*
Jericho, *Yĕrīchō*, also *Yĕrēchō*
Jeroboam, *Yārob'ām* (*Yorob'ām?*)
Jerusalem, *Yĕrūshalāyim*
Jesse, *Yishay*
Jethro, *Yithrō*
Jew, *Yĕhūdī*, pl. *Yĕhūdīm*
Jezebel, *'Izĕbel*
Jezreel, *Yizrĕ'ēl*, *Yizrĕ'ēl*
Joab, *Yō'āb*
Job, *'Iyyōb*
Jobab, *Yōbāb*
Joel, *Yō'ēl*
Johanan, *Yōchānān*, *Yĕhōchānān*
Jokmeam, *Yoqmĕ'ām*
Joktan, *Yoqtān*
Joktheil, *Yoqtĕ'ēl*
Jonadab, *Yōnādāb*, *Yĕhōnādāb*
Jonah, *Yōnā*
Jonathan, *Yōnāthān*, *Yĕhōnāthān*
Joppa, *Yāphō*
Joram, *Yōrām* (for *Yĕhōrām*)
Jordan, *Yardēn*
Joseph, *Yōsēph*
Joshua, *Yĕhōshū'ā*

Josiah, *Yōshiyyāhū*
Jotbatha, *Yōtbāthā*
Jotham, *Yōthām*
Jubal, *Yūbāl*
Judah, *Yĕhūdā*
Judith, *Yĕhūdīth*
Juttah, *Yuttā*

Kadesh, *Qĕdesh*
Kadesh Barnea, *Qādēsh Barnē'ā*
Kadmonites, *Qadmōnī*
Kanah, *Qānā*
Kedarenes, *Qēdār*
Kedemoth, *Qĕdēmōth*
Keilah, *Qĕ'īlā*
Kenath, *Qĕnāth*
Kenezite, *Qĕnizzī*, pl. *Qĕnizzīm*
Kenite, *Qēni*, pl. *Qēnīm*
Kerioth, *Qĕriyyōth*
Keturah, *Qĕturā*
Kidron, *Qidrōn*
Kir (Heres, Hareseth) *Qīr* (*Chĕrĕs, Chărĕseth*)
Kirjathaim, *Qiryāthāyim*
Kirjath Jearim, *Qiryath Yĕ'ārīm*
Kirjath Sepher, *Qirjath Sĕpher*
Kishon, *Qīshōn*
Kohath, *Qĕhāt*
Korah, *Qōrach*

Laban, *Lābān*
Lachish, *Lākhīsh*
Laish, *Láyish*
Lamech, *Lĕmekh*
Leah, *Lē'ā*
Lebanon, *Lĕbānōn*
Lehi, *Lĕchī*
Lemuel, *Lĕmū'ēl*

Levi, *Lēvī*
Levite, *Lēvī*, pl. *Lĕvīyyīm*
Libnah, *Libnā*
Lod, *Lōd*
Lodebar, *Lō Dĕbār*
Lot, *Lōt*
Lud, *Lūd*
Luhith, *Lūchīth*
Luz, *Lūz*

Maachah, *Ma'ăkhā*
Machir, *Mākhīr*
Madon, *Mādōn*
Magog, *Māgōg*
Mahanaim, *Machănāyim*
Makkedah, *Maqqēdā*
Malachi, *Mal'ākhī*
Mamre, *Mamrē*
Manasseh, *Mĕnashshĕ*
Manna, *Mān*
Marah, *Mārā*
Mareshah, *Mārēshā*
Mash, *Mash*
Masrekah, *Masrēqā*
Massah, *Massā*
Medebah, *Mēdĕbā*
Media, Medes, *Māday*
Megiddo, *Megiddō*
Melchizedek, *Malkīsĕdeq*
Memphis, *Moph*
Menahem, *Mĕnachēm*
Mephaath, *Mepha'ath*
Mephibosheth, *Mĕphībōsheth*
Merab, *Mĕrāb*
Merari, *Mĕrārī*
Merodach Baladan, *Mĕrōdakh Bal'ădān*
Merom, *Mērōm*
Meroz, *Mērōz*
Mesha (place), *Mēshā'*
Mesha (king) *Mēshā'*
Meshech, *Mēshekh*

222 LIST OF OLD TESTAMENT PROPER NAMES ACCOMPANIED

Micah, *Mīkhā*
Michael, *Mīkhā'ēl*
Michal, *Mīkhāl*
Michmash, *Mikhmās, Mikhmāsh*
Migdol, *Migdōl*
Migron, *Migrōn*
Milcom, *Milkōm*
Minnith, *Minnīth*
Miriam, *Miryām*
Mishael, *Mīsh'āl*
Mizpah, *Mispā*|
Mizpeh, *Mispĕ*
Moab, *Mō'āb*
Moabite, *Mō'ābī*
Moladah, *Mōlādā*
Mordecai, *Mordĕkhay*
Moreh, *Mōrĕ*
Moresheth Gath, *Mōrĕsheth Gath*
Moriah, *Mōrīyyā*
Moser, Moseroth, *Mōsēr, Mōsērōth*
Moses, *Mōshĕ*

Naaman, *Na'ămān*
Naara, Naaran, *Na'ăra, Na'ărān*
Nabal, *Nābāl*
Nadab, *Nādāb*
Nahalal, *Nahălāl*
Nahash, *Nāchāsh*
Nahor, *Nāchōr*
Nahum, *Nāchūm*
Naomi, *No'ŏmī*
Naphtali, *Naphtālī*
Naphtuhim, *Naphtūchīm* (pl.)
Nazarite, *Nāzīr*
Nathan, *Nāthān*
Nebaioth, *Nĕbāyōth*
Nebat, *Nĕbāt*
Nebo, *Nĕbō*
Nebuchadnezzar, *Nĕbūkadne'ssar;* in Daniel also *Nĕbū-*

kadnessar (in Ezekiel and several passages of Jeremiah the correct form *Nebukadre'ssar* is found)
Nebuzar-adan, *Nĕbūzar'ădān*
Necho, *Nĕkhō*
Nehemiah, *Nĕchemyā*
Nephtoah, *Nephtōăch*
Neriah, *Nēriyyā*
Nathaniel, *Nĕthan'ēl*
Nethaniah, *Nĕthanyā*
Netophah, *Nĕtōphā*
Nimrod, *Nimrōd*
Nineveh, *Nīnĕvē*
Nisroch, *Nisrōkh*
No Amon, *Nō 'Amōn*
Noah, *Nōăch*
Nob, *Nōb*
Nod, *Nōd*
Noph, *Nōph* (= *Mōph*, see Memphis)

Obadiah, *'Ōbadyā*
Obal, *'Ōbāl*
Oboth, *'Ōbōth*
Og, *'Ōg*
Omri, *'Omrī*
On, *'Ōn*
Onan, *'Ōnān*
Ono, *'Ōnō*
Ophel, *'Ōphel*
Ophir, *'Ōphir*
Ophrah, *'Ōphrā*
Oreb, *'Ōrēb* (raven)
Othniel, *'Othnī'ēl*

Pagu, *Pā'ā*
Paran, *Pā'rān*
Parvaim, *Parvăyīm*
Pashur, *Pashshūr*
Passover, *Pĕsach*
Pathros, *Pathrōs*
Pekah, *Pĕkach*

Pekahiah, *Pĕkachyā*
Peleg, *Pĕleg*
Peniel, Penuel, *Pĕnī'-ēl, Pĕnū'ēl*
Peor, *Pĕ'ōr*
Perazim, *Pĕrāsīm*
Perizzitte, *Pĕrizzī*
Pethor, *Pĕthōr*
Pharaoh, *Par'ō*
Philistines, *Pĕlishtīm* (pl.)
Pi-hahiroth, *Pī-hachīrōth*
Pisgah, *Pisgā*
Pison, *Pīshōn*
Pithom, *Pithōm*
Potiphar, *Pōṭīphar*
Pul, *Pūl*
Punon, *Pūnōn*
Put, *Pūt*

Raamah, *Ra'mā*
Rabbath Ammon, *Rabbath 'Ammōn*
Rab-Shakeh, *Rabshāqĕ*
Rachel, *Rāchēl* (ewe)
Rahab, *Rāchāb* (as poetical name for Egypt, *Rāhab*)
Ramah, *Rāmā*
Ramoth, *Rāmōth*
Rameses, *Ra'mĕsēs, Ra'amsēs*
Rebecca, *Ribqā*
Rechabites, *Rekhābīm* (pl.)
Reguel, *Rĕ-'ū-ēl*
Rehob, *Rĕchōb*
Rehoboam, *Rĕchab'ām*
Rehoboth (Ir), *Rĕchōbōth 'Ir*
Rephaim, *Rĕphā'īm*
Rephidim, *Rĕphīdīm*
Resen, *Rĕsen*
Reuben, *Rĕ'ūbēn*
Rezon, *Rĕzōn*

Rezeph, *Rĕ'ṣeph*
Rezin, *Rĕṣin*
Riblah, *Riblā*
Rimmon, *Rimmōn*
Riphath, *Rīphath*
Rogel, *Rōgēl*
Rogelim, *Rōgĕlīm*
Rosh, *Rō'sh*
Ruth, *Rūth*

Sabbath, *Shabbāth*
Sabta, *Sabtā*
Sabtechah, *Sabtĕkhā*
Salchah, *Salĕkhā*
Salem, *Shālēm*
Samaria, *Shōmĕrōn*
Samson, *Shimshōn*
Samuel, *Shemū'ēl*
Sanballat, *Sanballāṭ*
Sarah, *Sārā*
Sargon, *Sarĕgōn*
Satan, *Sāṭān*
Saul, *Shā'ūl*
Seir, *Sē'īr*
Sela (town) *Sĕla'*
Selah (musical sign) *Sĕlā*
Sennacherib, *Sanchērīb*
Sephar, *Sĕphar*
Sepharad, *Sĕphārad*
Sepharvaim, *Sĕpharváyim*
Seraiah, *Sĕrāyā*
Seraphim, *Sĕrāphīm*
Serug, *Sĕrūg*
Seth, *Shēth*
Shaalbim, *Sha'albīm*, *Sha'ălabbīm*
Shaleph, *Shĕleph*
Shalim, *Sha'ălīm*
Shallum, *Shallūm*
Shalman, *Shālĕmān*
Shalmaneser, *Shalman'ēser*
Shamgar, *Shamgār*

Shaphan, *Shāphān*
Sharon, *Shārōn*
Sheba (Benjamite), *Shĕba'*
Sheba (in Arabia), *Shĕbā'*; (in Ethiopia), *Sēbā'*
Shebna, *Shebnā*, *Shebnā*
Shechem, *Shĕkhĕm*
Shekel (coin), *Shĕqel*
Shem, *Shēm*
Shemaiah, *Shĕma'yā*
Sheshbazzar, *Shēshbaṣṣar*
Shiloh, *Shīlō*
Shimei, *Shim'ī*
Shinar, *Shin'ār*
Shisak, *Shīshaq*
Shittim, *Shiṭṭīm*
Shuah, *Shūăch*
Shunem, *Shūnēm*
Shur, *Shūr*
Sibmah, *Sibmā*
Siddim, *Siddīm*
Sidon, *Ṣīdōn*
Sihon, *Sīchōn*
Sihor, *Shīhōr*
Siloah, *Shīlōăch*
Simeon, *Shim'ōn*
Sinai, *Sīnay*
Sirion, *Shiryōn*
Sisera, *Sīsĕrā'*
So, *Sō'*
Sochoh, *Sōkhō*
Sodom, *Sĕdōm*
Solomon, *Shelōmō*
Sorek, *Sōrēq*
Succoth, *Sukkōth*
Susa(n), *Shūshan*

Taanach, *Ta'ănākh*
Tabor, *Tābōr*
Tabrimmon, *Tabrimmōn*
Tadmor, *Tadmōr*

Tahpanhes, *Tachpanchēs*
Tamar, *Tāmār* (palm)
Tammuz, *Tammūz*
Tappuach, *Tappūăch*
Tarshish, *Tarshīsh*
Tekoah, *Tĕqūă'*
Tel Abib, *Tēl .Ibīb*
Telassar, *Tela'śśār*
Tema, *Tēmā'*
Teman, *Tēmān*
Terah, *Tĕrach*
Teraphim, *Tĕrāphīm*
Thebez, *Tēbēṣ*
Tibni, *Tibnī*
Tiglath-Pileser, *Tiglath pil'ĕser* (also *pĕlĕser*)
Timnah, *Timnā*
Timnath Serah, *Timnath Sĕrach*
Tiphsach, *Tiphsach*
Tiras, *Tīrās*
Tirhakah, *Tirhāqā*
Tirzah, *Tirṣā*
Tob, *Ṭōb*
Tobiah, *Ṭōbiyyā*
Togarmah, *Tōgarmā*
Tola, *Tōlā*
Tou, *Tō'ū*
Tubal-Cain, *Tūbal Qáyin*
Tyre, *Ṣōr*

Ulai, *'Ūlay*
Uphaz, *'Ūphāz*
Ur, *'Ūr*
Uriah, *'Ūriyyā*
Urim and Tummim, *'Ūrīm vĕtummīm*
Uz, *'Ūṣ*
Uzal, *'Uzal*
Uzziah, *'Uzziyyā*, *'Uzziyyāhū*

Vashti, *Vashtī*

Zadok, *Ṣādōq*
Zalmon, *Ṣalmōn*
Zamzummim, *Zamzummīm*
Zanoah, *Zānōăch*
Zarephath, *Ṣārĕphath*
Zaretan, *Ṣartān*
Zebah (Midianite), *Zĕbach*
Zeboim, *Ṣĕbō'īm* and *Ṣĕbōyīm*
Zebul, *Zĕbūl*
Zebulon, *Zebūlūn*

Zechariah, *Zĕkharyā, Zekharyāhū*
Zedad, *Ṣĕdād*
Zedekiah, *Ṣidqiyyāhū*
Zela, *Ṣēla'*
Zemaraim, *Ṣĕmārăyīm*
Zephaniah, *Ṣĕphanyāhū*
Zerah, *Zĕrach*
Zered, *Zĕred*
Zereda, *Ṣĕrēdā*
Zerubbabel, *Zĕrubbābĕl*
Ziba, *Ṣībā*

Ziklag, *Ṣiqlag*
Zilpah, *Zilpā*
Zimri, *Zimrī*
Zinnah, *Ṣinnā*
Zion, *Ṣiyyōn*
Ziph, *Zīph*
Zipporah, *Ṣippōrā*
Zoan, *Ṣō'an*
Zoar, *Ṣō'ar*
Zobah, *Ṣōbā, Ṣōbā'*
Zorah, *Ṣor'ā*
Zuph, *Ṣūph*
Zuzim, *Zūzīm* (pl.)

V.

SURVEY OF THE COMPOSITION FROM DIFFERENT DOCUMENTS OF SEVERAL BOOKS OF THE OLD TESTAMENT.

PRELIMINARY NOTE.—The Hebrew Bible (differing from the arrangement of the Hebrew, Latin, German [and English] Bibles) is divided into the following three parts :—

1. Law (*Tōrā*). This comprises the so-called "Five Books of Moses."
2. Prophets (*Nĕbī'īm*), including
    a. The Former Prophets (*i.e.*, those which stand first in the Canon) : Joshua, Judges, Samuel and Kings.
    b. The Latter Prophets (*i.e.*, those which follow in the Canon) : Isaiah, Jeremiah, Ezekiel, the Book of the Twelve [Minor prophets].
3. Writings (*Kĕthūbīm*, by the Greeks called *Hagiographa*, *i.e.*, "Holy Writings"), in the following order, Psalms, Proverbs, Job, Canticles, Ruth, Lamentations, Ecclesiastes, Esther, Daniel, Ezra, Nehemiah, Chronicles.

The letter *a* with the number of the verse signifies the first half of the verse, *b* the second half. An asterisk signifies that a redactor's hand has meddled with the phraseology of the document in question. On the ground of more or less certain tokens the text of the several books is assigned to the different documents as follows * :—

The First Book of Moses (Genesis).

J^1 (Jahwist[1], p. 37 f.): IV. 16^b-24 (on v. 23 f. cf. p. 3). VI. 1-4. IX. 20-27 (omitting the gloss, "Ham, the father of," in v. 22). XI. 1-9, and from Chap. XII. onwards very much which now cannot be distinguished from J^2. "The Blessing of Jacob" (XLIX. 1^b-27, cf. p. 15 f.) was also undoubtedly adopted by J^1.

J^2 (pp. 31 f., 38 ff.): II. 4^b-9, 15—IV. 16^a. V. 29. VI. 5-6, 7*, 8. VII. 1-2, 3*, 4-5, 7-10, 12, 16^b, 17^b, 22, 23^{ac}. VIII. 2^b, 3^a, 6-12, 13^b, 20-22. X. 8, 10-15, 18^b, 19, 21, 25-30. XI. 28*-30 (?). XII. 1-4^a, 6-20. XIII. 1-5, 6^c-11^a, 12^c-18. XV. 1^{bd}, 2^a, 3^b, 4, 6, 9-12^a, 17-18. XVI. 1^b, 2, 4-7, 11-14. XVIII. XIX. 1-28, 30-38 (?). XXI. 1^a, 2^a, 7, 33. XXII. 20*-24. XXIV. XXV. 1-5, 11^b, 18, 21-26^a, 27-34. XXVI. 1^{ac}, 2^a (to "spake"), 3^a (to "land"), 6-14, 16-17, 19-33. XXVII. 1^a, 2-4^a, 5-10, 14-15, 17, 18^a, 20, 24-27, 29^{bc}, 30^{ac}, 31-32, 35-39^a, 40-41, 43, 45. XXVIII. 10, 13-16, 19^a. XXIX. 2-14, 26^b, 31-35. XXX. 3^c, 4^b-5, 7, 9-16, 20^b, 21, 22^c, 24^b, 25, 27, 29—XXXI. 1^a, 3, 21^b, 25,

---

* A really vivid picture of the manner in which the documents are interwoven cannot be given by merely stating the numbers of the verses. And it is just as impossible to state with each single verse or section whether it is assigned to the document in question by all investigators or by the majority or only by a few. In the Pentateuch and in the Book of Joshua it is only with regard to P that something approaching to unanimity has been reached. To see at a glance the manner in which the sources are mingled the best books to use are Haupt's Bible, mentioned above, on p. 35 (the so-called Rainbow Bible), the work also mentioned there, "Genesis mit äusserer Unterscheidung der Quellenschriften" (German translation in eight different types), and, finally, "Die Heilige Schrift des Alten Test.", by Kautzsch and others, where the various documents are indicated on the margin by letters (J, E, P, &c.).

OF SEVERAL BOOKS OF THE OLD TESTAMENT. 227

27, 38-40, 46, 48^a, 49^b-52. XXXII. 4-14^a, 23, 25-32.
XXXIII. 1-5^a, 6-10, 11^b-17. XXXIV. 1^b, 2^b-3^{ac}, 5, 7,
11-12, 19, 25*, 26*, 30-31. XXXVII. 3, 4, 21*, 25^{bc}-27,
28^b, 32, 33, 35. XXXVIII. XXXIX. 1*, 2^{ac}, 3^a, 4^{ac}, 5^{a*},
6^{bc}, 7^b-23. XL. 1^b, 3^b, 5^b, 15^b. XLI. 31, 41. XLII. 2^a,
4^b, 5 (?), 6^{ab}, 7, 27-28^{ab}, 38—XLIII. 13, 15-23^a, 24—
XLV. 1^a, 2^{ac}, 4^b, 5^{ac}, 10^a, 13, 14, 28 (?). XLVI. 1^a, 28—
XLVII. 5^a (v. 4^a, "they spake to Pharaoh," is repeated
from 3^b by mistake), 6^b (before 5^b, 6^a), 13-27^a, 29-31.
XLVIII. 2^b, 8^a, 9^b, 10^a, 13-14, 17-19. XLIX. 33^b.
L. 1-11, 14.

E (cf. pp. 32 f., 43 ff.): XV. 1*, 2^b, 3^a, 5. XX. 1-17. XXI. 6, 8-
32^a. XXII. 1-13, 19. XXVII. 1^b, 4^b, 11-13, 16, 18^b-19, 21-
23, 28, 29^a, 30^b, 33-34, 39^b, 42, 44. XXVIII. 11-12, 17-18,
20—XXIX. 1, 15-23, 25, 26^a, 27-28^a, 30. XXX. 1^b-3^{ab},
6, 8, 17, 18*, 19, 20^{ac}, 22^b, 23-24^a, 26, 28. XXXI. 2, 4-18^a,
19-20, 21^{ac}, 22-24, 26, 28-37, 41-45, 53—XXXII. 3, 14^b-22,
24. XXXIII. 5^b, 11^a, 18^b-20. XXXV. 1-4, 6^b-8.
XXXVII. 2^{bc}, 5^a, 6-8^a, 9-11, 19-20, 22, 28^{ac}, 29-31, 34, 36.
XXXIX. 2^b, 3^b, 4^{bd}, 5^b, 6^a, 7^a. XL. 1^a, 2, 3^a, 4, 5^a, 6-15^a,
16—XLI. 30, 32, 33, 37-40, 42-45, 46^b-50^a, 51—XLII.
1, 2^b-4^a, 6^c, 8-26, 28^c-37. XLIII. 14, 23^b. XLV. 1^b, 2^b,
3-4^a, 5^{bd}, 6-9, 10^{bc}-12, 15-18, 21^c-27. XLVI. 1^c-3^{ab}, 4, 5^a.
XLVII. 12. XLVIII. 1-2^a, 8^b-9^a, 10^b-12, 15-16, 20-22.
L. 15-22^a, 23-26.

JE (*i.e.*, Sections concerning which it cannot now be determined whether they belonged to *J* or *E*, or how they have
been constructed out of the two; cf. p. 33): XXXV.
16-22^a. XXXVI. 31-39. XXXVII. 2^b, 12-18, 23-25^a.
XLI. 34-36.

P (Priests' Code; cf. p. 106 ff.): I. 1—II. 4^a. V. 1-28, 30-32.
VI. 9-22. VII. 6, 11, 13-16^a, 17^{a*}, 18-21, 24. VIII. 1,
2^a, 3^b-5, 13^a, 14-19. IX. 1-17, 28—X. 7, 20, 22-23, 31-32.

15 *

XI. 10-27, 28*, 31-32. XII. 4ᵇ, 5. XIII. 6ᵃᵇ, 11ᵇ, 12ᵃᵇ.
XVI. 1ᵃ, 3, 15—XVII. 27. XIX. 29. XXI. 1ᵇ, 2ᵇ-5.
XXIII. XXV. 7-11ᵃ, 12-17, 19-20, 26ᵇ. XXVI. 34-35.
XXVIII. 1-9. XXIX. 24, 28ᵇ, 29. XXX. 1ᵃ, 4ᵃ, 22ᵃ.
XXXI. 18ᵇᶜᵈ. XXXIII. 18ᵃ. [XXXIV. 1ᵃ, 2ᵃ, 3ᵃ, 4, 6,
8-10, 13-18, 20-24, 25*.]* XXXV. 6ᵃ, 9-12ᵃ, 13ᵃ, 15,
22ᵇ-29. XXXVI. 6-8ᵃ, 40-43. XXXVII. 1, 2ᵃ. XLI.
46ᵃ. XLVI. 6-7. XLVII. 5ᵇ, 6ᵃ, 7-11, 27ᵇ, 28. XLVIII.
3-6. XLIX. 1ᵃ, 28ᵇ, 33ᵃᶜ. L. 12-13.

R Signifies additions, due to the redactor who blended *J* and
E into one work (*JE*ʳ; cf. p. 61 f.), or to the one who
united *JE* and Deuteronomy *JED*ʳ; cf. p. 94 f.), or finally
to the one who joined *JED* and *P* (cf. p. 119 f.): it also
signifies verses or sections originally belonging to *J*, *E* or
P, but subsequently transplanted by a redactor from
another context into their present position: II. 10-14. IV.
25-26. VI. 7*. VII. 3*, 23ᵇ. IX. 18-19. X. 9, 16-18ᵃ, 24.
XIV. (cf. the Note on p. 119). XV. 7-8, 12ᵇ-16, 19-21.
XVI. 8-10. XX. 18. XXI. 32ᵇ, 34. XXII. 14-18.
XXV. 6. XXVI. 1ᵇ, 2ᵇ, 3ᵇ-5,15, 18. XXVII.46. XXVIII.
19ᵇ. XXXI. 1ᵇ, 47, 48ᵇ, 49ᵃ. XXXII. 33. XXXIV.
26*, 27-29. XXXV. 5, 12ᵇ, 13ᵇ, 14. XXXVI. 1-5, 8ᵇ-
30. XXXVII. 5ᵇ, 8ᵇ. XXXIX. 1*. XLI. 50ᵇ- XLII.
28ᶜ. XLV. 19-21ᵃᵇ. XLVI. 1ᵇ, 3ᶜ, 5ᵇ, 8-27. XLVIII. 7.
XLIX. 28ᵃ. L. 22ᵇ.

The Second Book of Moses (Exodus).

J, to whom are almost unanimously ascribed: VIII. 4-10,
11*, 16-20, 24ᵇ-28. IX. 1-7. XI. 4-8. XII. 21-27*, 29,

---

* The ascription of these verses to *P* is disputed; others think that they belong to a still later time!

30, 34, 38? 39. The groundwork of XIII. 3-16, but revised by JE^r or JED^r (cf. above, on Genesis, under R), 21, 22. XIV. 5, 6, 11-14, 19ᵇ, 21*. XVI. 4, 5, 19-21*, 25-30? (others say P or else, in part [v. 28-30] JED^r). XVIII. 1ᵇ.

E: I. 15-20ᵃ. III. 10-15. VII. 20ᵇ, 21ᵃ. VIII. 21-24ᵃ. XI. 1-3. XIII. 17-19. XIV. 7, 16? 19ᵃ. XV. 1-18ᵃ (the so-called Song at the Sea; questionable whether it was received by E or not earlier than by a later redactor [JE^r?]), 20, 21. XVII. 8-16. XVIII. 1ᵃ, 2*, 3-27. XX. 18-21 (originally the continuation of XIX. 15-19). XXXI. 18ᵇ. XXXII. 1-6.

JE: I. 6, 7*, 8-12, 14*, 20ᵇ-22. II. 1-23ᵃ (v. 1-10 and 15 almost entirely E; v. 11-14 and 16-23ᵃ almost entirely J). III. 1-9, 16-22. IV. V. 1—VI. 1. VII. 14-18, 23-29. IX. 13-35. X. 1-29 (of which J claims most of 1-11, as well as 16-19, 28-29). XII. 31-33 (mainly perhaps E), 35-37 (the same), 42? XIV. 9*, 10*, 20, 24-28, 30, 31. XV. 22-27 (in 25ᵇ, 26, a clear trace of JED^r). XVII. 1*, 2-7. XIX. 2ᵇ-25 (mostly from E). XX. 1-17* (the Decalogue; cf. above, p. 7 f.; if already admitted by E into his document, it is however not without traces of JED^r and possibly [v. 11] $JEDP^r$). XX. 22—XXIII. 19*, the so-called "Book of the Covenant" [so called from XXIV. 7; cf. above, p. 29 f.]; the prevalent theory is that E had already admitted it into his document. XX. 22 and [on account of the address in the plural] XXII. 20ᵇ, 21, 23, 24ᵇ, 30 and XXIII. 9ᵇ, 13 are probably to be considered redactional additions. XXIII. 20-23 (mainly E, but with traces of revision by JE^r and probably also JED^r). XXIV. 1-14, 15*, 18*. XXXII. 7-14 (according to the prevalent view, composed by JE^r, according to others, touched also by JED^r), 15-20 (mainly E), 21-25. XXXIII. (7-11 certainly belong to E). XXXIV. 1-28 (mainly J, but with expansions; in v. 10-13 and 24 a clear trace of JED^r).

P: I. 1-5, 7*, 13, 14.* II. 23ᵇ ("then sighed, &c.")-25. VI. 2-13, 14-30 (late addition). VII. 1-13, 19, 20ᵃ (to "commanded"), 21ᵇ, 22. VIII. 1-3, 12-15. IX. 8-12. XI. 9—XII. 20, 28, 40, 41, 43-51. XIII. 1-2, 20. XIV. 1-4, 8, 9*, 10*, 15, 16? 17, 18, 21*, 22-23, 29. XV. 19 (redactional gloss on the Song at the Sea). XVI. 1-3, 6-8 (revised), 9-18, 19-21*, 22-24, 31-36 (v. 36 a later gloss). XVII. 1* (to "Rephidim"). XIX. 1, 2ᵃ. XXIV. 15*, 16, 17, 18*. XXV.—XXXI. 18ᵃ (in XXIX. 9 "Aaron and his sons" is a later gloss). XXXIV. 29-35 (if not a later addition). XXXV.—XL. (more recent parallels to XXV.—XXX).

The Third Book of Moses (Leviticus).

The contents of Leviticus in great part come from P (though not without supplements and glosses, as, *e.g.*, VI. 13 [*Heb.*, 20, *Eng.*, "in the day when he is anointed"], X. 16-20, XIV. 31 ["such as he is able to get"], XXVII., and traces of revision). Thus, as Benzinger's convincing analysis has shown, Chap. XVI. is composed of two laws: v. 1-4, 6, 11ᵃ*, 12, 13, 34ᵇ [29-34ᵃ], containing the older; and v. 5, 7-10, 14-28, the younger. H, the so-called Law of Holiness (see above, p. 100 f.), forms another leading constituent, but in it, too, it is impossible to mistake traces of later revision and subsequent blending with passages from P. Approximately, Chaps. XVII.-XXVI. are attributed to H. The most recent analysis by Driver and White, in P. Haupt's English edition of the Bible, attributes the following to H:—X. 10, 11; XI. 2ᵇ-23, 41-47; XVII.-XXII. (except the introductory formulas, such as

XVII. 1, 2; XVIII. 1, 2ᵃ; XIX. 1, 2ᵃ, &c., and a few other additions); XXIII. 10ᵇ-12, 15-20, 22, 39ᵇ, 40-43; XXIV. 15ᵇ, 16ᵃ, 17-21, 22ᵇ; XXV. 2ᵇ-10ᵃ, 13-15, 17-22, 24, 25, 35-40ᵃ, 43, 47, 53, 55; XXVI.

There are no traces in Leviticus of J and E or JE^r and JED^r.

The Fourth Book of Moses (Numbers).

J Amongst other passages : X. 29-32, XXI. 1-3.

E Amongst other passages: XXI. 4*, 5-9; XXXII. 16, 17.

JE: X. 33-36, XI. (mainly from J). XII. (probably E for the most part). XIII. 17ᵇ-20, 22-24, 26*, 27-31, 32*, 33. XIV. 1ᵇ, 3, 4, 8, 9, 11-25 (if from E; others hold that the passages come from JE^r or JED^r), 30-33, 39-45. XVI. 1ᵇ, 2*, 12-15, 25, 26, 27 -32ᵃ, 33, 34. XX. 1ᵇ, 3ᵃ, 4, 5, 7ᵇ, 8, 9, 10ᵇ, 11, 13-21. XXI. 11ᵇ-31, 32-35? (later addition to JE? perhaps rather to JED^r). XXII. 2— XXV. 5 (in Chap. XXII. 22-34 contains J's account; Chap. XXIII. comes chiefly from E., Chap. XXIV. from J. Only Chap. XXIV. 20-24 is regarded by almost everyone as a later addition). XXXII. 1ᵇ, 2ᵃ, 3, 5 (6-15, 20-27, in a later revised form, as also v. 31-33 probably is), 34-42 (probably in great part from E; in v. 38 the words "their names being changed" [in speech] is evidently a marginal gloss, required to avoid the word Baal).

P: I.-X. 28 (not without subsequent additions). XIII. 1-17ᵃ, 21, 25, 26*, 32*. XIV. 1ᵃ, 2, 5-7, 10, 26-29, 34-38. XV. (the close, v. 37-41, perhaps from H, see above, on Leviticus). In Chaps. XVI. and XVIII. two P-accounts are interwoven with *JE*'s (see above). To the one belongs, in the main: XVI. 2*, 3-7ª, 19-24, 27ª, 32ᵇ; XVII. 6-28; to the other: XVI. 1ª, 7ᵇ, 8-11, 16-18, 35—XVII. 5. Further: XVIII. 1—XIX. 22, XX. 1ª (to "month"), 2, 3ᵇ, 6, 7ᵃᶜ, 10ª, 12, 22-29; XXI. 10, 11ª; XXII. 1; XXV. 6—XXXI; XXXII. 1ª*, 2ᵇ? 4, 18, 19, 28-30; XXXIII. (compilation by one of the latest redactors, for the most part founded on *P*); XXXIV.—XXXVI.

The Fifth Book of Moses (Deuteronomy).

On the controversy respecting the extent of the so-called "Original Deuteronomy," cf. above, p. 63 f. The following passages are there regarded as constituents of the book in its older form (*D*): IV. 44-49; V. 1—X. 5, 10—XI. 28; XII.-XXVI. 15; XXVIII. 1-68; XXXI. 9-13.

These are regarded as later additions (*Dt*): I. 1—IV. 40; XI. 29-32; XXVII. 1-4, 8-26; XXVIII. 69—XXXI. 8, 24-30 [XXXII. 1-43; on which cf. above, p. 93]; XXXII. 44-47; XXXIV. 1ᵇ, 5, 6, 11-12. Some of the still later passages are XIV. 1-21; XXIV. 8, 9; XXVI. 16-19? XXXIV. 2, 3.

These must have come from *JE*: XXVII. 5-7 (to speak precisely, probably from *E*); XXXI. 14-23 (not without traces of revision) [XXXIII., see above, p. 40 f.]; XXXIV. 1ᶜ, 4, 10.

From *P*: IV. 41-43; X. 6-9; XXXII. 48-52; XXXIV. 1ª, 7-9.

The Book of Joshua.

J (Jahwist: see above, on Genesis), amongst other passages: XV. 14-19, 63; XVII. 11-18; XIX. 47.

E (Elohist): I. 1, 2*, 10, 11*. XXIV. (with numerous traces of a later, probably Deuteronomistic hand; thus in v. 1ᵇ, 2, 6, 7, 8, 10, 11, 13, 26ᵃ, 31; in v. 29ᵇ a trace of *P* must be found).

JE (See above, on Genesis, and cf. the remark below on *Dt*): II. 1-9ᵃ, 12-23. III. 1-3, 4ᵇ-6, 8—IV. 12, 15-18, 20. V. 2*, 3, 8, 9, 13 to VII. 26 (Chap. VII. substantially *J*, but, like Chap. VI., not without traces of *Dt*). VIII. 3-26, 28, 29. IX. 3-15ᵃ, 16, 22, 23*, 24-26. X. 1ᵃ*, 3-24 (in 12ᵇ and 13 a citation from the "Book of the Upright Ones"; cf. above, p. 2), 26, 27. XI. 1-9 (with traces of *Dt* in v. 2, 3, 6, 8), 11ᵇ. XIX. 9, 49, 50.

Dt (Deuteronomistic redactor, of whose hand there are manifold traces also in the passages assigned to *JE*): I. 3-9, 12-18. II. 9ᵇ-11, 24. III. 7. IV. 14, 21-24. V. 1. VIII. 1, 2, 27, 30—IX. 2, 27ᶜ (a dislocated clause). X. 1*, 2, 25, 28-43. XI. 10-20, 21-23 ? (or added later ?). XII.—XIII. 14. XIV. 6-15 (perhaps founded on *E*). XXI. 43-45 (in the Heb. text, v. 41-43, because 36, 37 are missing). XXII. 1-6. XXIII.

P (Priests' Code): IV. 13, 19. V. 10-12. IX. 15ᵇ, 17-21. XIII. 15-33 (with traces of a later hand). XIV. 1-5. XV. 1-12, 20-44, 48-62. XVI. 4-8. XVII. 1ᵃ, 3, 4, 9*, 10ᵃ. XVIII. 1, 11ᵃ, 12-28. XIX. 1-8, 10-46, 48, 51 (the entire chapter was revised by R, who worked with *JE* before him). XX. 1-3, 7-9. XXI. 1-11ᵃ, 13ᵇ-40. XXII. 9-34 (the text of *P* doubtless rests on an older foundation, but was revised by a more recent hand). XXIV. 29ᵇ.

R (Latest redactor and isolated later additions): III. 4ᵃ. V. 4-7. IX. 23*, 27ᵃᵇ. XV. 13, 45-47. XVII. 1ᵇ and 2 (founded on *JE*), 5 ? 6. XX. 4-6. XXI. 11ᵇ-13ᵃ. XXII. 7, 8.

In XV. 26-28 the names "Shema, Moladah, Beth-pelet, Hazar-shual, Beer-sheba, and the places belonging to them" were interpolated from Neh. xi. 26 ff., and therefore are not reckoned in v. 32. In XVII. 9 the second clause comes from another context.

The Book of Judges.

J (Jahwist; see above, on Genesis): I. 1^b-3, 5-7, 9-17, 19—II. 1^a, 5^b, 23? (this account of J's, which contains for the most part parallels to the Book of Joshua, is now transferred by the introductory words into the time after the death of Joshua. In II. 1^b, 5^a, the Jahwist's original narrative has been displaced by another).

H^1 (An older stratum of the ancient Hero-Stories *), constituting the nucleus of the Book of Judges; see above, p. 23): VIII. 4-10^a, (to "Karkor"), 11-21, 24-27^a, 29-32. IX. ? (in any case from a very ancient source).

H (Hero-Stories, from the early part of the Kingly period; see above, p. 21 ff.) : III. 15^b-26 (questionable whether from the same hand), 27 and 28? IV. 4-22. V. 1-31^a (Song of Deborah; see above, p. 4 f.). VI, 2^b, 3*, 4-6^a 11-32, 33*, 36-40? (perhaps stood originally after v. 17). VII. 1*, 2-11, 13-22, 23-25? (if 23, 24, 25^b were not from Ri). VIII. 1-3, 22-23? X. 8^a. XI. 1-11 (with traces of revision by Ri), 30—XII. 6. XIII. 2, 3, 5^b-7^a, 7^c-13^a, 14^b—XIV. 4^a, 5-18, 19^c—XV. 19. XVI. 1-31^{ab}.

---

* Part of the critics (see above, the footnote to p. 27) consider the various strata of H to be continuations of the Jahwistic (J) and Elohistic (E) sources employed in the Pentateuch.

ri (fragments of a list of Judges, from the later Kingly period; see above, p. 45): X. 1-5. XII. 8-15. XV. 20.

Ri (Compiler of the Deuteronomistic Book of Judges, which was constructed on the foundation of *II* and *ri*; see above, pp. 21 ff., 94 f.): II. 6-12, 14-16, 18-22.* III. 4-10, 12-15^a, 27 and 28? 29, 30. IV. 1-3, 23, 24. V. 31^b. VI. 1, 2^a, 6^b, 33^b, 34? 35. VII. 12. VIII. 10^b, 27^b, 28, 33-35. X. 6, 7*, 8^b-18. XII. 7. XIII. 1. XIV. 4^b. XVI. 31^c.

N and *N*^{1} (Pre-Deuteronomic compilers of a few narratives which now form the Appendix to the Book of Judges; see above, p. 24). The following must belong to *N*:—XVII. 1, 5, 7*, 8-11, 13. XVIII. 1^{bc}, 2*, 3-6, 7*, 8-10^a, 11-13, 14*, 15*, 16, 17*, 18*, 19, 20*, 21-29, 31. XIX. 1*, 2-30. Chaps. XX. and XXI. also originally came from this source, but have been thoroughly revised by a hand related to the Priests' Code (*P*). The traces of a duplicate narrative are clearly discernible in the accretions, XX. 11, 14 (probably a continuation properly of 3^a), 36^b (36^b-46 form an evident parallel to v. 29-35^a), 48. XXI. 9. In the older source the assemblies of the people take place at Mizpah, in the younger at Bethel. Budde (Die Bücher Richter u. Samuel, p. 151) attributes to the Mizpah-Source XX.

---

* Others hold that Chap. II. 16 ff. contains numerous elements from *E* (see the note on p. 234); Moore (Commentary on Judges, New York, 1895, p. 63 f.) assigns to that source v. 6, 8-10, 13, 14^a, 16, 17, 20, 21; III. 1^a, 3, 4; but v. 23^a, III. 2, perhaps, also 5 and 6 to *J*, and almost all the rest to the Deuteronomistic redactor. In the Gideon Histories he attributes to *J*, VI. 2-6, in part; 11-24, 34. VII. 1, 9-11, 13-15, 16-20, in part; 21, 22^{b*}. VIII. 4-21, 24-27^a, in substance; 30, 31. IX.: to *E* VI. 2-6, in part; 7-10, 25, 32, 33, 36-40, 35^a. VII. 2-8, 16-20 in part; 22^a, 22^{b*}, 23?, 24, 25. VIII. 1-3, 29. In Chaps. XVII. and XVIII., the account which we have followed—Kittel's analysis—in designating *N* is thought by Moore to belong in all probability to *J*, the original form of the narrative in Chap. XIX. ff., perhaps also being his work.

1ᵃ*, 1ᵇ, 3ᵇ-10, 3ᵃ, 14, 19, 29, 36ᵇ-38, 40-42ᵃ, and part of 43-48; to the Bethel-Source, 1ᵃ*, 2, 11-13, 15, 17, 20-28, 30-33ᵃ, 34ᵃ, 35-36ᵃ, and a part of 43-48.

N^1 XVII. 2-4, 6, 12. XVIII. 1ᵃ, 2*, 7*, 10ᵇ, 14*, 15*, 18*, 20*, 30.

R (The post-exilic editor or editors of our present Book of Judges; see above p. 120): I. 1ᵃ, 4, 8, 18. II. 1ᵇ-5ᵃ, 13, 17. III. 1-3, 11, 31. VI. 7-10. X. 7*. XI. 29. XIII. 4, 5ᵃ, 7ᵇ, 13ᵇ, 14ᵃ. XVII. 7*. XVIII. 17*. XIX. 1*. XX. 27, 28? XXI. 14ᵇ, 25.

The following are some of the latest glosses:—VI. 26, 28 ("the second"); XII. 4ᵇ ("Ye are fugitives of Ephraim," &c.: in v. 1 the Ephraimite attack is explained quite differently); XVIII. 17 (the words "came in thither, and took the graven image, and the ephod, and the teraphim, and the molten image," as well as "with the six hundred men girt with weapons of war").

? Passages of doubtful origin: XI. 12-28. XIV. 19ᵃᵇ.

The First Book of Samuel.

S (Saul-Source, a Judahite or Benjamite history of Saul, dating from the tenth or ninth century; cf. above p. 27 f.): IX. 1-8, 10—X. 7, 9-16. XII. 1-8ᵃ, 9-11, 15. XIII. 2-7ᵃ, 15ᵇ-18, 23. XIV. 1-46.

Da (David-Source; in all probability a Judahite history of David, contemporary with *S*, perhaps from the same hand; cf. above, p. 27 f.): XVI. 14-23. XVIII. 6ᵃᶜ, 7,

8ᵇ-11 (v. 6ᵃ and 8ᶜ, 10, 11 are not in the Greek Bible, and perhaps come from another source), 20, 21ᵃ, 22-26ᵃ, 27. XX. 1ᵇ-3, 11, 18-39. XXI. 1. XXIII. 1-5, 7-13, 19—XXIV. 13, 15-23. XXV. 1ᵇ-44. XXVII. XXVIII. 1-2, 4-16, 19ᵇ-25 (moreover the entire section, XXVIII. 3-25, should come, in order of time, after Chap. XXX.). XXIX.-XXXI.

SS (A considerably later history of Samuel and Saul, probably Ephraimite, a combination of diverse traditions, perhaps dating from the second half of the eighth century; cf. above, p. 45 f.): I. 1-5ᵃ, 6-28. II. 11-22ᵃ, 23-26. III. 1-21ᵃ. VIII. X. 17-24. XV. ? XVII. 1-11, 12-13, in part (the text there is in utter confusion), 14ᵃ—XVIII. 5. In part of this last section it is indeed questionable whether we have *SS*, especially in the verses and portions of verses not found in the Greek Bible, viz., XVII. 12ᵇ-14, 16-31, 38ᵇ, 41, 48*, 50, 55—XVIII. 5 (at XVII. 55 ff. it is evidently intended to narrate the first meeting of Saul and David, whilst according to XVII. 32 ff. there had already been a conversation before the fight. 54 and 57 also could not have stood side by side in *one* source). XVIII. 12-19 and 28-30 (in these two sections also the Greek text has not 12ᵇ, 17-19, 29ᵇ, 30). XIX. 1, 2, 4-17. XXI. 2-10. XXII. XXVI.

E (A narrative compiled in the kingdom of Ephraim in the ninth or eighth century; cf. above, p. 40)*: IV. 1ᵇ-18ᵃ, 19-21. V. VI. 1-14, 16, 18ᵇ—VII. 1.

---

* As in the Book of Judges, so here, several critics (Schrader, Cornill, &c., and last of all Budde in "The Books of Samuel in Hebrew," the eighth part of Paul Haupt's English Edition of the Bible, Lpzg., 1894), have apportioned the contents of the four ancient documents which we have distinguished above amongst the various strata of the Jahwistic (*J*) and Elohistic (*E*) sources which we have mentioned in connection with the Pentateuch and the book of Joshua. Thus Budde holds that the sources designated *S* and *Da* by us are in the main

238 SURVEY OF THE COMPOSITION FROM DIFFERENT DOCUMENTS

Ri (The Deuteronomistic editor of that form of the Book of Judges [see above, on the Book of Judges] the conclusion of which we probably now have in 1 Sam. xii.).

Dt (Deuteronomistic revision of the histories of Samuel, Saul, and David; see above, p. 94 f.): II. 27-31ª, 32ª, 33-36. VII. 2ᵇ-16. XIV. 47-51?

? (Passages of unknown origin): II. 1ᵇ-10. XVIII. 21ᵇ. XX. 4-10, 12-17. XXI. 11-16.

R (Redactional additions of various kinds, part of them probably early, and appended when the ancient sources were welded together, part of them not added till post-exilic times; see above, p. 120): I. 5ᵇ. II. 1ª. III. 21ᵇ. IV. 1ª, 18ᵇ, 22. VI. 15, 17, 18ª. VII. 2ª, 17. IX. 9. X. 8, 15-27. XI. 12-14. XIII. 1, 7ᵇ-15ª, 19-22. XIV. 52? XVI. 1-13. XVII. 12ª, 15. XVIII. 6ᵇ, 8ª, 26ᵇ. XIX. 3, 18-24. XX. 1ª, 40-42. XXIII. 6, 14ᵃᶜ, 15-18. XXV. 1ª. XXVIII. 3, 17, 18.

We regard the following as the latest additions (glosses):—II. 22ᵇ, 31ᵇ, 32ᵇ. VI. 19 (the words "fifty thousand men"). XI. 8ᵇ. XVI, 19* ("who is with the sheep"). XVII. 14ᵇ. XXIII. 14ᵇ. XXIV. 14. XXVIII. 19ª. XXX. 9ᵇ. XXXI. 7 ("and they that were beyond Jordan").

---

identical with J; our E (chaps. iv.-vi.) with E¹; SS with the Pentateuchal E², or (in many instances from chap. xvii. onwards) with E¹, less frequently (almost the whole of chap. xxii.) with J¹. In harmony with this a portion of the redactional additions are ascribed to the combiner of J and E (JEʳ). As to the rest, apart from the dispute whether the main documents reach to 1 Kings ii., considerable agreement has been reached in the analysis of the sources.

The Second Book of Samuel.

Je (Jerusalem-Source, an old history of David, written most probably in Jerusalem, in any case in Judah, dating from the time of Solomon or Rehoboam; see above, p. 25 ff)*: V. 3, 6^{ab}, 7^a, 8^a, 9-16. VI. IX.—XI. XII. 1-9, 13—XX. 22 (except some glosses; cf. on *R*).

Da (See on 1 Sam.): I. 1-4, 11, 12, 17-27 (on the Elegy, v. 18 ff., cf. above, pp. 2, 10 f.). II. 1-9, 10^b-12, 17—III. 1, 6^b-29, 31-39 (on the Elegy, v. 33^b f., cf. above, p. 10 f.). IV. 1-3, 5-12. V. 1, 2, 17-25. XXI. 15-22. XXIII. 8-39.

SS (See above, on 1 Sam.): I. 6-10, 13-16.

Dt (Deuteronomistic redactor): VII. 1-12, 14-29 (perhaps founded on an exemplar furnished by *Je*).

? (Passages of unknown origin): II. 13-16. III. 2-5. VIII. 1-6^a, 7-10, 13-14^a, 16-18. XXI. 1, 2^a, 3 (from "What")-14. XXII. 2^b-51 (of the same tenor as Ps. xviii.). XXIII. 1^b-7. XXIV.

R (See above, on 1 Sam.): I. 5. II. 10^a, 11. III. 6^a, 30. IV. 4. V. 4, 5, 7^b. VII. 13. VIII. 6^b, 11, 12, 14^b, 15. XII. 7^b-9^a? 9^b-12. XIV. 15-22? XX. 23-26. XXI. 2^b, 3^a (to "Gibeonites"). XXII. 1, 2^a. XXIII. 1^a.

These are probably to be considered as the latest additions (glosses): V. 6^c, 8^b. XIII. 8^a, 38^a (becomes

---

* Budde and others (see the preceding footnote) maintain that in this source also there are elements of the Jahwistic historical work.

superfluous if we put 37ª into its correct position after 37ᵇ). XV. 24* (additions: "and all the Levites with him" [instead of "and Abiathar"; cf. ver. 29], also "of the Covenant" [see v. 29!]; the words, "and Abiathar went up" are now incomprehensible). XXI. 9* (the words "at the beginning of barley-harvest").

The First Book of Kings.

Da (See above, on 1 Sam.): I., II. 13-26, 28-46.

Sa (Extracts from a biography of Solomon: the latter may have been part of the great Book of Kings, mentioned under K): III. 5-13? 16-28? IV. 1-4ª, 5-12, 13ª*, 14-19ª. V. 2, 3, 6? 7-15, 24, 25, 27, 28, 29-32? VI. 2-6, 8, 10, 15, 16*, 17, 23-27, 31, 33, 34, 36, 37, 38*. VII. 1-46, 51. VIII. 1-4*, 6*, 10-13 (on v. 12 and 13, cf. above, p. 2). IX.¦ 11ᵇ-18, 24? X. 1-10? 13? 16-20ª, 28-29? XI. 7*, 14-28, 40.

K (Extracts from the "Book of the Histories of the Kings of Judah," or "Book of the Histories of the Kings of Israel," which is cited by *Dt* for almost every king of Judah and Israel: on this so-called "great King's Book," cf. above, p. 70 f. We here partly put down to *K* certain sections, the origin of which from the "great King's Book" may be questioned, but which bear more or less of the stamp of authentic tradition): XII. 2, 1 (the transposition of these verses resulted from the interpolation of 3ª), 3ᵇ-11, 12* ("Jeroboam and" is an addition), 13, 14, 16, 18-20, 25. The basis of XIV. 1-18; [further] 25-28. XV. 16-22. XVI. 21-22, 24, 34? (on other traces of *K* cf. on *Dt*).

Dt (Deuteronomist: the principal compiler of our present "Book of Kings," who wrote under the influence of Deuteronomy; on this cf. above, p. 72 f.): II. 1-9 (v. 5-9 probably on an ancient groundwork), 27. III. 1, 2, 4, 14. IV. 13^b, 19^b—V. 1, 16-23, 26. VI. 7, 9, 11-14 (if not Z), 18-22, 28-30, 32, 35, 38*. VIII. 2*, 3^b, 9, 14-43, 52-64, 65*, 66. IX. 10, 11^a, 19-21, 25-28. X. 11-12? 14-15? 20^b-27. XI. 1-6, 7*, 8, 9^a, 11-13, 29-39 (perhaps founded on *K*; see above), 41-43. XII. 15, 26-31. XIII. 33^b, 34. XIV. 1-18 (founded on *K*).

From XIV. 23 onwards we ascribe to *Dt* all the formulæ which introduce or close the accounts of the individual reigns, although they contain all kinds of historical notices which doubtless come entirely from *K*: XIV. 19-24, 29-31 (after *K*: 20, 21, 30). XV. 1-5^{ab}, 7-15, 23-34 (after *K*: 2, 7, 10, 12, 13, 15? 23, 25, 27, 29, 33. XVI. 5, 6, 7? 8-11, 14-20, 23, 25-33 (after *K*: 8-11, 15-18, 23, 29. XXI. 20^b-22, 24. XXII. 39-54 (after *K*: 39, 42, 47-50, 52).

Dt^2 (The author, also Deuteronomistic, of certain additions to the Book of Kings compiled by *Dt*, dating from the second half of the Babylonian Exile; on this cf. above, p. 72 f.): III. 3, 15. V. 4-5 (or *Z*?). VI. 1. VIII. 44-51. IX. 1-9. XI. 9^b, 10. XVI. 12, 13.

? (Information additional to that given in the adjoining main account): IX. 23.

Pr (Histories of Prophets; extracts from a work relating to Elijah, dating from the ninth or eighth century; on it cf. above, p. 41): XVII. 1—XVIII. 30, 32^b—XIX. 9^a, 11* ("And Jahweh passed by," &c.), 12-21. XXI. 1-20^a, 27-29.

E (Ephraimite narratives; extracts from a historical work which appeared in the northern kingdom, dating probably from the ninth century; see above, p. 43) : XX. 1-12, 15-21 (in case 15-17^a, 19, 21^b are not to be ascribed to *Z*), 22, 23-25? 26-27, 29^a, 29^b and 30^a? 30^b, 31-34. XXII. 1-34, 35* (see on *Z*), 36, 37.

R (See above, on 1 Sam.) : II. 10-12.

Z (Subsequent additions. A part of them were perhaps adopted even by *Dt* or *Dt*^{2}. But most of them were doubtless not inserted till after the Exile in the King's Book arranged by *Dt* [or *Dt*^{2}] ; see above, p. 70 f.) : IV. 4^b, 13^a*. V. 4-5? VI. 16*. VII. 47-50. VIII. 1*, 2*, 4*, 5, 6*, 7-8? 65*. IX. 22. XII. 3^a, 12* (the words "Jeroboam, &c."), 17, 21-24, 32 — XIII. 33^a. XV. 5^c. XVI. 1-4? XVIII. 31-32^a. XIX. 9^b-11^a (to "stand upon the mount before Jahweh"). XX. 13, 14 (on 15-21 see above, on *E*), 22-25? 28, 29^b, and 30^a? 35-43. XXI. 23, 25, 26. XXII. 35* (the words "and the blood ran out of the wound into the bottom of the chariot"), 38.

The following are probably to be considered quite late glosses (and therefore for the most part are not in the Greek translation): IV. 4^b, 13 ("the villages of Jair, the son of Manasseh, which are in Gilead"). VI. 5 ("round about the walls of the house"). VII. 24 ("compassing the sea round about"), 42^c. VIII. 65 ("and seven days, fourteen days"). XI. 24 ("when David made the slaughter amongst the Aramæans"). XII. 27^c ("and return to Rehoboam, king of Judah"). 32 ("and he went up unto the altar" : cf. v. 33). XIII. 23 ("of the prophet who had brought him back"). XIV. 31 (cf. v. 21). XV. 6 (cf. XIV. 30). XVI. 11 ("he left him not a single man child," see XIV. 10). XVII. 6 (original

text: "bread in the morning and flesh in the evening").
XVIII. 19 ("and the four hundred prophets of the
Asherah"; cf. v. 22 and especially v. 40, where nothing
is said about the prophets of the Ashera). XXII. 28ᵇ
(from Micah I. 2, occasioned by an erroneous confound-
ing of the two prophets), 31 (the number 32 comes from
1 Kings xx. 24).

The Second Book of Kings.

K (See above, on 1 Kings): I. 1. VIII. 20-22. X. 32, 33.
XI. 1-9, 11, 12, 18ᵇ-20. XII. 5-16? 18, 19. XIII, 22,
24, 25. XIV. 8-14. XV. 16, 19, 20. XVI. 5-18.
XVIII. 17—XIX. 9ᵃ, 36, 37. XXIII. 29-30? 33-35?
XXIV. 1? (concerning other traces of K cf. on Dt).

K^2 The probably somewhat more recent parallel, XIX. 10
(from the second clause onwards)-20, 32-35, to the main
account in XVIII. 13 ff.

Dt (See above, on 1 Kings): I. 18. III. 1-3. VIII. 16-19,
23-29 (after K: 26). IX. 7-10ᵃ, 14, 15ᵃ, 28ᶜ, 29, 36*
("which he spoke, &c."), 37. X. 10? 17, 28-31, 34-36.
XII. 1-4 (after K: 2), 20-22 (after K: 21-22). XIII.
1-3, 7-11 (after K: 7). XIV. 1-7 (after K: 2, 5-7),
15-29 (after K: 19-22, 25). XV. 1-15 (after K: 2, 5,
10, 14), 17, 18, 21-38 (after K: 25, 29, 30, 33, 35ᵇ).
XVI. 1-4 (after K: 3?), 19, 20. XVII. 1-6, 18, 21-28),
41 (after K: 3-6, 24-28). XVIII. 1-13 (after K: 2, 4ᵇ,
7-8ᵇ, ? With v. 9-11 cf. XVII. 5, 6). XIX. 9ᵇ. XX.
(founded on an exemplar in K: v. 7 should follow v. 11).
XX. 1, 2, 16-26 (after K: 1, 18, 19, 23, 24). XXII. 1-4ᵃ,
5ᵇ, 8, 9ᵃᵇ, 10-14, 20ᵇ. XXIII. 1-4ᵃ (to "the keepers of
the door"), 6-7ᵃ, 8ᵃ, 9-13, 21-25, 28, 31, 32, 36, 37
(possibly 31, 36 are after K).

Dt^2 (See above, on 1 Kings) : XIII. 4-6 ? 23 ? XVII. 7-17, 19, 20, 29-34ᵃ. XXI. 7-15. XXII. 15-20ᵃ. XXIII. 26, 27. XXIV. 2-12, 15—XXV. 30.

? (See above, on 1 Kings) : XI. 13-18¹. XVIII. 14-16 (from a very good source). XIX. 21-31 (from a collection of oracles of Isaiah ?). XXIII. 8ᵇ, 15, 19, 20.

Pr^2 (A stratum of prophetical narratives relating to Elisha, probably from different hands, somewhat younger than the Elisha-Stories distinguished in 1 Kings under the symbol Pr ; see above, p. 41 f.) : II., IV.—VI. 23. VIII. 1-15. XIII. 14-21.

E (See above, on 1 Kings) : III. 4-27 ? VI. 24—VII. 17ᵃ. IX. 1-6, 10ᵇ-13, 15ᵇ-28ᵃᵇ, 30-36 (to " word of Jahweh "). X. 1-6ᵃ, 7-9, 11-16, 18-27.

Z (See above, on 1 Kings) : I. 2-17. VII. 17ᵇ-20. X. 6ᵇ? XI. 10. XII. 17 ? XVII. 34ᵇ-40. XXI. 3-6. XXII. 4ᵇ, 5ᵃ, 6, 7, 9ᶜ. XXIII. 4* (see above, on Dt.), 5, 7ᵇ, 14, 16-18. XXIV. 13, 14.

We regard the following as some of the quite late glosses (see above, on 1 Kings) :—I. 16 (" there is no God, &c.," inserted from v. 6). II. 15 (" in Jericho "). III. 19 (" and every choice city "). VI. 22 and 23 (" and two changes of raiments "). VIII. 1 (last clause). IX. 4 (" the servant of the prophet "). X. 19 (" all his worshippers," from v. 21). XI. 6, 7 (" about the king "), 11 (" by the king round about "), 13 (" the guard "), 15 (" the captains of hundreds " and " between the ranks "), 19 (" and all the people of the land "). XIII. 12-13 (at XIV. 15, 16, these verses are in their right place). XVIII. 17 (" the Tartan and the Rabsaris, &c." ;

cf. Isa. xxxvi. 2). XIX. 10ᵃ (to "Judah." The message consists of a letter!). XX. 11 ("to the steps which it had gone down"; from Isa. xxxviii. 8). XXII. 4, 8 and XXIII. 4: the original text no doubt ran simply, "the priest H.", as at XXII. 10, 12, &c.—XXIII. 33 ("that he might not reign in Jerusalem"; from 2 Chron. xxxvi. 3).

The Book of Ezra.

E (Verbal extracts from the Memoirs of Ezra; cf. above, p. 122): VII. 27—VIII. 34. IX.

e (Extracts from the Memoirs of Ezra in a revised form; cf. above, p. 122): VII. 1-10. X.

Q (Extracts from written sources and documents in the original phraseology; cf. above, p. 122): II. 1-67 (of almost precisely the same tenor as Neh. vii. 6 ff.).

q (Extracts of the same kind in a revised form: cf. above, p. 122): I. 1-4. II. 68—III. 1, 6. VI. 15.

Qa (The Aramaic source in Ezra, Chap. IV. ff.; cf. above, p. 122): IV. 8-23. V. 3. VI. 14ᵃ (except the late gloss in VI. 12ᵃ). VII. 11-26.

qa (Statements from *Qa* in a revised form; cf. above, p. 122): IV. 6, 7.

Ch (*Chronicler*, the redactor, or, as the case may be, the compiler of the Historical Work we now have as Ezra,

Nehemiah, Chronicles; as to the rest *Ch* also stands in those sections where the Chronicler has woven the notices which he may have found extant into a new representation: cf. above, p. 121 ff.): I. 5-11. III. 2-5, 7—IV. 5, 24— V. 2. VI. 14^b, 16-22. VIII. 35, 36.

The Book of Nehemiah.

N (Verbal extracts from the Memoirs of Nehemiah; cf. above, p. 122): I. 1—VII. 5 (on 6-69 and 70-73^a see below, on *Q* and *q*). XI. 1, 2, 20-24. XII. 31, 32, 37-40. XIII. 4-31.

n (Extracts from Nehemiah's Memoirs in a revised form; see above, p. 122: XI. 3-19).

e (See above, on Ezra!): VII. 73^b—X. 40 (amongst other things due to the Chronicler is the insertion of Nehemiah and the Levites in VIII. 9; as well as IX. 4, 5).

Q (See above, on Ezra!): VII. 6-69 (admitted by Nehemiah into his Memoirs). XII. 1-26^a.

q (See above, on Ezra!): VII. 70-73^a.

Ch (See above, on Ezra!): XI. 25-36. XII. 26^b-30, 33-36, 41—XIII. 3.

Later Additions to the Book of Jeremiah.

Z (cf. above, p. 85): III. 14-16? 17, 18.   X. 1-16.   XV. 13, 14 (from XVII. 3, 4).   XVI. 13, 14 (from XXIII. 7. 8), 18-21.   XVII. 19-27.   XXI. 11, 12.   XXVII. 7, XXIX. 10-15? 16-20.   XXX. 10, 11, 22-24.   XXXI. 38-40.   XXXII. 1-5, 17-23.   XXXIII. 2, 3, 14-26. XXXIX. 1, 2, 4-13.   XLVI. 27, 28 (cf. XXX. 10, 11). XLVIII. 47.   L. 1—LI. 58.   LII. (cf. 2 Kings xxiv. 18 ff.).

INDEX.

Amos, 50
Annals of the Kingdom, 71
Annalist of the Kingdom, 71
Aramaic Document in the Book of Ezra, 122; Aramaic Passages in the Book of Daniel, 139
Arrangement of the Books in the Hebrew Bible, 225

Balaam-Speeches, 16
Baruch, 84
Blessing of Jacob, 15
Blessing of Moses (Gen. xxxiii.), 19
Book of the Covenant, 7, 8, 29
Book of the Upright Ones, 2, 13, 15
Book of the Wars of Jahweh, 2, 15
Bow, so-called Song of the, 10

Calendar, 212 ff.
Chronicler, the Work of, 121 ff.
Chronicles, Books of, 123 ff.
Chronological Tables, 167
Chronology in the Book of Judges, 95; in the Books of Kings, 73 f.
Collections of Songs, 2, 3
Congregational Psalms, 147
Cubit, 206
Daniel, the Book of, 138 ff.
Daric (coin), 212
David, 25; a Psalmist? 11; David-Stories (*Da*), 28
Deborah, Song of (Judges v. 2 ff.), 5
Decalogue, 7, 8
Deutero-Isaiah, 96
Deuteronomist, 69, 94 f., 233 f.
Deuteronomy, 33, 34, 62 f., 94; chap. v., 7; xxxii., 94; xxxiii., 40
Deutero-Zechariah, 136 ff.
Division of the Kingdom, Consequences of, 18
Document Hypotheses, older and more recent (in Pentateuch criticism), 32 f.
Drachme (coin), 212

E-Source in the Pentateuch and Joshua (*see* Elohist)

Ecclesiastes, 162 f.
Elegy of David on Saul and Jonathan, 10; on Abner, 11
Elihu-Speeches in the Book of Job, 161
Elijah-Stories, 41
Elisha-Stories, 42
Elohist (see E), 32 f., 43 ff., 227 ff.
Epilogue to Deuteronomy, 66
Esther, Book of, 130
Exodus (see Moses, the Second Book)
Ezekiel, 86 ff.
Ezra, 106, 118
Ezra, Book of 121,
Ezra's Memoirs, 122

Fragments Hypothesis, 32

Genesis (see Moses, the First Book)
Gideon-Narratives, 21, 23 ff.
Grafian Hypothesis, 34

Habakkuk, 74
Haggai, 103
Hero-Stories in the Book of Judges, 21
Hilkiah, the Priest, 64
Historical Work, the Jahwistic, 35 ff.; the Jehovistic, 61; the Deuteronomistic, 94; the final redaction, 119 f.
Holiness, Law of, 100 f., 106
Hosea, 52

Isaiah, son of Amoz, 53 ff.; chap. i., 56; ii.-v., 56; vi., 56; xiii. f., 99; xv. and xvi., 50; xxiv.-xxvii., 135; xxxiv.-xxxv., 99

J-Source in the Pentateuch and Joshua (see Jahwist)
Jacob's Blessing, 15
Jahwist, 32, 33 f., 35; various strata of, 226
Jehoshaphat, Promulgator of the Book of the Covenant (?), 31
Jehovist, 61
Jeremiah, 76; the origin of the Book, 84 f.; additions to the Book, 85
Jerusalem-Source in the Second Book of Samuel, 25
Job, the Book of, 154
Joel, 133
Jonah ben Amittai, 134
Jonah, the Book of, 134
Josiah, Purification of the cultus under, 63 ff.
Joshua, the Book of, 94, 120, 232; x., 12 f., 2
Jotham's Fable (Judges ix., 8 ff.), 5
Judges, the Book of, 21, 45, 94, 120

King's Book, the great, 70
Kings, the Book of, 68, 96, 120; 1 Kings v. 9. ff., 13; xx., xxii., 2 Kings iii., vi. 24 ff., ix, f., 42

Lamentations, 91
Lamentations (Qinah)-Verse, 92
Lamech, Song of, 3
Lawbook, Ezra's, 106, 118
Legends, Remnants of Ancient, 5

Length (measure), 206
Levites, according to Ezek. xliv., 6, distinguished from the Priests, 90; in the Priests' Code, 117
Leviticus (see Moses, the Third Book)

Malachi, 105 f.
Measures of Capacity, 207
Measures of Length, 206
Micah, 57
Midrash on the Book of Kings, 127
Miriam, Song of (Exod. xv. 21), 2
Moab, Oracle on (Isa. xv. f.), 50
Money, 210
Months, Names of, 213
Moses, 6 ff.; the First Book of Moses, 226; iv. 23 f., 3; xiv., 119; xlix. 1 ff., 15. The Second Book of Moses, 228; chap. xv., 2; xvii. 14 ff., 7; xx. 7; xxxiv. 27 ff., 8. The Third Book of Moses, 230. The Fourth Book of Moses, 231; x., 35 f., 3; xxiii. f., 15. The Fifth Book of Moses (see Deuteronomy)

Nahum, 59
Nathan's Parable, 12
Nehemiah, 123
Nehemiah, Book of, 121
Nehemiah's Memorabilia, 122 f.

Obadiah, 132
Original Deuteronomy, 63 ff.

P—See Priests' Code
Parable of Nathan (2 Sam. xii. 1, ff.), 12
Pentateuch, 6, 119, 226 ff.
Pentateuch Criticism, on the History of, 31
Poetical Books, 141
Poetry, Popular, Remains of Ancient, 1
Priests' Code, or Priests' Document, 33, 106 ff. 227 ff.
Prologue to Deuteronomy, 66; to the Proverbs, 153; to Job, 157
Proper Names transliterated exactly from the Hebrew, 216
Prophets, Close of the Canon of, 137
Prophets, Mirror, of the, 41
Prophetism, 46 ff.
Proto-Zechariah, 104
Proverbs, Book of, 151
Proverbs, Them that speak in, 2
Psalms, Titles of, 141 f.; Number of, 141
Psalter, 141 ff.; Origin of, 143

Qinah-Verse (see Lamentations)

Rod, 207
Ruth, Book of, 129

Samuel, the Books of, 95, 120; 1 Sam. iv. 1 ff., 40; 2 Sam. i. 18 ff., 2; iii. 33, 11; xxii. and xxiii., 1-7, 11

Saul-Stories (*S*), 27; (*SS*), 45
Septuagint, 13
Sinai, Law of, 102
Song of Songs, 148
Supplement-Hypothesis (in Pentateuch Criticism), 32

Tell el-Amarna, Clay Tablets from, 173
Ten Commandments (*see* Decalogue)
Time, Computation of, 212
Titles of the Psalms, 142

Trito-Isaiah, 98
Triumphal Song of them that speak in Proverbs (Num. xxi. 27 ff.), 2

Weights, 208
Well, Song of the, 2
Wisdom Literature, 151
Writing, Art of, 10

Zechariah, chaps. i.-viii., 104; ix.-xiv., 136 ff.
Zephaniah, 61

www.ingramcontent.com/pod-product-compliance
Lightning Source LLC
Chambersburg PA
CBHW032146230426
43672CB00011B/2471